The Media Equation

The Media Equation

How People Treat Computers, Television, and New Media Like Real People and Places

Byron Reeves & Clifford Nass

CENTER FOR THE STUDY OF
LANGUAGE AND INFORMATION
STANFORD, CALIFORNIA

The book was set by CSLI Publications in Méridien and Frutiger, typefaces designed by the Swiss designer, Adrian Frutiger. The book was printed and bound in the United States of America.

Library of Congress Cataloging-in-Publication Data

Reeves, Byron, 1949–
The media equation : how people treat computers, television, and new media like real people and places / Byron Reeves and Clifford Nass.
xiv, 305 p. 23.5 cm.
Includes bibliographical references and index.
ISBN 1-57586-052-X
1. Mass media—Audiences. 2. Mass media—Influence. 3. Mass media—Psychological aspects. I. Nass, Clifford Ivar. II. Title. III. Series.
P96.A83R44 1996
302.23—dc20   96-20329
CIP

CSLI was founded early in 1983 by researchers from Stanford University, SRI International, and Xerox PARC to further research and development of integrated theories of language, information, and computation. CSLI headquarters and CSLI Publications are located on the campus of Stanford University.

CSLI Publications reports new developments in the study of language, information, and computation. In addition to books, our publications include lecture notes, monographs, working papers, and conference proceedings. Please visit our web site at
http://csli-www.stanford.edu/publications/
for comments on this and other titles.

to our families

Roxanne and Katherine
Byron, Phyllis, and Judiann

Barbara and Matthew
Jules, Florence, and Michael

Contents

Contents

Media and Form

Final Words

References

Preface

The Media Equation is the product of a collaboration that began in 1986 when the two of us arrived in the Department of Communication at Stanford University. Cliff had just finished a Ph.D. at Princeton, and Byron had been a professor at the University of Wisconsin-Madison. We had offices at Stanford that were two doors from each other, but we continued working on our separate research programs. Byron concentrated on viewer responses to television and film and Cliff on user responses to computers. Our different academic backgrounds and professional experiences, and our choices to study different media initially made any closer collaboration seem inappropriate. What could computers and television possibly have in common?

As we continued to talk, however, we realized that the answer was quite a bit. Indeed, one of the most exciting aspects of this project has been its convergence on topics that are usually kept separate. We are interested in computers and television, psychology and sociology, questionnaires and psychophysiology, new media and old media, fancy displays and plain text. These topics are often treated separately, in large part because each topic has its own vocabulary, journals, societies, training, and industries. Hopefully, this book demonstrates the strong links between them.

Over the last four years, our attempts to integrate media topics have accelerated. We have done studies, shared classes and students, created laboratories for joint research, and worked with media companies. And we have talked and talked about media, mingling ideas so much that the byline for this book was decided with the flip of a coin.

The basic ideas in this book and many of the studies it contains are the products of this collaboration. Much of the evidence for *The Media Equation*, however, is the product of a much larger group of colleagues and students that we have worked with, together and individually, over the last twenty years. We are greatly indebted to each of them. Indeed, this book would not have occurred to us absent their efforts.

The people whose ideas and results have contributed to this book are recognized in the Chapter References and the Author Index. The Chapter References also contain references to all of the academic papers that are the evidence for *The Media Equation*. The papers include extensive literature reviews, details about measurement, statistics and results, and qualifications, caveats and cautious claims. For this book, however, our intention was to write a bold statement about media that could serve as a counterpart to more guarded conclusions in academic publications. Our hope is that this will facilitate discussions about our results and make the research accessible to a larger audience.

There are several co-authors of the studies we report, and other teachers and colleagues, who have been particularly influential. We wish to acknowledge them in three groups: Those whom we worked with separately before our collaboration, and those who have helped us since.

Byron's Acknowledgments. There were several important colleagues in the School of Journalism & Mass Communication at the University of Wisconsin-Madison. Esther Thorson collaborated on many of the studies in this book and was a valued colleague. Several Ph.D. students at Wisconsin made important contributions, including Frank Biocca, Gina Garramone, Annie Lang, Guy Lometti, Dan McDonald, Jeanne Meadowcroft, Joan Schleuder, and Michael Shapiro. Each of these people now have important research programs of their own, and they continue to influence our work and the direction of research in mass communication.

Also at the University of Wisconsin, Jack McLeod had many important insights about this research and communication theory in general. Bill Blankenburg was a teacher and friend, and thoughts of his lectures to journalism students were responsible for any degree of clarity in the sentences that follow. Glen Broom and Dan Drew were valued colleagues and co-authors. Michael Rothschild in the School of Business was an important collaborator and the person who first proposed that we use brain-wave measures to study responses to media.

Research about perceptions of realism in media began for Byron while a graduate student in the Department of Communication at Michigan State University. Bradley Greenberg and Charles Atkin were teachers there and early collaborators, and some of the work done with them is reported here. Gerald Miller, Edward Fink, and Joseph Woelfel were influential teachers, and Mark Miller, a fellow graduate student, helped piece together theory and methods and make graduate school fun.

Cliff's Acknowledgments. Cliff's study of communication technology began at Princeton. The greatest intellectual influence there was Jim Beniger. His course on technology and society, taken because easy credits were needed to fill the schedule, changed the direction of a career. Jim took a computer scientist and made him a social scientist. He continually created opportunities and recognition, and provided outstanding training and criticism. Jim's wife, Kay Ferdinandsen, was a guide throughout graduate school.

Also at Princeton, John Sutton introduced the work of Max Weber which solidified social science as an intellectual home. Marvin Bressler, John Darley, Walter Wallace, and Bob Wuthnow proposed new ways of thinking. Among Ph.D. student peers, Hilary Bok, Karen Cerulo, David Garfinkle, Robert Gutstein, Patricia O'Reilly, Norman Ramsey, and Marsha Witten were particularly influential.

Shared Acknowledgments. Most recently, we have both benefited from several students and faculty colleagues in the Department of Communication, and at the Center for the Study of Language and Information (CSLI) at Stanford. In the department, Don Roberts and Ted Glasser have been quick and intelligent conversationalists about psychological responses to media and the larger academic context for our work.

One departmental colleague at Stanford, Steven Chaffee, deserves special mention. At different universities and at different times, but for each of us from the first day of our academic careers, Steve has been advisor, mentor, co-author, and reviewer. Our project is indebted to his ideas and support.

John Perry, Director of CSLI, encouraged us to write this book, and he has offered unfailing intellectual support. George White, Director of the Industrial Affiliate Program at CSLI, has been an enthusiastic supporter. Three other faculty associated with CSLI—Herb Clark and Barbara Tversky of Psychology and Terry Winograd of Computer Science—have made important comments about our research.

Many faculty at other universities have also been influential through their writings and advice. Particularly important to our work were Margaret Bradley, Steve Bulick, Dan Gilbert, Sara Kiesler, and Peter Lang. Writers, not mentioned earlier, whose books have influenced our own thinking include Ellen Langer, Paul Messaris, Donald Norman, Roger Shepard, and Sherry Turkle.

At Stanford, several students have collaborated with us on research. They include Michael Basil, Barbara Brown, Paul Carney, BJ Fogg, Seth Geiger, Nancy Green, M. Gens Johnson, Lisa Henriksen, Eun-Young Kim, Glenn Leshner, Matt Lombard, Edward Maibach, Laurie Mason, Geetu Melwani, Youngme Moon, John Morkes, John Newhagen, Peter Orton, Rozilyn Pierson, Gemma Rowley, Caroline Schooler, Shyam Sethuraman, Sara Spears, Michael Slater, Jonathan Steuer, and David Voelker. We greatly appreciate their work on these projects, and the insights they brought to our team. Many are currently directing their own research programs, and they all continue to influence our work in the Stanford laboratories they helped build.

One doctoral student in psychology who later worked with us as a post-doctoral fellow was Chris Dryer, currently at IBM. We benefited greatly from his knowledge of the literature in psychology and statistical methodology, his industriousness, and his interest in media.

Barbara Kataoka has administered our research and the Department with aplomb. Charles Kearns and Mark Urbanek helped with lab hardware and software. Gigi Pasquil, Lola Romero, Martha Sanchez, and Terese Weinlader provided the organizational support needed to permit us to focus on research.

Several colleagues provided extremely useful reviews of earlier drafts of this book. They were Bill Blankenburg, Janice Bradford, Steve Chaffee, Karen Fries, Patrick Jackson, Annie Lang, Debbie Lieberman, Dan Ling, John Morkes, Russ Neuman, John Perry, Don Roberts, Ellen Wartella, and George White.

Without the support of communication companies, our research would not have been possible. The research has been generously supported by Apple Computer, ATR (Interpreting Telephony Research Labs), Bell-Northern Research Ltd., Boeing Computer Services, Cable & Wireless Innovations, Capital-Cities ABC, Compaq, CPI, Fujitsu Ltd., Hewlett-Packard, Hitachi Ltd., IBM, Institute of System Science, LG Electronics, Matsushita Electric, Microsoft, NEC, Nippon Telephone and Telegraph, NTT Data, Novell, Pixel Instruments, SRI International, Stewart Filmscreen, Texas Instruments, US West, and Xerox PARC.

These companies have been much more than formal organizations. We have met several people in each of their research and product departments who have been intellectually supportive, and who have challenged us with real-world problems to which our research might apply.

We are particularly indebted to the Microsoft Corporation. We have worked with many product and research groups there, and have had the great pleasure of seeing some of our work included in their products. Many conversations we had there are reflected in this book. Karen Fries, Dan Ling, and Barry Linnett deserve special mention. Their creative and technical talents and their enthusiasm about the possibilities for research to inform practice are uncommon. We learned a great deal from them.

We received outstanding support from both CSLI Publications and Cambridge University Press. Dikran Karagueuzian at CSLI Publications has been the ideal editor, intellectually committed, enthusiastic, and accommodating. For Cambridge University Press, Alan Harvey and Peter-John Leone were responsive and helpful. John Morkes edited early chapters and thought of the title of the book. Cynthia Benn copy-edited, Copenhaver Cumpston designed the cover, Tony Gee designed the book, and Jeff Moores created the cover art. All did outstanding work.

B.R.

C.N.

I

Introduction

1

The Media Equation

The screen shows a bag of popcorn on a table. Several kernels have fallen from the bag. An adult, watching with preschool children, asks a question about the picture: "What will happen to the popcorn if I pick up the television set and turn it upside down?" A lot of kids say that the rest of the popcorn will spill out of the bag.

While interesting, this mistake is not really surprising. Children often take television literally. They'll soon be older, and will be wise enough to know better.

A novice computer user, excited about getting a new machine, sits down to try some new software. When the application is started, an animated dog on the screen greets the user with a smile and a big "Hello," then asks, "What would you like to do today?" When the dog appears, the user grins and says "Hello" back.

The smile isn't really so surprising, either. Computer novices like special treatment. Experts, however, don't seem to need or respond to on-screen social niceties.

In a televised presidential debate, members of a studio audience asked the candidates questions. One of the candidates began a response by leaving his place at the podium and walking toward the person who asked the question. On television, the candidate appeared to narrow the distance between himself and each viewer watching at home. Many viewers responded quite favorably to his comments, not because of what he said, but because he seemed to move physically closer to the viewers.

Surprising? Not really. Distracted by the task of following a debate, viewers might forget that a screen image isn't a real person. If they thought about it for a moment, it seems unlikely that they would be influenced by the candidate's apparent entrance into their personal space.

A research team from an artificial intelligence lab demonstrated a new robot to a group of computer specialists. They described a one-legged hopping machine that had memory, could learn new instructions, was bred for intelligence, could focus attention, could accept punishment and reward, and even had a personality. No one at the meeting noticed that they were using the vocabulary of human psychology to describe the abilities of a collection of wire, silicon, mechanical joints, and computer code.

The language used to describe the robot is also not surprising. The researchers thought they were just using the metaphor of the human mind as a useful tool for analyzing intelligent systems. No one at the meeting seemed to think that the robot was a real person or had human attributes; they just found it convenient to talk about the robot as human.

How Different Are Media and Real Life?

These stories show that there are good reasons why some people might confuse media and real life. Children do it because they're young, and novices because they don't have enough experience. People engaged in a difficult task may be confused because they are too distracted to notice otherwise and smart people may do it because it's a useful metaphor. All of these dismissals have one other thing in common, however. They all suggest that the confusion of mediated life and real life is rare and inconsequential, and it can be corrected with age, education, or thought.

We have collected a great deal of evidence that shows this conclusion is not true. Equating mediated and real life is neither rare nor unreasonable. It is very common, it is easy to foster, it does not depend on fancy media equipment, and thinking will not make it go away. The media equation—*media equal real life*—applies to everyone, it applies often, and it is highly consequential. And this *is* surprising.

The media equation comes from a research project that we call Social Responses to Communication Technologies. In short, we have found that individuals' interactions with computers, television, and new media are *fundamentally social and natural,* just like interactions in real life. The key word is "fundamentally." Everyone expects media to obey a wide range of social and natural rules. All these rules come from the world of interpersonal interaction, and from studies about how people interact with the real world. But all of them apply equally well to media.

Testing the Media Equation

Consider this research example, a prototype of our work on the media equation. If either of us called you on the phone to ask how well you liked this book, you would likely be polite and say that it was fine. But if *someone else* were to make the same phone call, the evaluation might be less positive. This is an example of a simple *social* rule: People are polite to those who ask questions about themselves.

We found that this same rule applies to media. When asked to evaluate the performance of a *computer,* people gave more positive answers about how well a computer performed if it asked questions about itself than if a different computer asked the same questions. People are polite to computers, too.

The same equation—media = real life—works for pictures as well. For example, in the real world, motion demands attention, especially if what moves is coming toward us. This is a simple natural rule. The presence of motion determines how attention is allocated, and ultimately, what is remembered about an experience.

We found that this rule applies to media as well. Motion in *pictures,* especially motion that appears directed at the viewer, stimulates

5

physical activation in the brain as if the moving objects were actually present. Pictures, too, are natural experience.

Evidence for the media equation now includes thirty-five studies that have recreated a broad range of social and natural experiences—but with media taking the place of real people and places. All of the studies go far beyond pleading with a computer or yelling at a television. We have looked at everything from interfaces that flatter to the personalities of cartoon characters, from talking computers to movies on home theaters, from pictures of objects thrown at the viewer's face to faces that cover a wall, from super-high-resolution images to fifth-generation home video, and from questionnaires that ask people what they think to brain-wave measures that tell us what people could not otherwise describe.

The consistency of responses in all of these studies led us to the media equation: Media equal real life. But that's not where we started.

Intuitions to the Contrary

The media equation is not intuitive. In fact, the equation competes with ideas about media that seem much more obvious. What seems most obvious is that media are *tools*, pieces of hardware, not players in social life. Like all other tools, it seems that media simply help people accomplish tasks, learn new information, or entertain themselves. People don't have social relationships with tools.

Likewise, pictures *seem* to be merely symbols that represent people and places that are not actually present. People seem to attend to media with detachment and they seem to focus on *in*equalities between images and the real world. Everyone seems to believe that media are special, and everyone has pet theories, personal experiences, stories, and complaints about media that bolster the belief that media are unique.

Many of these ideas characterized our own thoughts about media when we began our research. We believed that people might occasionally confuse media and real life, but the confusion wasn't pervasive, and most important, it was curable. Along with many participants in our research, we were tempted to think that the results were curious but personally irrelevant. *I* know that computers don't have feelings. And *I* can certainly distinguish between life on the screen and the real thing.

We now think our intuitions were wrong, however, and this led us to a second important conclusion: People respond socially and naturally to media even though they believe it is not reasonable to do so, and even though they don't think that these responses characterize themselves. This conclusion is, by definition, counterintuitive, and it significantly complicates research. Participants in our experiments were not aware that they equated media with real people and places. Therefore, attempts to verify the media equation can't rely solely on talking to people, listening to their stories, or asking them questions on a survey. Social and natural responses to media are not conscious, and as a consequence, people are not able to confirm the media equation, even if they'd like to help. This means that our research story is also about how to observe what people cannot themselves describe.

The media equation tempts many qualifications, but few are needed. One tempting qualification is that people might be fooled, but only by the niftiest of new media—virtual reality systems, IMAX theaters, or full-motion holography of the future. Our research suggests otherwise. Even the simplest of media are close enough to the real people, places, and things they depict to activate rich social and natural responses. Many of our studies generate these responses with rather pathetic representations of real life: simple textual and pictorial material shown on garden-variety technology. The equation still holds, however. Mediated life equals real life.

Moreover, the media equation is not limited to a particular type of person. While it might be tempting to assign the confusion between media and real life to problems of age, knowledge, distraction, or convenience, our research shows that social and natural responses are remarkably common, and true for every group we have tested, including children, college sophomores, people in business, and technology experts. *All* people automatically and unconsciously respond socially and naturally to media.

Are there times when the media equation doesn't apply? Of course. People are quite capable of thinking their way around it. People can treat media as tools or as images that only represent the real world but are not real themselves. But these responses, all highly thoughtful, share many surprising characteristics: They require a lot of effort, they tend not to occur when people are tired or when other things compete for their attention, and they are always difficult to sustain. The automatic response is to accept what seems to be real as in fact real.

People have done some amazing things in our labs. They have taken great care not to make a computer feel bad, they've felt physically threatened by mere pictures, and they've attributed to an animated line drawing a personality as rich as that of their best friend. It eventually occurred to us that people were not doing these things because they were childish, inexperienced, distracted or because they needed a metaphor. We had to acknowledge that these responses were fundamentally human, and we had to acknowledge that they were important.

Benefits of Considering the Media Equation

An understanding of the media equation accomplishes four things, all of them important, and each difficult to obtain otherwise.

Improving the Design of Media

The first benefit of the media equation is practical. If human-media interactions are social and natural, then there are a number of unexpected ways to improve the *design* of media. Many of these applications stem from one important conclusion: Humans are experts on social relationships, and they are experts on how the physical world works. Rules for using media as tools, on the contrary, are often arbitrary and must be learned. When media conform to social and natural rules, however, no instruction is necessary. People will automatically become experts in how computers, television, interfaces, and new media work.

Because people have a strong positive bias toward social relationships and predictable environments, the more a media technology is consistent with social and physical rules, the more enjoyable the technology will be to use. Conforming to human expectations means that there is instant expertise just because we're human, and there are positive responses, including feelings of accomplishment, competence, and empowerment.

All of the chapters to follow include design rules that are based on our experiments, and on the larger social science literature in the area being discussed. These rules include simple ways to give personality to a computer; when to use multiple voices in an interface; how movement can guide visual attention; the trade-offs between visual and audio fidelity in video-conferencing; how to make effective advertisements; and general principles for making interactive multimedia presentations more polite, friendly, or arousing.

Evaluating Media

The second application of the research concerns judgments about media and especially worries about new media. If media can do harm, then the explanation for how that process works will depend on the *psychology* of the people who use them, not just the technologies per se, nor the industries that make the appliances and produce the content. Psychology is at least as important in the evaluation of media as economics, policies, laws, and the media industries themselves. And it is from the perspective of psychology—the study of how people think and feel—that the media equation comes.

Media have evolved to capitalize on fundamental human responses to them. This is true of everything from negative political advertising, to the development of chatty "happy-talk" news, to discussions about computer agents. By trial and error, people who design media are gradually discovering the intricacies of how media work. The media equation helps to organize these principles and to form a basis for a critique of media.

Useful discussions of how to change what we don't like about media need to consider that not all responses to media are obvious; some are constrained by unconscious thoughts and feelings. In the chapters to follow, we discuss implications of the research for communication policy, ethics, activism, and even personal media habits. These discussions include ideas about how media affect political cynicism, worship of media personalities, violent behavior, shyness, and even deviant sexual behavior.

New Methods for Research

The third benefit of the research concerns the *methods* used to find out new things about media. Our experiments use the same methods that psychologists use to determine how people respond to each other and to the physical world. The biggest advantage of borrowing these methods is that they differ substantially from other techniques that are currently used to study media. Many popular methods, especially focus group techniques, rely heavily on the assumption that people can be introspective about media experiences. This is an assumption that we think is frequently wrong.

Many of the procedures in the studies we have conducted are uncommon, and many of them require elaborate or unusual ways to record responses. We have tried to indicate the advantages of each method in relation to more traditional techniques for studying media, and we have tried to provide enough detail about the research methods and results to enable readers to evaluate evidence for the media equation.

Big Issues

The fourth benefit of the media equation is the opportunity to reconsider big issues related to media. These are ideas, most often discussed in universities, that have often assumed too much about how people interact, watch, listen, and read. The first is the idea that media are predominantly tools, and that people consciously use media tools to serve their needs. Rather, we think our research shows that media are perceived as real people and places, and that human responses to media are determined by the rules that apply to social relationships and navigating the world. Responses to media are not primarily governed by rules about how to use appliances more akin to a hammer or car.

Another common assumption about technology is that when people treat media as human, they are guilty of anthropomorphism, a mistaken belief that inanimate objects are human. Anthropomorphism, however, is rare and is not the basis for the media equation. Social responses are commonplace, even when people know that the responses are inappropriate.

There is also a strong tendency in discussions about media to consider the *real* similarities between media machines that think and the thinking done by humans. The consequence of this confusion is a bias toward ideas about "hardware" similarities between media and people, for example, the similarity between neurons in the brain and neural networks in a computer. This view, however, underestimates a critical human tendency to confuse what is real with what only *seems* to be real. For example, people are not only deemed intelligent because they think well; they are also intelligent because they *appear* to think well, quite apart from the real merits of their mental capacity. Because of this, we should not worry as much about whether media are the same as their real-world counterparts, and instead think more about whether media are *perceived* as identical. Perceptions alone can alter a broad range of human behavior.

The media equation also challenges the cherished assumption that words and pictures in media are *symbolic representations* of things that are not actually present. When information is mediated, we often assume that people only think about *who* sent the information and *why*, and most importantly, what the information *means*. Our research shows that this view can assume too much. When a picture threatens, we don't think about who made it, what they intended, and what it all means; we often think only about what we should *do*.

Why Do People Respond Socially and Naturally to Media?

In a recent U.S. congressional hearing, entertainer Shari Lewis answered questions from senators about television violence and children. She brought her hand-puppet, Lamb Chop, with her. At one point in the hearing, the story is told, Lamb Chop the puppet made a statement (through the projected voice of Shari Lewis) about television violence. A senator then said, "Miss Lewis, do you agree with Lamb Chop?"

If it took you a moment to laugh at this story, you are in good

11

company. None of the senators laughed right away either. Everyone sitting in the hearing room seemed to think that it was perfectly reasonable for a puppet to give testimony, and it was perfectly reasonable to ask the puppeteer if she had a *different* opinion than the puppet. A puppet is a natural conversational partner. The hard part, once engaged, is to think of it as anything else.

How is this possible? The answer is that people are not evolved to twentieth-century technology. The human brain evolved in a world in which *only* humans exhibited rich social behaviors, and a world in which *all* perceived objects were real physical objects. Anything that *seemed* to be a real person or place *was* real.

During nearly all of the 200,000 years in which *Homo sapiens* have existed, anything that acted socially really was a person, and anything that appeared to move toward us was in fact doing just that. Because these were absolute truths through virtually all of human evolution, the social and physical world encouraged automatic responses that were, and still are, the present-day bases for negotiating life. Acceptance of what only *seems* to be real, even though at times inappropriate, is automatic.

Modern media now engage old brains. People can't always overcome the powerful assumption that mediated presentations are actual people and objects. There is no switch in the brain that can be thrown to distinguish the real and mediated worlds. People respond to simulations of social actors and natural objects as if they were in fact social, and in fact natural. A puppet, while obviously different from a human when people *think* about it, is close enough to a human to fool our old brains, especially if we are otherwise engaged or running on automatic. So, did Shari agree with Lamb Chop or not? That's the question.

People often don't scrutinize their actions or their environment. People frequently live life mindlessly and with little introspection.When our brains automatically respond socially and naturally because of the characteristics of media or the situations in which they are used, there is often little to remind us that the experience is unreal. Absent a significant warning that we've been fooled, our old brains hold sway and we accept media as real people and places.

With effort, people can perhaps think their way out of primitive, automatic responses. This is effective, for example, at a scary movie. A mental reminder that "it's only a movie, it's only a movie," does offer an escape. But this strategy makes it hard to follow the plot, and is not typical or usual. The default is to automatically and unconsciously ignore fabrication and expect reality, as if the technology itself were invisible. The fact that the movie scared us in the first place is good evidence that media are real first, and false only after we think about it. There are vestiges of old brains in modern thinking.

How We Did the Research

If media and real life are similar, then knowledge of how people respond to *real* people and places should reveal a lot about how people respond to media. The place in the library for this information is the social science section, especially psychology, sociology, and communication.

Social science is not an obvious place to start. A reference librarian might suggest a hundred other places first. An interest in media machines or interfaces gets you to electrical engineering, computer science, or to a media laboratory; an interest in media content and production might get you to the fine arts section or to a film school; and an interest in media jobs could get you to journalism, broadcasting, or to a newspaper.

An interest in how people work, however, is the province of social science, and it is this area that has the best information with which to leverage the media equation. What social scientists know about how people respond to each other can be used to explain how people respond to *media*. But there is even more reason to land in the social sciences: Not only do social scientists know about social and natural responses, they are also good at measuring them, especially when the responses cannot be known through intuition, casual observation, or introspection.

The social science section of the library contains results of a century of research about how people respond to each other, about how they respond to their natural environment, and about how to measure both.

Our strategy was to borrow, as outlined with simplifying overstatement, using the following steps.

Step 1: Pick a social science finding about how people respond to each other or to the natural environment. This might be a finding about how people express politeness, how they respond to personalities different from their own, how people negotiate interpersonal space, or how they stereotype by gender. On the natural side, this could be a finding about how people respond to motion, how they regulate emotional states, or how what people hear influences what they see.

Step 2: Find the place in the report where a social or natural rule is summarized. For example: "People like to be praised by other people, even if the praise is undeserved"; "people like other people who have personalities that are like their own"; or "the onset of motion elicits intense focus."

Step 3: Cross out the words "person" or "environment" in the studies, and substitute media. The substitution could be a media machine, some exemplary content, or an interface. For example, if the interest is computers, the rule that people like other people who flatter them becomes this: People will like *computers* that flatter them. If the rule is that people feel strong emotions when another person comes close to them, then people will feel strong emotions when a *picture of a person* comes close to them. If people orient visually to movement in the natural environment, then people will orient to movement on a *screen*. The result in each of these cases is a prediction, complete with accompanying explanation, about human interaction with media.

Step 4: Find the part of the report that describes how the rule was *tested*. For the flattery rule, for example, a study was done that observed students who were praised by a tutor. In the personality study, two people talked across a table, and tried to solve a puzzle. In the motion study, orienting responses were measured by recording brain electrical activity.

Step 5: Cross out, again, one of the people or the description of the environment, and substitute media. Instead of a human tutor in the flattery example, you now have a *computer* tutor. Instead of two people solving a puzzle, you would have a person and a *computer* solving a puzzle. Instead of measuring brain activity in relation to actual movement, brain activity is measured relative to moving *pictures*. This substitution provides a method for testing the prediction.

Step 6: Run the experiment. This is important. To arrive at the media equation, we made no *assumptions* about whether the results would be the same for real people and places, and their mediated counterparts. Rather, people were asked to visit a laboratory, and to experience media. We gathered data that were summarized, statistically analyzed, and interpreted using the same standards that were used in the original experiments. When an experiment is successful, the results of the media study match the original study.

Step 7: Draw implications. We are interested in how media should be discussed, and this includes the ways the experiments can inform designers, producers, directors, critics, regulators, owners, and consumers. A desire to apply social science in these areas is one of the reasons that we started the project in the first place. We also draw implications for the theory of human-media interaction as well as implications for the social sciences more generally. But always, we try to apply the theory.

A lot of steps, but nothing terribly complicated. In the chapters that follow, we will show how this method, and the media equation that resulted from its use, can frame and organize some surprising things that people do with media.

Media and Manners

2

Politeness

The three-term mayor of New York City, Ed Koch, used to ask a simple question: "How am I doing?" His question closed speeches, greeted crowds, and made a great sound bite. Imagine that the mayor, exuding enthusiasm and smiling brightly, turned to you with his question, "How am I doing?" Is your first impulse a critical evaluation of his political agenda? Likely not. "You're doing swell, Mr. Mayor!"

Imagine that in the evening, a pollster from the *New York Times* calls with the same question. "How is the mayor doing?" Without hesitation, your answer might be more truthful: "Not so well."

What explains your two different responses? Was the first a lie? Not really. Instead, it was *polite*, a virtue not a vice, even in New York City. Trying to make people happy is the norm, and it generally works well. When the mayor asks about how he's doing, he's implicitly telling listeners what would make him happy—receiving a positive answer. When someone *else* asks the same question, however, the mayor's feelings are not at stake; honesty prevails.

We don't all carry an etiquette handbook, but everyone seems to know good manners. Although violations exist, most people are polite most of the time. The level of conformity is striking, a fact blurred by vivid memory for occasional lapses. Politeness is ubiquitous, and it's practiced automatically. Communities encourage it, and the rules are a centerpiece of childhood socialization. Politeness, even more than early mastery of letters and numbers, is a genuine mark of an educated child, as any kindergarten teacher can attest.

The example of the mayor's question helps identify one important politeness rule. When people ask about themselves, they will usually receive more positive responses than when an independent person asks the same question. That is, if the person in the question also asks it, politeness reigns.

There is still some chance, however, that a response could be negative. After all, the mayor just asked a question; he didn't give explicit instructions about what the response should be, nor did he mention the response that he would like to hear. The desired response must still be inferred. This is likely, but something could still go awry, especially if the respondent were tempted to think too much about politics. If you were the mayor, is there a way to gain even greater control?

Yes, there is. Imagine the response if the mayor looks you in the eye and says, "I think I'm doing great! How do you think I'm doing?" Now the stakes are even higher. The mayor isn't relying on an assumption that you will be polite. He's giving you an explicit prompt about just what you should say. If you don't answer positively, you are at odds with his expressed self-opinion. That's really impolite.

The subtleties of politeness rules, however, are not fully exposed yet. Consider again the pollster from the *Times*. She is not only going to hear more negative responses about the mayor, she will also hear more varied responses. The mayor himself, since people are likely to be polite, is going to hear pretty much the same thing from everyone: "Things are fine, Mr. Mayor." But the pollster, since she is more likely to hear the truth, will hear a range of responses: some good, some bad, some in between. This suggests another rule: When people ask about themselves, the answers will be more homogeneous than when someone else asks the same questions.

Politeness has received a great deal of attention from psychologists. Their results lend credence to the rules that the mayoral example summarizes. While the scientific experiments confirm an important set of rules for social behavior, they are not surprising. Most people could easily imagine responding in similar ways. Our question was whether the same rules might apply to media. Are people polite to computers?

Politeness Rules for Humans vs. Politeness Rules for Computers

Millions of dollars are spent each year trying to make computers friendly and polite. Sometimes it works, sometimes it doesn't, but in any case, it is a useful exercise because there are humans at the other end who will recognize and appreciate the effort. Designers want people to like media machines, and politeness is one way to ensure this.

But what about manners in the other direction? Do computer users actually reciprocate? Do people try to be polite to machines? If the answer is yes, we could make the following predictions, substituting computers for the mayor and the *New York Times*:

Rule 1: When a computer asks a user about itself, the user will give more positive responses than when a different computer asks the same questions.

Rule 2: Because people are less honest when a computer asks about itself, the answers will be more homogeneous than when a different computer asks the same questions.

What "social scene" do these predictions suggest? Imagine that you have just used a computer to do some work. Afterward, the machine, using simple text, praises its abilities. The same machine then asks for an evaluation. Are you polite (as most were to the mayor) instead of truthful? Would you be more likely to tell the truth if you wheeled your chair over to a second computer that asked for the same evaluation? And would the collection of responses to the second computer, because the truth was more likely told, represent a greater variety of opinions?

Many people would answer no to these questions. First of all, computers do *not* have feelings, so it would be foolish for users to be polite to them. Whose feelings would be spared, anyway? Second, it would be quite unusual to think of two different computers as two independent people. What is it that they are independent of? Certainly not each other. Finally, people are trained to be honest to computers, not to humor them. There is good evidence that when people are interviewed about sensitive topics, they are more likely to tell the truth to a computer than to another person.

The two politeness rules may sound silly when you think about their application to media. Thinking about it, however, is exactly what people may not do. We predicted that people would still be polite, media notwithstanding.

Our rationale was this: Computers, in the way that they communicate, instruct, and take turns interacting, are *close enough* to human that they encourage *social* responses. The encouragement necessary for such a reaction need not be much. As long as there are some behaviors that suggest a social presence, people will respond accordingly. When it comes to being social, people are built to make the conservative error: When in doubt, treat it as human. Consequently, any medium that is close enough will get human treatment, even though people know it's foolish and even though they likely will deny it afterward.

Observing Polite Interactions with Computers

To determine whether our predictions were accurate, we conducted several laboratory experiments. In all respects possible, they were similar to the experiments done by psychologists who study politeness in human-human interaction. The only difference was that participants in our studies worked with a *computer* rather than a person.

Here is how the first experiment worked. We invited twenty-two people to a laboratory and told them they would be working with a computer to learn about various topics. We told them that at the end of the work session we would ask them to evaluate the computer that they used. They would have to tell us how they felt about the computer and how well they thought the computer had performed during the session.

One person at a time sat down in front of the computer to be tutored about various statistical profiles of Americans. The computer, a black NeXT computer with a 21-inch black-and-white monitor, was placed on an office desk in front of each person. The only thing that the computer displayed was text and graphical buttons: no pictures, no voices, not even an icon.

Twenty facts were presented in each session. Here is an example: "According to a Harris Poll, 30% of all American teenagers kiss on the first date." After the presentation of each fact, the computer asked the users if they knew anything about the fact they had just read. Using a mouse for input to the computer, participants indicated whether they knew "a great deal," "somewhat," or "very little." Participants were told that the computer would provide some additional facts based on how much they said they already knew. In reality, however, everyone received the same information presented in the same order.

After participants finished hearing the facts, the computer gave them a test and then told the participants which answers were right and which were wrong. Then the computer told each user what it thought of its own performance; in all cases, the computer said that it had done a great job.

The participants were divided into two groups to evaluate the computer's performance. Half were assigned to answer the evaluation questions on the same computer that had just praised itself. The other half answered the identical questions on a different computer located on the other side of the room.

In the evaluation, participants were asked how well different adjectives described their session with the computer. The adjectives were chosen to capture how well each person thought the computer performed, as well as how much they liked the interaction. Twenty-two adjectives were used to evaluate the computer, including *accurate, analytical, competent, fair, friendly,* and *helpful.*

People Are Polite to Computers, Too

If machines don't deserve our positive regard, there should be no differences in evaluations of the computers based on which one asked the questions. If computers are social actors, however, then participants who responded to the *same* computer that taught them should be polite, and uniformly so, just as if the machine were a real person with real feelings.

What happened? As predicted, the participants who answered questions on the same computer gave significantly more positive responses than did participants who answered on a different computer. The computers got the same treatment that people would get. The respondents who interacted with the same computer throughout the experiment rated it more positively on twenty of the twenty-two adjectives presented. Based on statistical tests, we can be confident that these results did not occur by chance.

The variance in responses also conformed to the prediction. Evaluations made on the same computer had a significantly smaller range of responses than did evaluations made on the other computer. Participants felt freer to be honest when an independent computer asked the questions, and this increased the variance in evaluations of the computer's performance.

What did the participants themselves think about these results? When we told them what we predicted (after the experiment was over, of course), all of them said confidently that they did not, and never would, change their evaluations just to be polite to a computer. From these comments, we concluded that social responses to media were unconscious and automatic.

When research results are first discussed, colleagues often ask tough questions. The questions in this case were about alternative explanations for these social responses. One issue was the definition of "other." In the first experiment, the "other" asking the questions was a different computer, set up on the other side of the room from the first computer. Could there have been something about the particular placement of the computers that caused the differences, rather than a perception on the part of users that a computer was a social entity that warranted polite treatment?

To test this, we decided to see if the same results would occur if we made the "interviewer" something other than a computer. We did the experiment again, and this time we made the "other" a paper-and-pencil questionnaire instead of a computer.

The participants who used a paper-and-pencil questionnaire to evaluate the tutoring sessions were less favorable in their evaluations of the computer than the participants who completed the same questionnaire on the computer that had just instructed them. The questionnaire elicited significantly more varied responses as well, as had the second computer in the first study. The conclusion: The paper-and-pencil questionnaire, like a different computer, was perceived as an "other" that did not require a polite response.

Both studies used computers that showed only text. We wondered what would happen if the social presence were more explicit. What if the computers were fancier and even more suggestive of human presence? To answer this question, we decided to repeat the experiment using voices rather than text. We wanted to find out whether voices would accentuate politeness when compared with text.

In the voice experiment, the facts and other information were presented with human speech coming from a small speaker attached to the computer. All participants heard a single voice on a single computer that tutored and then praised itself. One group of participants heard the same voice on the same computer ask for an evaluation. A second group heard a different voice on a different computer request the evaluation. A third group gave their evaluation with pencil and paper.

We found the exact same differences with voices as we did in the earlier studies that used only text. When a voice on a computer asks about itself, people are more positive and less honest than when they are questioned by a different voice on a different computer or when they give their responses on a questionnaire. The conclusion: Users are polite to computers whether they use text *or* voices.

One final result tells something about how impressed we should be with the newer capabilities of media. The result is actually a *lack* of differences. Voices did not make the interaction any more social than text. The presence of voices was apparently no big deal, at least as far as creating a social presence. It doesn't take virtual reality to create the sense that another person is present; people don't need much of a cue to respond socially.

How Should One Think About Media?

People were polite to computers. Not only were the computers in these experiments tools for learning new information, they were social actors that people reacted to with the same polite treatment that they would give to another human. This certainly adds a new dimension to an understanding of human-media relationships.

Before radically altering how we think about media, however, a reasonable question is whether there is a chance that this conclusion is wrong. Several questions about the research could be raised, and our answers to the questions are particularly important because they apply not just to the present studies, but to virtually all of the research in the book. Here are some things to keep in mind.

First, it's important to remember that all participants did exactly the same things in the lab. Everyone received the same facts, the same test, and the same evaluation, and they used identical interfaces on identical machines. The only difference was which computer asked the questions. So the results must be attributable to that one difference.

In laboratory experiments, there is also a danger that participants will figure out what is being studied and then try to help by telling the experimenters what they want to hear rather than what they really think. This didn't happen in the computer experiments, however. When asked, none of the respondents guessed that the number of computers had anything to do with the experiment, and no one guessed that the experiment had anything to do with politeness. Everyone believed that the study was about how people use computers to learn.

What if participants believed that computers *really did* have human capabilities? To make sure this wasn't true, we selected subjects who would be least likely to hold this opinion—everyone in the experiments had extensive experience with computers. They all were daily users, and many even did their own programming. If anyone should have known that computers don't have feelings, they should have. Old brains, however, have not yet caught up with new media.

Another possibility is that people were merely impulsive. Many people occasionally yell at a newscaster or quarterback on television, or plead with a computer to give back a disk. These responses, however, are instantaneous, and they are rarely sustained. In our experiments, the social responses lasted much longer than an instant—they characterized an entire learning session. Polite responses were related to the entire experience. Hence, social responses to media are more than impulses that punctuate more thoughtful moments.

Another question about the experiments is familiar in the humanities. Maybe people *willingly suspend disbelief* when they encounter media. Perhaps people make a conscious decision to "make believe," in this case, pretending that a computer is a person. In exchange, a user might be better able to understand a presentation (or in the case of entertainment, have a better experience). However, no one said that they were making believe that the computer was real just for fun or because it was helpful. So if there was a suspension of disbelief, it certainly wasn't *willing* or conscious. Indeed, it is *belief*, not *disbelief*, that is automatic.

One of the most interesting responses to the politeness studies is this: "I'd be polite to a computer, but I'm not thinking of the computer as a person, I'm merely responding to the person who wrote the computer program. And that person *is* real!" Perhaps the use of social rules is reasonable because the technologies are created by humans, and hence, they warrant human treatment.

This explanation can be ruled out for two reasons. First, no one in the experiments said that they were using social rules for *any* reason. Moreover, when asked specifically about whether they had considered the programmer when they made their evaluations, not one person said they had.

Is it then possible that people were *subconsciously* thinking about the programmer? This is not likely the case either. If there were a subconscious orientation to a programmer, then the people who used two computers would have had to think about two *different* programmers, one for each machine. However, when the people who used two computers were questioned about whether they thought the machines were programmed by the same person or different people, they all said that they assumed there was a single programmer (and they were right).

What Do Polite Responses to Media Mean?

We think that these experiments demonstrate, against the intuition of many scholars, and counter to the verbal reports of the participants, that social rules apply to media. In this case, the medium was a computer, but not one capable of virtual reality or any other obvious display of social presence. The computer showed plain text on a plain black-and-white screen. It is not necessary to have artificial intelligence or full-motion video to be social. The nerdiest of media, a computer that looks like it came from NASA control, is close enough to being human to trigger rich scripts for social interaction. Computers are social actors.

Social responses to media are not obvious, however, to those who exhibit them. The participants in the experiments denied that they had been intentionally polite to a computer, and we believed them. Instead, the responses occurred without conscious awareness. They were automatic and mindless. A significant part of the human brain works on unconscious responses, and that work is often completed without the results being available for analysis by those parts of the brain responsible for thoughtfulness and introspection.

At the broadest level, these studies demonstrate the viability of the media equation. Findings and experimental methods from the social sciences can be applied directly to human-media interaction. It is possible to take a psychology research paper about how people respond to other people, replace the word "human" with the word "computer," and get the same results.

Designing Polite Media

Initially, it may seem that these studies have more implications for what humans do with machines than for what machines should do with humans. Actually, the two are quite related. The reason is that polite behavior, as well as many other social behaviors, is part of an *interaction*. Social behaviors are not accomplished in isolation from the responses to them—social means reciprocal. This is pivotal for the design of interactive media, because the biggest reason for making machines that are polite to people is that people are polite to machines. Everyone expects reciprocity, and everyone will be disappointed if it's absent.

When media violate social norms, such as by being *im*polite, the media are not viewed as technologically deficient, a problem to be resolved with a better central processing unit. Rather, when a technology (or a person) violates a politeness rule, the violation is viewed as social incompetence and it is offensive. This is why we think that the most important implication of the politeness studies is that media themselves need to be polite. It's not just a matter of being nice; it's a matter of social survival.

Grice's Maxims for Politeness

How can designers ensure that computers are polite? Again, our answer is to borrow from the researchers who study politeness—the social scientists. Perhaps the most general and powerful politeness rules that media could obey are *Grice's Maxims*. H. Paul Grice, a philosopher and psychologist, viewed conversation as an exercise in which people try to be helpful. Grice argued that *all* people feel that conversations should be guided by four basic principles that constitute the rules for polite interaction: quality, quantity, relevance, and clarity.

Quality. Speakers should say things that are true. This is the one Gricean maxim that computers obey pretty well. They may be insensitive in delivery or too quick to disappoint, but at least they tell the truth. It is important to remember, however, that accuracy is a shield and not a sword. Accuracy can breed frustration because of a perceived lack of cooperation. If someone stops his or her car to ask, "Where am I?," the answer "in a car" is accurate but quite impolite. In Grice's terms, the driver is annoyed not because the answer was inaccurate, but because the comment wasn't cooperative.

Quantity. Each speaker in an interaction should contribute only what the conversation demands, not too much or too little. This rule is frequently violated by interactive media. For example, most menu systems present a single word or at most two words for each option, and this is true no matter how complex the action. The result is that users often feel that the program is not cooperating. Why is that computer not giving me the whole story? The outcome is frustration.

Can icons, the favorite exemplar of brevity, solve the problem of quantity? Not all the time. A single icon that represents a complex task can be just as frustrating as a single word. The use of plain English (full sentences or at least multiple words in logical phrases) would make an enormous difference in understanding and satisfaction. The success may be traded against time, but almost by definition, politeness takes time. In real life, most of us would choose politeness over brevity, even at work, and even in our most productive moments.

Another way to solve the problem of quantity is to use people's ability to elaborate abbreviated messages with information that they already have. Messages are often too much or too little for *someone*, but over time, people can learn that a short message stands for a larger response. As two people get to know each other, there are times when politeness can be abbreviated (e.g., "Hi" substitutes for "Hello, how are you to-day?" once people get acquainted). Familiarity can also bring opportunities to elaborate (e.g., "I've been meaning to tell you..." substitutes for a stifled "Fine"). A polite system will give information at a level of detail that matches the user's social expectations.

In the same vein, providing users with technical abbreviations (e.g., "Drive Error: Abort, Retry, Fail?") or pages and pages of detail violates the quantity rule. Much better are systems that allow users to set a level of sophistication that determines the amount of information that they would like. With a tracking system on the computer (i.e., a function that counts various occurrences), a computer could know how often a particular message has been delivered, for example, and adjust the quantity of information accordingly.

Relevance. What people (and media) say should clearly relate to the purpose of the conversation. A good example of this rule is the disabling of menu options, depending on context. An interface shouldn't say anything about things it can't do at the moment. Icons that represent possible actions could be highlighted, for example, and the icons for impossible actions dimmed or removed from the screen.

One aspect of relevance that is ignored in interfaces is response to user *goals*. The early days of television provide an excellent example of the consequences of this mistake. In early television, producers assumed that people watched the news to gather information. They thought that viewers were civic-minded, and consequently, the news was presented as seriously and efficiently as possible. However, research began to show what now seems obvious: People turn on the news for all kinds of reasons. These reasons include the desire to be entertained or merely to feel socially connected. The recognition that viewers had several different goals initiated several new concerns: the attractiveness of anchors, design of the news set, and enough "happy talk" to maintain interest.

The same thing is likely true for computers. Someone writing a letter, even on the most sophisticated word processing package, is likely to have multiple goals. One goal may be to complete a task; that is, write the letter. But it's hard to imagine writing a letter and not also doing some combination of the following: blowing off steam, clarifying feelings, impressing the boss, avoiding boredom, and so on. Why shouldn't computers modify interactions in relation to these goals? Interfaces that provide a *single* way of presenting information, without taking into account multiple goals of users, risk violating the rule of relevance. Anger and frustration could be the result.

Clarity. Contributions to an interaction should not be obscure. Designers often remove ambiguity so that a message can have only one meaning. This is desirable, but it comes at a price. To avoid ambiguity, highly technical language is often necessary, and much of that language is obscure. In an example close to home, one of us is ashamed to admit authorship of the following sentence: "The coercive, mimetic, and normative forces in the institutional environment homogenize the garbage-can decision processes." One might argue that several paragraphs would have been required to achieve the same precision with more commonplace words. But that's silly. There wasn't a single reader who wouldn't have gladly traded precision for simplicity.

The upshot of this rule is that it would be better to have a statement with even three meanings than to have one that is precise but unknowable. This is especially true if the ambiguity can be resolved in later exchanges. It would be worrisome if the user consistently resolved the ambiguity incorrectly, because the computer would then seem incompetent. User testing, however, can determine the most common way that ambiguity is understood; if most users resolve it incorrectly, it can certainly be rewritten. Furthermore, highly technical language, even if precise, can actually lead to *more* guesswork for users. Interactive media should not be obscure *or* ambiguous; but too often, interfaces have opted for the former.

A key point about Grice's maxims is that people will assume that violations have social meaning. If a speaker violates any of the rules, the listener will assume that the speaker is not paying attention, or is being sarcastic, or is being intentionally unpleasant. All of these conclusions lead to negative consequences for media, because people will ascribe meaning to failure, whether the entity that fails is a person or a machine.

It's Impolite to Reject

Media increasingly provide the ability to change how they look and work during an interaction. When you change something, however, you reject one option in favor of another. If the rejection is aimed at socially meaningless features, such as changing the color of the computer desktop, this is no problem. But when you change features that are more obviously social (e.g., a voice or a picture that represents a helper), the rejection is also more social. In the social world, rejection is significant; it is impolite.

Although it seems a bit weird, people can feel the same inhibitions when rejecting social representations on a screen as they would rejecting a real person. For example, imagine that you have been working with software that uses a character to help complete tasks on the computer. After a while, you become tired of the character, and you're aware that the software offers an option to change characters. Our research suggests that it is difficult to simply replace the old character with a new one. People don't want to be impolite by making the current character feel bad.

What to do? Use the tried and true solution that works in real life. A polite invitation for change might go like this: "It's been really fun working with you, but some people like to change characters on occasion. Would you like to do that?" There are three advantages of this statement, and the accompanying question: (1) The statement legitimates the change, (2) it makes the decision impersonal, thereby limiting the need for a polite response, and (3) it doesn't reveal the feelings of the character asking the question.

Rules of Etiquette

There are many more popular sources for politeness rules than the psychology literature we have discussed so far. We recommend them all highly. We have both laughed mightily thinking about a bunch of computers dutifully taking notes while listening to Dale Carnegie or reading Emily Post and Miss Manners. But humor aside, that is exactly our prescription. If mediated and real-life conversations are more on a par than previously imagined, then media should be judged by their *social* as well as *technical* sophistication. Consider the following simple rules, even though they seem more suited to a handbook of etiquette than to a Computer Science 101 course.

It's Polite to Say Hello and Good-bye

How do you enter or leave a social situation? In any face-to-face conversation, people don't turn around and leave. First, they indicate intent and then ask permission to leave, at least implicitly. The opportunity to break this rule in media is legendary. In a famous interface project, a character suddenly disappeared from the screen due to a bug in the program. Users became disturbed, the designers noted, because they felt that the character was angry and had left as a result. Users did not view the disappearance as a problem with the technology. Characters that leave the screen should always take leave by saying "good-bye" or at least making a sound or gesture. They shouldn't evaporate into the digital ether.

It's Polite to Look at People When Speaking

Humans, as well as many other animals, are sticklers for eye contact. Eyes are the number one place to look to size up a partner, understand his or her feelings, or predict what will come next. When people look at faces, half their time is spent watching eyes. When we can't see someone's eyes, we get worried, and this is likely why it is impolite not to show your face. The same is true for faces on a screen. Dan Rather and Mr. Rogers understand this well. They never turn their backs, and instead stare right into the camera. Their counterparts in computing, however, often do not make eye contact.

A media character should never turn its back without an announcement, especially during an interaction. For example, in a prototype for a children's multimedia product, a character turned away from the user whenever it wanted to "see" something on the screen. This seemed reasonable to the designers, who intended the character to appear to look *with* the user at something important. But it was also impolite. To allay the user's discomfort, the character could have said, "Let's see what else we can find" before turning. Admittedly, this is another action in a domain where the fewest lines of code carry the day, but here as always, politeness does have some cost. The gain is more important: The user didn't have to wonder what the character was doing.

It's Polite to Match Modality: Answer a Letter with a Letter

It is polite to respond to friends using the same method that they used to contact you. A letter gets a letter in return, a phone call gets another call, and so on. We suspect that this applies to human-computer interaction as well. It is the rule of "matched modality."

There is asymmetry when a user receives information in one medium but answers in another, but in computing there often is no way to circumvent this mismatch. For example, some computer products ask questions verbally but accept only text or mouse input. This can be uncomfortable because the computer actually forces an impolite response.

What to do? If an interface accepts only text input, perhaps it should produce only text output. If the user can respond with voice, then a voice-based interface might work better. In any case, the criterion for choosing an appropriate way to respond should not merely be the most sophisticated mode available; it should be the one that allows for politeness between user and machine.

Politeness and Product Testing: Eliminating Positive Bias

The politeness studies also apply to product testing. One implication is that the same computer should not present products and then ask for evaluations. People who give opinions to the same computer that just demonstrated a product will likely react more positively than they really feel. It would be better either to use a paper-and-pencil questionnaire or simply to have another computer ask the questions.

A second implication extends the results of the politeness studies to real people associated with a product during testing. If an interviewer helps a person use a media product, the user will want to be polite to the interviewer as well. There is a good solution, however. First, two products can be presented, and the interview can focus on the differences between them. Not only is this a good measurement idea, since people are great at comparing things, but when focusing on the comparison, respondents are not thinking about what the polite response should be. This should encourage truthfulness.

A final point about product testing is that we should be suspicious of verbal responses. Many of the most important reactions and responses of users are those that are not conscious, and hence not available for verbalization. The people in our experiments assure us that they are not being polite to computers—but our data say otherwise. Subjects often do not know how they really feel or how they really will behave in a given situation. If what people said they wanted was what they actually liked, all of network television might look like public broadcasting. This ignorance is not necessarily a human deficiency; it is simply a human fact.

Politeness across Cultures: Differences and Similarities

Most guides to good manners caution readers about cross-cultural differences in politeness, and international consultants earn a good living offering insurance against major *faux pas*. Cultural differences are certainly no secret to the companies that have a multinational business. They know that language translation is not the whole story. People also have to negotiate interpersonal space, wait the appropriate amount of time before talking, address each person in a proper manner—and the rules vary from country to country and from culture to culture. It is interesting, therefore, that the translation of language is often the *only* consideration for internationalizing media products. Mistakes in manners are a frequent result.

This point, while important, is not novel. What is not well understood, however, is how much importance we should attach to cultural differences. We think they are a bit overrated (which *doesn't* mean we think they are irrelevant). The differences are overrated mostly because they focus attention away from what is common to all human beings: *Everyone* is polite. This certainly does not mean that the specific behaviors that constitute politeness are exactly the same in every culture; they are not. But it does mean that everyone recognizes politeness, everyone tries to obey politeness rules, and everyone feels bad when they are broken. In a rush to celebrate cultural differences, we are often too quick to concentrate exclusively on those differences.

As children are taught by adults, being polite costs very little, and the benefits are enormous. Should we ask less of media and their makers?

3

Interpersonal Distance

When people interact, space matters. Spatial arrangements determine what people say, how they say it, and even whether it's necessary to say anything at all. The space between two people can determine the duration of an interaction and its emotional tenor. Everyone uses distance to tell other people what he or she thinks about them and what he or she thinks about the current situation. Not only is this true in all cultures, it's true for most species.

There are rules for interpersonal space. The parameters of these rules can vary across cultures (e.g., close proximity in conversation is more acceptable in Latin America than in the United States), but everyone knows what distance means. A polite response delivered at close range means more than the same from afar. In fact, it is hard to think of any social behavior that doesn't change in meaning, at least a bit, when the distance between people changes.

Social scientists have shown that violations of distance rules can cause all kinds of problems. This is especially true when strangers are the culprits. Unwanted advances induce anxiety, negative characterizations of the invader, and even hostility. If you don't like someone at a distance, it only gets worse up close. On the positive side, incursions into the personal space of another, when invited or desirable, can invoke everything from curiosity to the most extreme excitement that people can experience.

Interpersonal distance dictates the *intensity* of responses. Standing close turns up the volume knob and heightens concerns about personal pleasure and pain. Close is arousing. When arousal increases, people are more focused on the cause of the excitement, they are more attentive, and they remember more. There are also physiological preparations for possible action. None of these responses, however, are triggered by conscious control. Rather, people are built to attend automatically to things that arouse.

When people *at*tend to a person who is close, they focus on what the person *in*tends. The quickest way to make that judgment is to look at the face. By observing the eyes, mouth, and eyebrows of another person, people can assess the person's plans. When arousal is high, as when a person is physically close, people accent the processing of facial features. As a result, responses to strangers when they first approach often depend more on whether their faces appear threatening or friendly than on the words they speak.

What happens when people encounter mediated representations rather than real people? Does interpersonal distance still matter? Admittedly, this sounds far-fetched. We can all safely say that real people don't reside inside of media or on a screen, so it shouldn't matter whether *images* of people make them appear close or far away. If a pictured person appears too close, it is obviously because of the position of the camera, the size of the screen, or the position of the viewer. None of the pictorial cues that represent distance are cause for any action on our part. After all, it's only a picture.

Representing Interpersonal Distance in Pictures

Our prediction was that the media equation extends to expressions of manners even more primitive than politeness—it extends to the apparent physical distance between viewers and the screen. If people recognize polite and impolite computers, then the same automatic responses could cause people to bestow the same equivalence to pictures. Changes in the spatial arrangements between people and the pictures they view could be as social as the communication of manners through text and voices.

Replacing "a person" with "a *picture* of a person," we made the following predictions:

Rule 1: When viewers see a picture of a person who appears close rather than far, their evaluations of the person in the picture will be more intense.

Rule 2: Viewers will pay more attention to pictures of people who appear close rather than far.

Rule 3: Pictures of people who appear close will be remembered better than will pictures of people who appear far away.

Invading Personal Space with Pictures

To test the predictions, we conducted an experiment that resembled psychological studies done with real people and real spaces. In those studies, researchers vary the actual physical distance between subjects when they interact. This can be accomplished by having someone on the research team stand either close to or far from the participants, and then having someone else ask participants to describe their feelings about the interaction.

This is a tough simulation with pictures. Media can't actually walk up to someone and start talking. There are several ways, however, that a mediated person can *appear* to be close or far. The key to distance cues in pictures is visual field or the extent to which any image fills the space the eyes are capable of seeing. When something takes up a large portion of the visual field, one of two things must be true: The object must be close or the object must be large. Since all faces are approximately the same size, people will conclude that faces that take up a large portion of vision must be close.

A picture can take up space in the visual field in three ways. Viewing distance is the simplest. People on a screen could be perceived as near or far (i.e., fill more or less of the visual field) because of the physical space between the viewer and the screen. Just as one person can stand near or far from another, a person can view a screen image from near or far.

In the case of television, viewing distance is determined by room architecture (distance constrained by walls) or personal preference (where you place your favorite chair). In the case of computers, the variance in viewing distance is more limited because most computing is done within arm's length.

A second way to vary perceived distance is the size of the screen that shows a picture. The same images on a large screen may appear closer than those on a small screen because the latter takes less space in the visual field. Modern media permit the exact same picture to appear on everything from a hand-held portable screen 2 inches high, to a wall-sized home theater with a picture from floor to ceiling, to an IMAX screen 40 feet tall. People can't easily correct for the size of a screen, because throughout evolution, small and large things were just that. Size was absolute. Only recently have humans developed ways to make big and little pictures that represent things substantially different from their real-life size.

A third way to vary perceived distance is the type of camera shot used to compose a picture. Faces appear closer when a camera frames a face so that the entire height of the screen includes *just* the face, as opposed to the entire body. Even when the distance to the screen and the size of the screen are the same, the camera has closed the distance to the subject in the picture. Close shots are compelling because more attention is focused on the eyes, mouth, and eyebrows—the most significant features in an interpersonal encounter.

Meeting People in Pictures Who Appear Near and Far

The goal of our media experiment was to allow people to experience each of the three methods for making people on a screen seem near or far. If pictures are like natural experience, then viewers should respond differently to faces on a screen depending on how close the people in the pictures seem. Faces that seem near should cause more intense evaluations, they should receive more attention, and they should be better remembered. These responses should be true even though the faces are nothing more than fluorescent light rendered on a piece of glass.

We invited thirty-two men and women to participate in the experiment. One at a time, each person was asked to watch several faces in several combinations of screen size, shot size, and viewing distance. The distances and sizes in the experiment were selected to resemble, as much as possible, variations in pictures that people experience in the real world. The close viewing distance was 4 feet from the screen; the far distance, 10 feet. The large screen size was 41 inches; the small, 15. The close-up shot framed people from chin to top of head; the long shot showed people from head to toe.

Participants had a chance to see pictures in all combinations of the three parameters. To make sure everyone got a chance to experience each combination fully, we showed five faces in each of the eight combinations of distance, size, and shot-type. The people who appeared in the pictures were from 20 to 40 years old; half of them were men and half were women; and they were shown on the screen for 10 seconds as they talked about their favorite restaurant or their last vacation.

Measuring Responses to People in Pictures

We measured evaluation of the pictures as well as attention and memory. Evaluation was the most straightforward to measure. We merely asked participants to rate the people in the pictures using adjectives that described liking and personality. The questions began with "Does this person seem …". Some of the items were *calm/anxious, pleasant/unpleasant, competitive/cooperative*, and *violent/gentle*.

The questionnaire wasn't appropriate for studying attention and memory, however. For these outcomes, we borrowed techniques from the researchers who study responses to real people.

Attention

There is not much to observe in humans that indicates the intensity of attention. Unlike rabbits, people don't perk up their ears when engaged. Asking people how much attention they gave to a message, especially when the question comes some time after the attention is given, doesn't work well at all. Self-reports about mental effort are tough even if people are willing to help. It's possible to know where people are looking by tracking their eyes, but beyond this assessment of selective attention, it is quite difficult to know how much *effort* they invest after the selection.

Psychologists have developed techniques for measuring attention that help overcome these problems, but the techniques are not obvious. One method is called the secondary reaction-time task. This measure assesses mental engagement without requiring people to talk about their behavior after the fact. To study mediated messages, we stole this method lock, stock, and barrel from psychology. Here's how it works.

When the mind is engaged in a primary task, it has trouble adding other tasks without compromising performance on the original one. For example, it's difficult to continue walking quickly after a friend poses a hard question, and sometimes, it's even hard to continue walking at all. We slow down or stop the primary task (walking) to perform the secondary task (answering the question). Conversely, when people are more intent on the primary task, it takes longer to address the secondary task. Compromises in performance are especially true when any one of these tasks becomes demanding. People can allocate their mental effort in many different ways, but they can't increase their total energy beyond some finite point. Mental capacity is *limited*.

The secondary-task method takes advantage of this limitation. Participants are invited into the lab, and they're asked to watch something on a screen. They are asked to pay close attention to the screen because they will be questioned about what they see after they view. This ensures that watching television is the primary task. We then tell participants to listen for audio tones during the presentation, and this becomes the secondary task. When viewers are highly engaged in the primary task (watching the screen), they have less capacity left over to process the audio tones (the secondary task).

Participants are told to press a button on a joystick as quickly as possible when they hear one of the tones. The tones occur at random points in the television program, about one every 15 seconds. A computer then records the time, in milliseconds, that it takes to respond to the tone. The resulting data are reaction times to the secondary task, hence the name of the measure. When participants are paying attention to the video (the primary task), their reaction times to the tones are slower because they have less mental effort left over to process the tones. When reaction-time scores are slow, we conclude that attention to the screen was high.

This measure is not a standard one in research about media. One reason is that it's a bit of a nuisance. You have to hook up a reaction-time device to a computer. Also, there are some tricky statistical issues which complicate the analysis of data. Consequently, it's important to know the rationale for the extra effort.

The biggest advantage of the secondary-task method is that attention is measured with a system that does not require introspection. Viewers do not have to be *aware* that they are pressing the button slower or faster—and in fact, they are not aware. People don't think that their speed pressing the button is related to their attention to the screen. Even experienced researchers have little sense of when their own response times change, and they find it difficult to "beat" the system even though they know how it works. When something interesting is on the screen, reaction times reliably get slower—and this rule seems to apply to everyone.

Memory

Memory is a huge concept in psychology, and it has many definitions and measures. One of the most important distinctions in memory is the difference between recall and recognition. Recall refers to the ability to access information in our minds without help. When information is recalled, it is dredged up merely through thought. We recall the name of a friend (without any help); we recall the route to her house (without looking at a map); and we recall what she said last night (without any reminders).

Recognition memory is different. It is the ability to match something that a person sees, hears, or reads with a previous experience. Even if you can't recall a name, you'll *recognize* it when you hear it. You can't recall the directions to a house, but you'll recognize the street when you pass it. You can't recall what someone said, but if you hear a snippet, you can construct the rest of the conversation.

In this experiment, we focused solely on recognition memory. (Recall is too difficult to study for facial memory because there is no good way for a viewer to demonstrate recall short of a long written description or by drawing a picture.) After participants had finished viewing the faces, we measured recognition memory with a standard test. We quickly flashed pictures of several faces on the screen, and asked participants whether they had seen each face during the experiment. Of the thirty-two faces in the memory test, half of the faces had been seen earlier; the other half were new pictures of faces that viewers had never seen before. The score for each participant's recognition memory was the number of faces that he or she could identify accurately.

A Viewer's Personal Space Can Be Invaded

The first social rule that we thought participants would apply to pictures was that evaluations of the people in the pictures would be more intense when the faces seemed close. That is indeed what happened. The close faces (especially those framed with a close shot), were evaluated more intensely than the faces that seemed farther away. For both positive and negative evaluations, scores were more extreme for close images than for distant images.

Attention and memory were also enhanced when pictures seemed close. Participants paid more attention (had slower reaction times) to the close faces than the far ones. This was especially true for faces on the larger screen and for faces framed with a close shot. On average, viewers took about 10 percent longer to respond to the tones when the pictures were close, which is a significant difference with reaction times. Just as in human-human interaction, participants focused more attention on faces that seemed close.

Recognition memory was also better for the close faces, especially those that were viewed from a close distance and faces framed with a close shot. On average, participants accurately identified 12 percent more of the faces that seemed close.

Other Explanations

The results of this experiment show that mediated manners extend well beyond the manners that people are taught. People have a primitive or innate interest in the physical arrangements that define an interaction, and they respond automatically, even to pictures.

The responses do seem weird, however. These are, after all, only pictures. Is there any room for skepticism? It may seem so, but there are several points that should lessen doubts about these results.

First, the experimental design used in the study ensures that all participants have exactly the same experience when they come to the lab. The only difference in the presentations related exactly to what we were studying—the apparent distance between viewer and picture. We can also safely say that no one in the experiment guessed what the study was about and then changed his or her responses to please the experimenters. Even if people could guess, it would have been difficult for them to control their reaction times precisely.

Could media experts have done better or worse than media novices? Likely not. When it comes to viewing video, virtually everyone is an expert. All of the participants in the study had ample experience with television and film, and everyone knew that all of the faces shown on the screen were, in real life, approximately the same size. Social responses don't depend on instruction, nor can they be extinguished with experience.

One critique of studies like this one is that the results might be related to the *particular* content presented. For example, it is likely that some of the faces shown in the research might have been more arousing or memorable than others, regardless of how close they appeared in the experiment. This would be similar to liking a movie with one actor, but hating it if a different actor were substituted.

How can we be sure that the characteristics of particular faces didn't account for the differences in the present study? We presented a lot of *different* faces to each participant in the study, and we mixed and matched faces with viewing distance, screen size, and shot type. In this study, it meant that we collected a total of forty different faces, and we randomly picked five different faces to show each person in each of the different conditions. Essentially, we created a unique video production for each participant. This is a burden, but it pays off. The results of the experiment are not attributable to the particular faces that were shown.

The Media Equation Extends to Physical Space

What does all this mean for theories about media? Several things. Once again, human responses to media are social even though media supposedly offer only symbolic representations of people in the real world. The creation of space, even if accomplished with illusory tricks possible only with modern technology, is consequential in media as well as in real life. There is no "discount" for pictures.

This evidence also shows that social responses to media are not limited to *feelings* about the technologies themselves. When people were polite to computers, those responses, while quite social, were particular *attitudes* toward the machine. Changes in the perception of physical distance, however, determine very different psychological responses—from the mental energy required to pay attention to the ability to remember what had been seen. Social responses to media are part of a complex web of influence that extends from attitudes and evaluations to attention and memory.

This study also suggests that three different visual tricks, most often treated *separately* by professionals, are really quite similar. Viewing distance is controlled by the viewer (or constrained by the viewer's environment). Screen size is a characteristic of the appliance (and is determined when it is purchased). And shot type is controlled by the director (at least until we have TVs that allow us to zoom in on objects of interest). From the point of view of industry, then, the three distance cues are radically different, and it would be surprising to find these three techniques grouped together in any discussion of media. But from a psychological perspective, as demonstrated in the present study, the three cues *should* be grouped, because they all elicit similar responses from viewers.

Implications of Distance Cues for Making and Evaluating Media

If the distance cues in pictures make us think that people are actually close or far, how should people think differently about how media are evaluated and created? The most important implication is that people presented in media are perceived as actually present. This perception is not only a primitive reaction; it is influential across a broad range of psychological life. Viewers evaluate faces on a screen, and they prepare to respond to the faces, in the same ways that they would for actual people. This is true even though the responses may seem improbable to the people doing the responding.

Implications for applying this part of the media equation to several important media issues are discussed in the next paragraphs.

Meeting People through Pictures versus Words

Pictures of faces, because they are processed as if they were people in actual interpersonal encounters, may be more different from words than previously imagined. It may be impossible for a person to appear in a picture without the baggage of primitive social cues, and with the good chance that those cues will influence how viewers respond to the pictures. People are not able to ignore pictorial social cues any more than they can ignore the same cues in real life. It's no wonder that it is difficult to concentrate only on what is said.

Consider this example of interpersonal distance at work on television. In a recent presidential debate, one of the candidates answered a question by saying that he would pledge to try and meet the needs of voters by emphasizing political issues, not images. The other candidate responded that he would also make the same pledge, and he added a personal comment: He was sick of having to start every day by figuring out how to defend himself.

Imagine reading a transcript of the exchange. It's possible to *read* spoken comments free of any influence from the physical situation in which the comments were generated (e.g., who stood where and how close they were to each other and to the audience). A video of the same interaction, however, adds a thousand words. The visuals contain a lot of information about the *social* arrangements between the speakers, and between the speakers and those watching at home.

The exchange in the debate started with relatively long shots of both candidates, from their waists to the top of their heads. The second speaker, however, didn't stand still when he talked. When he gave his personal comment, he moved toward the camera. Essentially, he moved directly toward every single person watching him on television. This led to a more tightly framed shot of the candidate for the remainder of his time on camera. The added sense of presence almost demanded that the viewer form some opinion about the intrusion, and since the candidate was smiling and speaking softly at the time, we can assume that many of the opinions were positive.

If we apply to the video of the debate the experimental results regarding attention and memory, we could also assume that people paid more attention to the speaker who advanced toward the audience (or at least more attention to his physical presence, if not to his words). We can also assume that viewers would better remember his picture. In contrast, the speaker who remained still, even though his picture certainly contained more information than could be inferred from reading the words he spoke, was visually much less present.

A minor point concerns persuasive strategies in a televised debate: To engage an audience, occasionally move toward it. Moving closer will work even if the audience is in front of a computer or TV screen. To stand still is to relinquish audience attention to other parts of the stage.

A more important implication is that pictures, especially pictures of people, add a lot to linguistic expression. Pictures focus attention on primitive social cues, potentially to the detriment of other information.

Pictures may help with memory, but at the expense of taking away time for people to decide what things mean. It's difficult to think about how a candidate stands on an issue if you have to simultaneously monitor his physical presence in your personal space. The effort needed to process his presence and his comments comes from a single and limited reservoir of mental energy.

Pictures, because they look like the things they represent, require less mental effort to translate between referent and reality. Pictures give information that is more familiar and easy to process, and this may promote more passive thinking. It is much easier for people to determine if they like a speaker based on how close the speaker stands than it is to actually listen to what the person has to say. Should it be a surprise, then, that any citizen, regardless of political sophistication, feels quite comfortable judging the personal qualities of a candidate once he or she has seen the candidate's picture?

The same process likely applies beyond politics. People feel quite comfortable thinking about media personalities as friends, confidants, and villains as well as doctors, detectives, lawyers, or other characters they portray. The basis for all of these relationships may be the primitive and real experience of another person's presence, even though it is pictorial. We can laugh at ourselves for the apparent gullibility, but our brains respond otherwise. Consider an extreme case: Would you feel comfortable naked in front of an anchor on the evening news? If not, why not?

Which Picture of Which Face?

Imagine that the experiment with faces and distance had been done with a single picture of one person. And imagine we found the same results. Could the study be easily criticized? The answer is yes. Our research, and most other studies that use pictures of people (or just about anything else), find *different* results for different pictures. There may be an overall trend, but the results for any one picture could easily be different from the rest.

This means that *casting* is critical. There are considerable differences

49

between faces, differences that are determined by a hundred important qualities besides the distance of the face from a viewer (e.g., attractiveness, facial expressions, age, gender). If you produce media, however, you can present only one face at a time. Therefore, choose faces carefully.

Casting can obviously affect the success of a film or television show. Its influence is less obvious, however, for new media. When characters are used in computer interfaces (for example, as agents who help with the tasks of computing), the most likely first question is whether the character makes the experience better than the same experience with no character at all. This may not be the best question, however. Almost always, there will be *some* characters that are better than no character, and *some* characters that are worse. The better question is *which* character is best. The answer can come only from a screen test, no less appropriate for multimedia and computing than for film or television.

Scaling Physical Space

Directors in film and television usually have a good idea about how people and objects will be displayed to their audiences. That's useful, because media can be designed, even if unconsciously, to conform to the interpersonal arrangements of a given display. Movies are on big screens, television sets are much smaller, and there are unofficial rules about how to shoot and frame people within each medium. The biggest problem so far has been the need to create material that can be shown on a small television *and* on a large screen in a theater.

The problem of scalability is increasing. Moreover, production for newer technologies requires even greater thought about display formats, because size and shape can vary tremendously. Today, the same video data can be displayed in a two-inch window on a computer monitor or on the very large screen of a home theater. For the smaller picture, a full head shot might create a sense of intimacy. For the home theater, the camera might be better placed at a distance, with the people in the pictures framed head-to-toe. As one producer of IMAX films commented, Mick Jagger's face, 20 feet high, is frightening: Best to use a long shot when the screen is huge.

One solution to the problem of multiple displays might be to allow viewers the chance to frame their own shots. Viewers could change where they stand or sit relative to the people in the picture by manipulating the visual signals. If viewers wanted to get closer, they could zoom in on the picture or change the focal length of the lens that rendered it. If people wanted to withdraw, they could make a person appear smaller by reversing the process. This flexibility could enhance the feeling of lifelike interaction.

Face Size across Media

The power of approaching and withdrawing is not lost on film and television directors; they use it with great skill. Over the last thirty years, they have increasingly closed in on faces when the display of emotions is critical. When an interviewer has a con man on the ropes, for example, or when emotion is at its height, faces are framed to fill the screen.

Almost since its introduction, television has been steadily moving in on the personalities who deliver news. Close is intimate, intimate is engaging, and engaging means more viewers. An effective method in all of these examples is to exaggerate closeness by *changing* the distance between viewer and viewed—start with a long shot, and then slowly move closer.

People assume that a picture of a face, regardless of its size, is merely a symbol that stands for someone not actually present. But it is more. The size of a face can broadly influence psychological responses—from the mental energy required to attend, to the ability to remember what was seen, to thoughtful judgments of character.

4

Flattery

A graduate student recently heard the two of us present our work, and afterward he delivered the following comment to the one of us still in the lecture hall: "*Your* presentation was absolutely superb! *You* really changed the way I think about research!" The one who heard the praise felt great. Unable to contain his pride, he revealed the compliment in the office the next day. The other responded, "Don't feel so special; he said the same thing to me in the hallway."

We laughed at our gullibility. This guy was simply a flatterer who praised everyone. But interestingly, we both *still* felt better about our presentations than we would have without him. And although one might think that academics are unique in their naivete, everyone is a sucker for praise, whether it's deserved or not. Flattery, it turns out, will get you everywhere. Even though we can point a critical finger at those who ingratiate, research shows that people like working with flatterers, and people generally think better of them than they do those people who make no evaluation at all.

Even if insincere praise is better than none at all, people assure themselves that they truly value the real thing and that they can tell the difference. But can they? Studies have shown that the effects of flattery look very much like—if not identical to—those of sincere praise. Everyone likes interacting with and thinks as well of people who praise sincerely as those who flatter. Humans accept praise and they enjoy it, wherever and whenever they can get it. Sincerity, if it is important at all, is *assumed* when the news is good.

What about when the news is bad? The opposite story is true. There is a big difference between warranted criticism and calumny, and people are eager to make the distinction. If the flattering graduate student had been critical instead of positive, we would have been quick to ponder the merits of the remark. If the criticism was *un*deserved, we would likely dismiss it; why should we listen to someone who makes baseless remarks? But if validity could be established, then we'd have to feel bad.

The summary is that an important asymmetry exists between praise and criticism. If the news is good, we have no motivation to distinguish the sincere from the insincere; it feels good either way. If the news is bad, however, we look for ways to dismiss it. If the bad news is unwarranted, it is happily ignored.

Why might people respond differently to praise than to criticism? One reason is that people have a self-serving bias. People like to see themselves in the best possible light. When a person hears praise, it's an opportunity to serve him or herself. The person can easily rationalize his or her own uniqueness by saying, "Sure, they say that to everyone, but I bet they really *did* see something special in me." People don't have much of a motive to examine the validity of the remark. On the other hand, negative information will be scrutinized for flaws because negative information challenges the desire for positive self-evaluation. Insincerity gives people an opportunity to dismiss.

Praise, Criticism, and Computers

When a computer is substituted for a human, the following social rules about praise and criticism should apply.

Rule 1: People will believe that they did better on a task when they are flattered by a computer than when the computer doesn't give any evaluation.

Rule 2: People will like the computer more and believe it did a better job when they are flattered by the computer than when the computer says nothing about their work.

Rule 3: Whether praise is warranted or not will have no effect on what people think about the praising computer.

Rule 4: People will believe that they did a better job when the computer criticizes them without basis than when the criticism is warranted.

Rule 5: People will like the computer more and think the computer is better when it praises them than when it criticizes them.

If some of these rules sound foolish when applied to people, they sound more so when applied to computers. In human-human interaction, we can imagine people rationalizing acceptance of praise. But computers can ignore everything, so a user who is told a computer's evaluation is unwarranted should not be moved by the computer's comments.

The media equation, however, suggests something different. If a computer gives an evaluation, it must be a social actor, and if it is social, then all the familiar rules apply. We decided to test whether the equation applied to flattery and calumny.

Testing Flattery on Computers

The participants in this test played a computer game similar to "Twenty Questions." There's nothing magical about this game compared to others, but it did provide a familiar and casual context for people to interact with a computer. Most important, it allowed each participant in the study to receive comments that could be praised or criticized, and with justification or not.

To start the game, a computer asked the participant to think of an animal. The computer would then ask a series of yes or no questions to which the subject would reply by typing in "yes" or "no." Eventually, the computer would try to identify the animal.

If the computer guessed the animal (which happened rarely), then the subject would start over and think of a new animal. When the computer failed to guess the animal (which we caused to happen most of the time), participants were asked to type a better question into the computer. Participants were told that their suggestions would then be used by the computer to ask better questions in the future. The main purpose for soliciting the questions was to allow each person to perform a task that could later be evaluated as helpful or not.

Sixty participants played the game, one at a time. Here is an example of a typical game. The person first thought of an animal, in this case, a zebra.

Computer: "Does the animal have four legs?"
Person (via a keyboard and mouse): "Yes"
Computer: "Is the animal a reptile?"
Person: "No"
Computer: "Is it an elephant?"
Person: "No"
Computer: "This computer cannot guess what the animal is. Please provide a question that would help this computer distinguish this animal from the other animals in the database."
Person: "Does the animal have stripes?"

At this point, each person was placed into one of three groups. For one group, the computer went immediately on to the next game after each person had typed in a question. No feedback, just another game.

Participants in the other two groups got feedback, one group positive and the other negative. Participants in the group that was praised were complimented for their questions. For example, these participants might read: "Your question makes an interesting and useful distinction. Great job!" The group that was criticized got the opposite, for example, "The addition you made complicates the game unnecessarily. That was a bad decision." Each person in the three groups played the game twelve times, so by the end of the session, everyone was clear about the direction of the computer's comments.

There was one more important part of the experiment. We had to make sure that for some participants, the responses were perceived as warranted, and for others, that the responses were undeserved. We did this by telling participants *how* the computer decided whether the suggestions were good ones or not.

Half of the participants were told that the feedback they got was warranted. They were told that their questions would be evaluated using algorithms derived from the responses of hundreds of people who had played the Animal Game since it was created in 1991. If the computer said a question was good or bad, there was a reason: It was better or worse than others in the database.

The other half of the participants were told not to believe a word the computer said. We told them that the computerized evaluation system had not yet been developed. Consequently, they would receive random comments that had absolutely nothing to do with their actual performance. These comments were simply examples of comments that would be used when the system was completed.

After playing the games, everyone completed a paper-and-pencil questionnaire. There were thirty questions that measured one of three basic evaluations: how well each person thought he or she did on the game, how much each person liked the computer, and how well each person thought that the computer did playing the game.

Responses to Mediated Praise and Criticism

The results showed that people loved to be flattered, and that they were impressed by the flattery—even though the flatterer was a piece of communication hardware producing random responses. Participants who were flattered thought they did significantly better at picking questions than did those who received no evaluation. The evaluation, even though it was baseless, was not dismissed. In fact, quite the opposite. Praise from a computer worked better than no evaluation, regardless of the apparent *in*sincerity of the comments.

Flattery also paid off for the computer. Participants whom the computer had flattered said they liked the computer more than did participants who received no evaluation at all. The flattered participants thought that the computer played the game better as well. This means that the effects of flattery go beyond the recipient; they bounce back to the flatterer. Finally, there were clearly no differences on any of the evaluation questions based on whether the computer's comments were warranted or not.

How do we know that subjects didn't just forget that the flattery really was baseless? When we asked participants about the experiment after they completed the evaluation, everyone remembered whether the praise they received was random or not. Participants were pushovers for praise, even when it was unambiguously irrelevant.

If computers are social actors, then the opposite findings should be true for criticism. As expected, participants dismissed criticism that was undeserved. When criticism was unwarranted, participants thought that they did better and they thought that the computer did better than when the criticism was warranted. When participants were genuinely criticized, they believed that their performance was not as good.

A characteristic of flattery is that it's better to be dishonest than to say nothing. You can make people feel good, even if you don't mean what you say. For criticism, however, it's even better to be dishonest than honest: Participants thought the computer's performance was poorer when criticism was sincere compared to times when the criticism was unwarranted.

Not surprisingly, given these results, participants liked the computer more when it praised than when it criticized. Praise is always positive; criticism is at best ignored. A praising computer, sincere or not, is perceived as better and more likable than one that criticizes.

Keep in mind some important features of the experiment. All of the participants in the study performed identical tasks, and they all received identical praise or criticism. No one guessed that the experiment was about praise, criticism, or the justification for either; everyone thought it was just a game. Everyone was an experienced computer user who had no difficulty whatsoever understanding that computers can produce random statements. In fact, many of the participants could have written the program to generate them.

Thinking about Sincere and Insincere Evaluations by Media

One important idea supported by this study is that praise and criticism are powerful. Evaluations affect people's feelings about their performance, the evaluator, and the interaction, and this is true whether the evaluations are justified or not.

A second important idea is the *asymmetry* between praise and criticism. In the case of criticism, people operate logically. They take legitimate comments much more seriously than unwarranted ones. In the case of praise, though, there is no difference between the reactions to warranted praise and flattery.

These findings, all consistent with the psychological literature about the same concepts in human-human interaction, lend confidence to the media equation: People automatically use social rules from real life to guide interactions with media.

Designing Media that Flatter

What do these results mean for those who design media? The rules can all be summarized in a simple adage: "You catch more flies with honey than with vinegar." Computers and other media should praise people frequently, and they could do so even when there may be little basis for the evaluation. People will enjoy it and believe it anyway. Conversely, computers and other media should criticize infrequently, and if criticism ever is warranted, the critique should be gentle.

This advice could be easily panned as condescension. It sounds a bit simple and smug for something as sophisticated as a computer to bother to say something nice. If people need praise, it could be argued, they shouldn't be using sophisticated technology. We think this reaction is wrong, however. Experts as well as novices respond socially to media, so the feelings associated with praise and criticism do not evaporate with more and better instruction in technology. Experts as well as novices are humans, and they love to be flattered, regardless of the source.

The flip side of this criticism is a charge of immorality. Since computers can't *really* care about user's feelings, why should they behave in a way that *seems* as if they do? Our answer is that politeness and manners aren't always about sincerity; they're about making people feel comfortable. If insincerity is good enough for colleagues, teachers, friends, family, and especially children, why isn't it good enough for *mediated* versions of the same? We all feel fine telling children that they shouldn't criticize others, and we feel fine praising them often, sometimes even when it's undeserved. Making people feel good is a virtue, and media shouldn't be excluded.

The opportunities to apply the simple rules of praise and criticism are numerous, much more so than it seems given the apparent distance between the worlds of social behavior and high tech. Many of the rules are already staples in traditional media, especially rules about flattery. Performers end shows with praise ("You've been a wonderful audience"), video exercise coaches keep people engaged with constant commentary ("You're doing great"), and of course, flattery works well with children. Barney the Dinosaur and Mr. Rogers, stars of popular children's shows, both turn to the camera and tell each child in the audience, "You are special."

These comments work, though admittedly they are often fodder for stand-up comics. We can all thoughtfully recognize the potential for insincerity, but we all love to be praised by media nonetheless—and that is *automatic*. So far, however, these ideas have not made many inroads in the world of new media. Here are some provocative ways to include flattery in advanced technologies, presented with unabashed enthusiasm.

The Ideal Spell-Checker

It is rare for a computer program to praise someone, even though there are plenty of opportunities. Consider spell-checkers. The typical spell-checker highlights all the words that are spelled wrong, and even those that *might* be wrong. The result? There is no praise, and a great deal of (frequently unwarranted) criticism. If you happen to use a word that is not in the dictionary, the computer says it is misspelled even if it's really correct. When the checker is done, it simply says, "The spell-check is completed."

Now consider a spell-checker that substitutes sugar for vinegar. At the end of the check you read, "Your spelling was significantly above average. You should be commended for your work." Intermittently during the check, it also says, "You spelled this difficult word correctly. Congratulations." At the end of the spell-check, you read: "It's unusual for people to spell the following words correctly," followed by a list of words. Even if the words were not particularly difficult, such unwarranted praise will often have a positive effect, especially if users were not confident of their spelling.

Some people will read this idea and immediately cringe in the name of efficiency. "Now I don't just have to write the memo, I've also got to listen to gratuitous remarks that interrupt my work." Remember, however, that a significant part of every day is taken up with similar protocol. Much of our interpersonal communication merely lets other people know how we are doing or that we like being where we are. These comments have little to do with the business of the day, strictly defined. But they are not merely a waste of time or unnecessary customs. People like to know that everything is all right. They want to know that the people they are with are not angry or threatened, and they want to be understood and liked.

New Media Can Flatter at Every Opportunity

No doubt, praise can be overdone, but that threshold has yet to be reached in new interactive technologies. Praise should be more frequent, and it can be leveraged even when it's not justified.

Here are some other examples. If on-line users find a Web site that isn't known to most users, they could be congratulated for finding interesting and undiscovered information. Callers who negotiate a complicated messaging system could be praised for their help in efficiently routing information to the proper sources. And after you've successfully ordered a movie on your new interactive cable system, you could be praised for your aesthetic taste, as well as your interface talents. Happiness and liking of the software and content would be the result in all of these cases.

Changing Criticism to Praise

Unfortunately, many opportunities to praise in media are not only missed, they are often replaced with something worse—criticism. There is little payoff, however. Criticism should be given out sparingly. We realize that the application of this comment is often obvious, and fortunately, there aren't that many cases where debasement or calumny is a media goal.

When criticism seems warranted, however, there is often an opportunity to turn criticism into an offer of help. For example, user education, a seemingly positive goal, is often presented more as criticism than help. If the computer says, "Here's an easier way to do your work," this is an implicit criticism. A better comment might be, "You have found a good way of doing this task. Here is another way to do it that some people prefer." Note that the same content is transmitted, but in the latter case, the computer has changed criticism to praise, and likely with positive effect. Even if people think that everyone gets the same comment, they will *still* feel better about the interaction.

Notification about errors could be handled similarly. In traditional computer systems, many of the messages are notices that the user has made a mistake. When everything is working, the computer simply performs the task and says nothing. When something is wrong, however, the computer usually blames the user. In stark contrast, the people we most enjoy working with tend to mix praise with criticism, recognizing that the more criticism, the more important it is to offer praise. Media should produce positive comments to balance the stream of inevitable bad news.

Experts Also Like Praise

The psychology literature says that flattery will work best with people who are less confident about their performance. This means that it's probably good to flatter novices quite broadly. They will appreciate the encouragement. Experts, on the other hand, should be complimented more subtly by picking out more intricate material and by noticing detail. This will discourage experts from interpreting praise as deceit.

People should not make the mistake, however, of underpraising or overcriticizing experts, especially computer experts. The reason is that experts, just like novices, are humans first and a particular category of humans second. *All* people—experts and novices, young and old, women and men—love to be praised and hate to be criticized. And this is true regardless of whether the evaluation comes from a person or a machine.

5

Judging Others and Ourselves

Writing a book with a friend is more than an intellectual task. It is also decidedly social. You not only have to form and evaluate your own ideas, you've got to communicate them to another person, and deal with his ideas as well, good ones and bad ones alike. There are an impressive number of opportunities to impress, insult, enthuse, and reject, and we now have a better appreciation for why some people write alone. Since we are studying something that we do every day, we've had some good laughs categorizing our own strategies for the conversations and debates that have resulted in these pages.

One strategy we use is to praise each other. What would you think if you overheard this praise? The psychology experiments about this are clear: You'd think that the person being praised was doing good work, and you'd think that the person praising was nice.

People think better of those who are praised just because something good was said. Humans are powerfully biased to accept information as true, even if we know the source of the information has little expertise. One of us could have been a plumber, a pilot, or a preacher and the praise of research skills would have been nearly as effective as it would if the source was Dr. Science himself.

The opposite strategy, criticism, is equally simple, but tougher to deliver and hear. There are times in our discussions when criticism comes out. When it does, anyone listening would likely think the person who is criticized and the work they had done just got worse. And as with praise, it doesn't matter if the critic had a license or not; criticism is viewed as true, at least until there is time to think otherwise. If you heard the criticism, you'd think that the person criticized was inferior. Also, according to the psychological research, you'd think the critic wasn't very nice, even if you thought he or she was accurate.

Imagine you were listening to one of our debates, and one of us delivered a particularly critical barrage. We've already noted that the critic wouldn't be well liked, but there would be one other response that is more positive. You would perceive the source of the criticism as more intelligent than if he or she had praised. Research has shown that critics are perceived as smart.

The effects of praising and criticizing other people are relatively straightforward. If you hear people praised, you'll think the better of them; if you hear people criticized, you'll think the worse.

These strategies do not represent the trickiest strategies that people use for winning arguments, however. Subtlety abounds when praise and criticism are directed at *oneself*, and the nature of positive and negative comments changes substantially.

There are times when it's impossible to resist bravado—self-praise. "These pages are the best I've ever written." The response to this is to ask to see the draft. The reason? The listener is thinking, *"I'll* be the judge of that!" Self-praise is often met with suspicion.

How can you get around skepticism? Occasionally, before one of us makes a claim that he has done good work, or even instead of making the claim at all, he gives the pages to others, hoping that they will really like them. The more rascally version of this strategy gives the pages to someone who the person *knows* will love them. Then the author can say, "I wrote these pages, and John thought they were great." Or better yet, he can have John deliver the message himself.

The summary, again confirmed by psychological experiments, is that praise from others is far more influential than self-praise. This is a standard that explains everything from independent testing to personal testimonials. Humans are built to be suspicious of a person when the self-interest of that person is apparent; people like confirmation from disinterested others. You would likely be much less impressed if you were to hear us praise ourselves than if you heard someone else do the praising. Also, you would probably not like the self-praiser as much as the person who praised another.

One other strategy is modesty—aim criticism at yourself. As we now recall, compliments and critiques that we've directed at each other are often preceded by the following: "The problem I see here, which occurs in my own writing as well, is that you …". While this comment may not make our critiques more believable, it certainly limits bad feelings. People who criticize themselves are liked a lot better than those who criticize others.

Writing is certainly not the only activity where these social rules work. People do similar things all the time, and in many different contexts. Rules about praise and criticism—and the consequences of each—regulate marriages, child rearing, advertising strategies, and more. In all of these contexts, people ask themselves two important questions: Is the remark positive or negative? And to whom is it directed—the person speaking or the one listening?

Our research goal was to add one more context to this list: human-*media* interactions. Will the same rules work with computers?

Assessments of Media That Praise and Criticize

When media use the same guidelines as we did while writing, we should be able to make several observations. In our predictions, we substitute a computer for a person, continuing the sequence of experiments that tested the various ways in which interactive media are social actors.

Here are the rules:

Rule 1: A performance praised by a computer will be perceived as superior to a performance criticized by a computer.

Rule 2: When a computer praises itself, the praise will be perceived as less valid than when the praise comes from an independent computer.

Rule 3: A computer that praises another computer will be liked more than a computer that praises itself.

Rule 4: A computer that criticizes another computer will be liked less than a computer that criticizes itself.

Rule 5: A computer that criticizes another computer will be perceived as more intelligent than a computer that praises another computer.

Once again, some of these rules, while reasonable for human-human interaction, seem absurd when applied to an interaction with media. For people, the rules make sense because everyone can tell the difference between "self" and "other." In fact, this distinction is often considered a key difference between humans and animals. People also have a strong desire to present themselves in the best possible light, but they have less motivation to do the same for other people. This is commonly recognized, even if this thoughtful acknowledgment makes people seem more calculating than we'd like.

It may seem strange to apply these talents to media. Computers do not have a sense of "self," nor is it logical to think of computers in terms of "self" versus "other." Similarly, computers do not have an inherent desire to put themselves in the best possible light, because they have no desires at all. Consequently, just as it seems strange for computer users to change behavior to protect the "feelings" that machines obviously don't have, it seems silly for users to be concerned about a computer's "motivations."

Observing Mediated Praisers and Critics

To examine reactions to computers that praise and criticize, we once again used a task where participants were tutored and evaluated on computers and then asked to assess their interactions. Participants were invited to the laboratory, and they were told that they would work with a computer to learn about various topics. The forty-four participants were also told that we were interested in how well the computers performed and in the feelings that each person had during the interaction.

Each session had three parts. First, participants were tutored by a computer that had an audio speaker attached so that information could be presented with voice as well as text. The recorded voices were three male graduate students. Each of the machines had a different voice, and the voices were rotated among machines.

During the tutoring session, participants were presented with twenty facts, for example, "The more wire a computer has, the slower it runs." After each fact, the computer asked participants how much they already knew about the fact. The users then indicated whether they knew "a great deal," "some," or "very little." They were then told that the computer would provide later facts based on their answers to this question, but in reality everyone got the same facts in the same order. We were merely trying to make participants feel that they were part of an interaction.

After the tutoring session, the participant moved his or her chair in front of a different computer. This second computer, using a voice that was different from the first voice, then administered a fifteen-question, multiple-choice test.

Next came the evaluation session, and it was here that we simulated the different versions of praise and criticism directed at self or other. In this session, the computer went through each question on the test, telling whether the participant got the answer right or wrong. More important, each participant was told whether the tutoring computer had done a good job or not. For half of the participants, the tutor's performance was praised, for example, "The tutoring session provided extremely useful facts for answering this question. Therefore, the tutoring computer performed extremely well." The performance of the tutoring session was criticized for the other half of the participants, for example, "The tutoring session did not provide useful facts for answering this question. Therefore, the tutoring computer performed very poorly."

The other experience that differed among subjects was the source of the evaluations. We wanted half the participants to think that the tutor had praised or criticized *itself,* and the other half to hear the evaluation from a neutral source. To simulate *self*-praise and *self*-criticism, we had participants go back to the original computer to hear the evaluations. In these cases, the first machine taught the participant something, and then told him or her how it did as a teacher. For the other half of the participants, the evaluation was done by a *third* computer in yet a different voice. An interesting point about this design is that it was the first experiment ever to study the distribution of tasks across computers.

The combination of praise versus criticism, and same versus different computers resulted in four types of experience: other-praise, self-praise, self-criticism, and other-criticism.

After the session was over, participants were asked to indicate how well various adjectives described the sessions. We wanted to know how participants perceived the performance of the computer, and how much they liked the interaction. Adjectives were used to evaluate the qualities of the tutoring session, including words like *competent, analytical, intelligent,* and *friendly.* For the evaluation session, we asked about *accuracy, friendliness,* and *intelligence.*

Different Computers Are Different Social Actors

For praise and criticism, participants believed the assessments. For all of the adjectives that described the tutoring session, participants thought the computer did better when it was praised than when it was criticized.

The effect for praise was so strong that it even affected perceptions of participants' *own* performance. When the tutoring session was praised, participants thought that on average they got two more answers right on the test, a powerful demonstration that subjective experience turned into concrete impressions.

Did the results depend on "self" versus "other"? For the adjectives that were used to assess the tutoring session's performance, participants thought the computer performed better and they thought the evaluation was more accurate when it was praised by a *different* computer than when it praised itself.

The rest of the results followed in kind. The sessions with the computers were liked significantly more when praise came from a third, independent computer. Participants also distinguished between "self" and "other" when assessing criticism: They disliked a computer significantly more when it criticized another machine than when it criticized itself. It seems that the participants in the experiment were watching a social interaction, not a bunch of networked hardware.

The results for "intelligence" were icing on the cake. When we were designing this study, we didn't actually know that critics were perceived as more intelligent than people who praise. When the experiment was running in the lab, a graduate student predicted this result, and he turned out to be right: Participants thought that a computer was significantly more intelligent when it criticized others than when it praised.

Like participants in all of our computer experiments, the participants in this one were experienced computer users who said that notions of "self versus other" certainly did not apply to computers. All of the participants performed identical tasks and they received identical evaluations. No one guessed what the experiment was about, and no one said it made a difference which computer produced the evaluations. Social responses to media, while powerful, are not obvious to the people who are being social.

Thinking about the Judgments That Media Make

What do these results mean? First, people draw strong inferences from the source of an evaluation. Media are perceived as less competent and less likable when they praise themselves than when something (or someone) else does it. The evaluation itself is also less believable without an independent source. Media are liked more when they praise rather than criticize others, and when they criticize rather than praise themselves. Even the relative intelligence of praise versus criticism was dependent on the source of the evaluation. Consequently, we can now extend the media equation to times when people are *observers* of social interactions between media, as well as times when they are recipients of the same.

This study demonstrates that people will use the idea of "self" and "other" when assessing the performance of computers. What stands out here is the *breadth* of use of the self/other distinction. Differences in the source of an evaluation, as represented by a computer box and voices that came from it, influenced how much people liked the computers as well as how they thought the computer performed. And just as in real life, the results reversed when "self" was substituted for "other:" Praise is better from others than self; criticism is more likeable from oneself than from others.

Designing Media that Praise and Criticize

One of the most appealing reasons to leverage media manners is that it doesn't require extensive disk space or complicated audio and video production. For example, one current software product presents video images of two financial experts. In the product, the two speakers describe themselves as experts, and tell about their own extensive experience. These experts would be more compelling and more likable if they had described *each other* as experts. Not one extra line of code would have been required, but there would have been a significant psychological advantage in being careful about the source of praise.

When designing media, however, perceived competence and liking may have to be traded. Media that praise themselves are more competent but less likable than self-critical media. Similarly, critical media are less likable yet more intelligent than counterparts that are positive. That is, neither of the aphorisms "Modesty is the best policy" nor "Self-praise is better than none" can guarantee universal acclaim. They are both true, and they are competitive.

We suspect that when intelligence and likability compete, designers will go with smarts most of the time, especially for new interactive media and computers. Intelligence is a holy grail. But this may be short-sighted. When you think about the teachers that you value the most, are they the ones who were most intelligent, as in raw intellectual horsepower, or those who knew enough, *and* were nice—those with high social as well as traditional IQs?

Media and Personality

6

Personality of Characters

Our collaboration, so we're told by psychologist friends, is one of different personalities. One of us, at least some of the time, likes to take command and make decisions. In most interactions, he will speak first, do much of the talking, and make absolute statements with great confidence. The other person is more reserved, at least some of the time. In conversation, he'd prefer to respond rather than speak first, do less than half of the talking, and be cautious in his claims, often ending sentences with questions.

What's interesting about these different combinations of behavior and preferences is that they seem, at least to the people experiencing them, as if they describe two very complex people, both unique and unpredictable. All the snippets of behavior that come with the two descriptions seem to be necessary even to begin an accurate description of either person.

Psychologists, however, try to find simplicity where others find complexity. Their job is to describe people via the *fewest* possible principles. To this end, they have tried to reduce infinitely rich personalities to a few simple types. They do this not to abbreviate what is complicated, but rather because they think people may actually be less complex than they appear. Consequently, a psychologist might look at the two of us and say that we are at opposite ends of a single dimension of personality called *extraversion* or *dominance/submissiveness*.

Beyond the two of us, psychologists have demonstrated that all personalities can be categorized into a few basic types, describable using only a few words. This abbreviation seems to rob people of individuality; to describe a whole personality, it seems that you'd need a long list of words. But psychologists have shown that the word list is smaller than we think. Personality *can* be reduced to a basic set of categories, in spite of injury to a sense of uniqueness.

To reduce personality to its essentials, psychologists start with hundreds of adjectives. People are asked to choose the adjectives that best describe themselves or other people. Then, via a series of statistical procedures that cluster similar adjectives, a final set of descriptions is defined. For instance, people who describe themselves as "dominant" also tend to describe themselves as assertive, aggressive, competitive, and self-confident. People who describe themselves as submissive also tend to describe themselves as shy, timid, and yielding. As a result, a single distinction—dominant versus submissive—captures a wide range of quite similar traits that appear special, but really are not.

Researchers have discovered that all of the personality adjectives can be neatly organized into five basic dimensions. Although all five dimensions are important, there is also good evidence that the first two are the most critical. Dominance and submissiveness represent the first dimension, and friendliness is the second. Friendliness is defined on one end by the words friendly, warm, and sympathetic, and on the other end by disagreeable, hard-hearted, and cold. The three other dimensions are conscientiousness, emotional stability, and openness.

These dimensions come from many empirical studies, and importantly, they appear across cultures. There are several ways to *express* each personality trait, and the expressions *are* unique to individuals and cultures, but the underlying traits are the same. The five basic dimensions are so useful that they appear in almost all of the popular personality tests used in schools, workplaces, and self-help literature. Personality psychologists call the dimensions "the Big Five."

Not only are the Big Five the dimensions that psychologists use to identify people, they are also the ones that *all* of us use to identify one another. Everyone is an expert at quickly pinning down these traits in the people we meet. This is an important ability, as personality strongly determines how people will behave and respond in a wide range of situations.

Mediated Personalities

What happens when personalities are mediated? Do the same traits apply? The assumption in many analyses of media is that people who are actually *in* the media are unique. Media people can have personalities that look nothing like real life. Their identity is surely not constrained by the same personality types that describe regular folks. Mediated people can't affect our lives directly, and there is no urgency to understand how they will behave. Doesn't this make them different?

The media equation suggests otherwise. Everyone, mediated or not, has a personality, and personalities come in a limited number of categories. It may be too much to expect that an entirely different way of analyzing personality will be applied just because the personalities are experienced via media.

If the media equation applies to personalities, we should be able to observe the following:

Rule 1: The two most important categories of media personalities are dominance/submissiveness and friendliness/unfriendliness.

Rule 2: Media personalities are readily identified by the people who experience them.

Study 1: Personalities on Television

Our first study of personalities in media was done almost twenty years ago, well before we had any notion about an equivalence of real and mediated worlds. At that time, and still, the differences between the two worlds received more attention than the similarities. Consequently, when this first personality study began, we expected that viewers might use different personality attributes to describe television personalities than they would use to describe real people.

The simple goal of the first study was to compare the personality traits that emerged from descriptions of television people against the traits used to describe people in real life. We began by studying children. At the time, we thought that children would be the group most likely fooled into thinking that media were special. We even thought that children might come up with their own traits because media people were substantially different from those experienced in real life.

The study was done with two hundred students in the third, fifth, and seventh grades. They were each asked to describe fourteen television characters. The particular characters used in the study may challenge memories about television in the seventies, but they represented a range of personalities and program types, and all of them were quite popular.

The question in the study was this: Will the kids use familiar traits (dominance and friendliness) to evaluate popular television characters? Or will other traits emerge, less associated with real people and more geared to television? The problem, and a huge one, was how to ask children these questions.

If you ask people, whether children or adults, to describe television characters using the attribute of friendliness, for example, they'll gladly oblige by rating the friendliness of any character presented to them. From the answers to this question, it's easy to show that some characters are perceived as friendly and some are not. What you cannot know is whether friendliness is an important attribute in the first place. There is no certain relationship between the *ability* to recognize a trait and the *importance* of that trait in social life.

The trick is to find a way to let the various attributes emerge naturally *without* suggesting them in the first place. One method is to ask people to describe the characters, tape and transcribe all the comments, and then count the number of times that different traits are used. This method has the advantage of not biasing evaluations in favor of the attributes that the researchers chose, but it is quite difficult. First, people have to be willing to make the descriptions, which is a bit of an undertaking. It also means that respondents must be aware of a particular trait in the first place. There is a great temptation for respondents to make up evaluations that sound good, even if they don't describe their actual judgments.

We overcame these problems by using a technique called multidimensional scaling. With this method, people are asked only one type of question: How similar is each character to all others in the study? People are not asked to apply traits that the researchers think are important. This technique is based on the idea that a judgment about *similarity* is the most fundamental psychological question possible.

By asking this simple question, it is possible to determine the basic elements that differentiate characters. The first step is to gather similarity ratings for all possible pairs of a sample of characters. Respondents are told that they can think about whatever they'd like when they make the similarity judgments. The magic of multidimensional scaling is the remarkable degree of homogeneity in the responses. Different people have quite similar criteria for judging similarity, even though each may be wholly unaware of how they make the judgments.

Next, the psychological similarities are turned into physical distances between the characters. We assume that people imagine a kind of physical distance as a way to tag psychological differences; a mental ruler places things that are more similar closer together. Once the physical distances between the characters are known, the characters can be placed in an actual physical space (or at least a picture of one), represented by a graph with axes, that is as consistent as possible with the judgments that people provided. The characters located next to each other in the space are most psychologically similar—thus, Steve Austin (a bionic hero who fought bad guys in *The Six Million Dollar Man*) was placed next to Marshall Dillon (a Western hero who fought bad guys in *Gunsmoke*).

The dimensions in the space represent the fundamental ways in which television characters are different. Naming the dimensions describes how the children thought about the characters.

We thought that personality traits might describe the axes. This was not obvious at the time, however, because this technique opens up all kinds of possibilities for dimensions. Television people might differ in a lot of ways, and personality might not rank high on the list. More likely dimensions might be the programs themselves (characters from police shows versus those from comedies), occupations (detectives versus cowboys versus mothers), or even whether the characters were animated or not.

Personality was, however, quite apparent in the location of characters in the space. This identification was accomplished in several ways. One method was just to look at the placement of the characters, and to try to think up attributes that were consistent with their placement on the dimension. We wanted to find ways to distinguish the characters who were high on each dimension from those who were low. On dimension 1, we wanted to know how Steve Austin was different from the young girl Laura in *Little House on the Prairie*. On dimension 2, Marshall Dillon was at one end, and Fred Flintstone (the lead character from the animated comedy, *The Flintstones*) was on the other.

For dimension 1, a good first guess was that one end of the dimension represented macho strongmen, compared to the female characters and the boyish John Boy from *The Waltons* on the other end. This is consistent with the personality trait dominance. Because this was the first dimension (the most important dimension statistically), dominance was the single most important trait that distinguished the characters. This is in spite of all other differences between the characters, including gender, and in spite of the fact that the people were from television.

On dimension 2, friendly characters were on one end, and more serious characters were on the other. The summary: Without any prompting, the two basic personality traits defined how media people were similar and different.

We didn't just look at the graphs to make this claim, however. After the similarity judgments were completed, we also asked participants to rate each character on the basic personality traits as well as several other attributes. The basic personality dimensions were strongly and significantly related to the dimensions just described. And if that isn't enough, we did the study again with a different group of kids and characters, with the same results.

This study is another piece of evidence for the media equation, even though the study is twenty years old. Mediated personalities are not unique, although the particular cues that describe the personalities may be. Steve Austin, for example, manifested his dominance with bionic limbs as well as conversational style. Consequently, his dominance was *expressed* in a fashion only possible in an *un*real world. But regardless of the particular expression, the same fundamental attributes still applied.

The results of this study were one of the first clues that media might not be as special as we often assume. Unfortunately, the results were not seriously applied to conclusions about adults (in retrospect, an error), because we then assumed, like others who commented on the study, that children would soon outgrow what was thought to be a childish tendency to take media at face value. Adults, everyone thought, would surely think differently, and better.

Recently, we gave adults a chance to do just that. We did a similar study with adults and changed some other things as well. Instead of real actors, we asked adults to evaluate animated animals and objects, and instead of familiar characters, we made some up.

Study 2: Adults and Novel Cartoon Characters

This study used line drawings of nonhuman characters. The drawings were in color, but they were quite simple and had no shading. We had dogs, bugs, cats, turtles, dinosaurs, and even a pencil, plant, and a book. All had eyes and other features that suggested life, but none had any quality that suggested they were worthy of *human* evaluation. All of the characters were original drawings created by five artists, so there were no worries about prior familiarity, and this time, the participants in the study were forty-two adults between the ages of twenty-five and sixty.

Each person was asked to rate the similarity of all pairs of the characters. From that information, we found four dimensions that represented the similarity judgments quite well. The first dimension separated the characters that were animals (e.g., the cat, cow, dog, and sheep) from characters that were nonliving objects (e.g., the pair of shoes, a book, and a pencil). The second dimension distinguished one artist from all the others. That artist had used a particularly sophisticated style, and participants (unconsciously) noticed that it was different from the more familiar cartoon style.

The third and fourth dimensions were the most interesting. They were the two basic personality traits. Dimension 3 was dominance. Those characters high on dominance were the alligator, piranha, hippopotamus, wolf, and a sharp-toothed dog. All were big and aggressive animals, both in the drawings and in real life. On the submissive end of the scale were a cat, a frightened bird, and a balloon-sculptured dog. It's doubtful that any of those characters would be the first to speak in a conversation with any of the characters on the dominant end of the scale. The fourth dimension was friendliness. There were smiles on one end, and grimaces on the other.

In short, adults applied the same basic personality dimensions to novel, animated animals and objects. Not one of the adults, of course, could describe with any confidence *how* they had made these judgments, and if confronted with the traits they actually used, all would likely deny that *human* personality entered their minds at all. Even if participants made an effort to suspend disbelief, or just tried to please the experimenter, it would have been virtually impossible for them to adjust their responses to correspond with the goals of the study. Indeed, it is likely that the participants had not even *heard* of the basic personality dimensions.

What Do These Studies Reveal about Media?

These studies provide strong evidence for the psychological equivalence of real and mediated worlds. The studies elaborate the media equation in three ways. First, the area of *personality* psychology, as well as rules already taken from *social* psychology, are applicable to the study of media. This is important because personality, like ideas about manners, is always discussed as something profoundly human. Second, the studies show that social responses are not just applied to the appliances that deliver media; they also apply to fictional representations, human or otherwise, that appear on a screen. Finally, the research demonstrates that personality is socially powerful. Give anything eyes and a mouth, it would seem, and personality responses follow.

Designing Characters with Basic Personalities

Fictional people, and even inanimate objects with eyes, do not have a special set of psychological traits. The ability to assign personality traits, whether to humans, animals or shoes, is constrained by something quite basic and automatic. The same dimensions that exist in the real world apply to media—apparently without exceptions, and without additions.

Why are the basic personality traits important to know? Several important responses depend on them. Personality governs the nature of the affiliations that we have with other people, and people presented in the media aren't any different. Personality will determine *who* we like in the media and what we *expect* from those we encounter, and it can even influence how groups of people (i.e., several media people plus a viewer) will get along together. How we think and behave depends fundamentally on the fact that there is only one notion of personality—mediated or not.

Unique Expressions of Personality

Some things, however, *are* unique to mediated personalities. Those who create media characters can express personality with great flexibility. In media, you can be a dominant personality because you have supernatural strength (e.g., a bionic arm) or an unusual role (e.g., captain of a starship), as well as via more traditional markers available to the rest of us.

Another advantage that mediated personalities have is the ability to control the situations in which they appear. This allows for a rich expression of personality without the constraints of real life. Characters, unlike the rest of us, are not forced to be in situations that might disguise or moderate the strength of a personality. For example, in real life, dominant people often find themselves in situations, such as sitting at a lecture, in which it is impossible to act decisively or speak first. With media characters, it is possible to create characters that are constantly in situations where their personalities can be clear. For example, dominant characters can be allowed to aggressively confront one crisis after another.

Preference for Obvious Personalities

The ability to present media personalities more *purely* is an important advantage for media characters. People *like* identifiable personalities, even if they might not like the personality once it's identified. Quick assessments are valued, and undiluted personalities are more quickly and accurately considered. Complicated people are just that: Who knows what they'll do next?

The implication for creating personalities is simple (and hardly novel in the world of literature and theater): Make personalities strong and reliable. Strong personality is the starting point, whether it is a character in a television story or a computer agent that will assist in cyberspace.

What Comprises a Personality?

Information about personality can come from anywhere. Humans are quite comfortable with personality judgments based on nothing more than how people walk, or how quickly they move. There may be sounds that communicate personality or merely subtle differences in word choice. A crucial implication of the complexity of personality expression is this: Even though personality can be assessed with limited information, inconsistencies in the presentation of characters will diminish the purity of personality, and thereby contribute to confusion, and even dislike. A character who looks dominant, behaves shyly, speaks with a forceful voice, and offers uncertain claims will appear inconsistent—someone we might want to avoid unless we have a lot of time to parse the inconsistencies.

Creators of a character must "get to know" it (that is, know its personality) before it can be fully developed. The expressions of personality can be quite creative, even totally novel and irreproducible in the real world, but all actions, appearance, language, and attitudes must be consistent. Substantial coordination is required to end up with a believable presentation. That's why the credits for Disney animated films are often organized by characters.

None of the above should be taken to mean that characters cannot have flaws. In fact, flaws *add* to believability. A character could easily be dominant, friendly, *and* a bit neurotic. This is quite different from an *inconsistent* personality, such as a character who is sometimes very friendly and sometimes very unfriendly. Media personalities can profit from negative components, but not from inconsistency.

Line Drawings Are Rich in Personality

What is the amount of information needed to convince people that a personality is present? The answer, clear from the research, is that very little information is needed. Simple line drawings of objects (as long as they have eyes or even a hint that they are alive), are quite enough to activate psychologically rich responses. *Perceived* reality does not depend on verisimilitude: A character doesn't have to look anything like a real person to give and receive real social responses.

This fact is crucial and, we think, counterintuitive. What *seems* likely is that until representations of characters actually look like real people (until they are photorealistic, 3-D, life size, or viewed through virtual reality goggles), personality will be either irrelevant or different. This is clearly not the case. Many people will *say* that media characters aren't like other people, but people will often react to them and interact with them in exactly the same way that they would with real people.

Distribution of Personalities

How many people have each type of personality? This is a key difference between mediated and unmediated personalities. In the real world, psychologists have found that there are about as many dominant personalities as there are submissive ones, and the same number of friendly and unfriendly ones. Media personalities need not follow this fifty-fifty distribution, however, and they tend not to. The most prominent and best-liked characters in media are those that are both dominant and friendly, or at least rank high on one of those attributes. Despite exceptions (irreverence and shyness are trademarks of several popular characters), these attributes prevail, from the anchors on the evening news to Mickey Mouse.

An emphasis on dominant, friendly people has an unexpected consequence. The world of media overrepresents dominant and friendly personality traits. To the extent that *any* representation in media is equated with real life, perceptions of real-world personalities could become biased in favor of personalities that are the most numerous. More submissive or less social people may be wondering why they are so outnumbered, while their outgoing and friendly counterparts are thrilled that there are so many people in the world who are like them.

The distribution of personalities in media may influence how we judge people in the real world. Whenever there is not enough information about the real people we meet to make a confident personality judgment, we begin to make inferences. Media influence our inferences about ambiguous personalities because the mental database of personality information that everyone carries can be skewed by the tendencies of media to create dominant and friendly characters.

The possibility that media personalities prime the evaluation of new people was the subject of one other study we've done about television personalities. The experiment was done with children, but it illustrates the potential of media to influence the way everyone categorizes other people. In the experiment, elementary school children were introduced to a new person in their school by showing them pictures. A brief background story was told about each of the pictured children, but every attempt was made to describe the new children ambiguously with respect to basic personality traits.

The children were then assigned to one of two groups. One group watched several segments of television programs that featured typical and popular television characters (i.e., ones that were dominant and friendly). The children were unaware that this part of the experiment had anything to do with the subsequent evaluations of the pictures. The other half of the children did not watch any television. Both groups were then asked to evaluate the personalities of the new children after they looked at the pictures, and after they had been told the stories about each of them.

Those kids who watched television before doing the evaluations were more likely to evaluate the new kids as dominant and friendly. That is, the popular media figures served to *prime* personality evaluations of real people in favor of the television personalities. The attributes of media personalities were activated in the minds of those who watched television, and what is active in the mind has a great chance to influence the present, even if the activation comes from media. Media characters, rather than constituting a special class of personalities irrelevant to our personal lives, are influential in *any* personality assessment.

7

Personality of Interfaces

When people write about science, they have to make tough choices about how strongly to communicate the results of research. Even though there is precise math to describe degrees of uncertainty, at some point, if the data are to be useful, the writer has to translate the numbers into words. Two writers looking at the same numbers quite often choose different words. One might say: "This study absolutely proves...," and consequently, "You should definitely do the following...". The other, staring at exactly the same data, might say: "This study suggests the possibility that...," and consequently, "Perhaps you might want to consider the following...".

When you read such differing claims about research, you probably have no trouble deciding which set of comments you like the best. It's tempting to think that the choice is a scientific one: "Without bold claims, science will never be useful" or "It's more appropriate for science to be conservative." But the issue may not be a scientific one at all. Rather, it's about personality.

The first set of comments in the opening paragraph above reflects dominance, unambiguous certainty about what is true. The other reflects submissiveness, caution and reserve about what is true. If this seems obvious, there are two corollaries that are not. First, if you liked one set of comments better because of the personality it conveyed, this means that personality can be perceived in the most minimal of places—a simple English sentence. As you read the comments, there were no pictures of people, not even an animated character. There were no objects that looked or acted human and no extended interaction to discover the nuances of temperament. Rather, a full-blown personality was created on a pinhead.

The second corollary is that you probably liked one set of comments more than the other because of *your own* personality. People like to interact with personalities that resemble their own. In psychology, this is known as the "law of similarity-attraction." Despite the folk wisdom that opposites attract, there is strong empirical support for attraction based on similarity. People prefer strangers with personalities like their own to strangers whose personalities are different. The same is true for friendships, as well as relationships that are arranged, such as college roommate assignments. In countless studies on spousal relationships, marital satisfaction is largely attributable to congruent rather than reciprocal dispositions.

How might these characteristics of personality apply to media?

Personality and Computers

For years, academics and researchers in human-computer interaction have thought about how—and whether—one could give personality to computers. Most people assumed this would be a good thing, so good that the call to "give computers some personality" has become a design mantra. The simplicity of the call, however, has been met with complicated responses. Most people think a computer can have a personality only with the help of computer agents or guides, sophisticated pictorial representations, complicated artificial intelligence, or programs that follow the rules of natural language.

Many of these complicated features may eventually give machines some personality, but none of them takes advantage of the ease with which humans automatically identify personality. Psychology offers far simpler strategies than many currently being pursued. If media and real life are not as different as they seem, then perhaps the psychological realities caused by old brains should get some attention while engineers figure out more advanced technologies.

We decided to test these ideas in an experiment. The plan was to find a simple way to give a computer personality (we started with dominant and submissive ones), and then see whether those personalities evoke the same response in users that psychologists attribute to personality in real life. If we're right, a computer that initiates interaction and uses language confidently should be perceived as dominant, and a computer that does not should be perceived as submissive. People should be able to identify the personality of a computer rapidly, and they should respond to the computer in ways that are consistent with the similarity-attraction hypothesis. We would expect dominant users to prefer dominant computers over submissive ones, and submissive users to prefer submissive computers over dominant ones.

Applying the social rules from human-human interaction to human-computer interaction, we predicted the following:

Rule 1: People will perceive a computer that uses dominant text as having a dominant personality, and a computer with submissive text as having a submissive personality.

Rule 2: Dominant people will say that the dominant computer is more like them than the submissive computer, and submissive people will recognize the submissive computer as more like them than the dominant computer.

Rule 3: Dominant people will prefer the dominant computer, while submissive people will prefer the submissive computer.

When we first wrote down these predictions, they seemed a bit strange. The notion of "personality," so profoundly human and hopelessly complex, did not seem applicable to computers. Even when people speak of computers being "user-friendly," they certainly don't mean the same thing as when they say a person is "friendly." How could limited information about personality elicit strong responses? Here's how we answered this question.

Endowing a Computer with Personality

For our experiment, we needed people *and* computers that were either dominant or submissive. The easier of the two to find was people.

First, we asked two hundred people to answer a personality questionnaire that is a standard test to measure levels of dominance and submissiveness. The test asked them to indicate how well adjectives such as "assertive," "timid," and "outgoing" describe them.

Our goal was to find two groups of people, one that was definitely dominant, and the other definitely submissive. To do this, we selected the twenty-four people who scored highest on dominance, and the twenty-four people who scored highest on submissiveness. We now had participants who were clearly dominant or submissive, although we told them nothing about how they scored on the test. Several weeks after taking the test, they were invited to the lab to interact with computers.

When participants came to the lab, we wanted them to work with either a dominant or a submissive computer. We created these two computer personalities by changing four features of the machines. Each feature was taken straight from the psychology literature about personalities and people.

The first place we put personality was in the language style of the interface. The dominant computer expressed itself strongly in comments phrased as assertions and commands. This is consistent with a dominant person's tendency to make decisions for others, and to direct the action of other people. In contrast, the submissive computer used unassertive language expressed in the form of questions and suggestions.

Though the language styles used for the two personalities were different, we kept the information the same. In the experiment, participants were asked to discuss items that might be useful for survival in the desert. For example, in a discussion about sunglasses, the dominant computer would say: "In the desert, the intense sunlight will clearly cause blindness by the second day. Without adequate vision, survival will become almost impossible. The sunglasses are absolutely important." The submissive computer was more tentative: "In the desert, it seems that the intense sunlight could possibly cause blindness by the second day. Without adequate vision, don't you think that survival might become more difficult? The sunglasses might be important."

The second place for personality was the level of confidence expressed by the two computers when they made comments. Here, we decided to use numbers in addition to language. Whenever the computers would make a comment, they would also display a ten-point confidence scale, with one of the points highlighted to indicate the confidence level for that suggestion. The dominant computer displayed an average confidence level of 8, with the scores ranging from 7 to 10 on a 10-point scale. The submissive computer displayed confidence scores that averaged 3, and ranged from 1 to 4.

The third expression of personality was the sequencing of the interaction. The dominant computer always went first, discussing each issue before the user. Dominant machines, like dominant people, lead. Conversely, the submissive computer always went second, discussing issues only after the user had a chance.

Finally, we gave the dominant computer and submissive computer different names. The dominant computer was labeled "Max," and the submissive computer was labeled "Linus," names that we knew were associated with different personalities.

All other aspects of the computers and the interactions were identical. The dominant and the submissive computers both gave the same type and amount of information. There was no artificial intelligence in the software, and there was no attempt on the part of the computer to understand the comments or personality of the user.

Testing whether Computers Have Personalities

Our next decision was about the nature of the interaction. What should participants do with the machines? Our goal was to find a task that would put participants on an equal footing with the computers, and one that would encourage participants to work cooperatively with the computer on an interesting problem.

The task we decided to use is called the Desert Survival Problem. Participants were asked to imagine that their airplane had just crashed in the desert. There was no sign of water, but some items had been salvaged from the wreckage. Participants were asked to rank these 12 items for their survival value: a flashlight, a jackknife, a sectional air map, a plastic raincoat, a magnetic compass, a compress kit with gauze, a bottle of salt tablets, a quart of water, a book entitled *Edible Animals of the Desert*, a quart of vodka, a topcoat, and a cosmetic mirror.

This survival problem works well for group problem-solving, because people find it interesting and fun. Everyone has information to contribute, and conversations are easy and lively. The task also has the advantage that answers are not obviously wrong or right. We did tell participants, however, that a group of survivalists had come up with a "correct" ranking, and we intended to evaluate their performance based on how closely they could match the experts.

Participants began the task by using pencil and paper to write down their first thoughts about the ranking of the items. When they finished, they went to another room to work with the computer. Half of the participants with a dominant personality and half with a submissive personality were assigned to the dominant computer; the other half were assigned to the submissive computer. We told everyone they would have a chance to exchange information with the computer about each of the twelve survival items. After completing the exchange, participants were told that they would then have a chance to change their initial rankings of the items.

At this point, participants exchanged comments with the computer via a terminal on the other side of the room. The dominant computer made assertions (as opposed to the suggestions of the submissive computer), discussed an item first (as opposed to second), and indicated a high level of confidence (as opposed to a low level of confidence).

When the interaction was over, participants went into another room and made a final ranking of the twelve items. Then they filled out a questionnaire that asked for evaluations of the computer and evaluations of the interaction. The answers to these questions were the basis for determining whether participants responded to the computer's personality in the same way that they would respond to a human who had the same personality.

First, participants were asked to describe the computer they worked with using a list of descriptive adjectives. Some of the adjectives, such as *assertive* and *timid*, related to the dominant versus submissive personality categories. These were used to check the manipulation of personality, because we had to make sure that participants really did think that the computers had the same personalities that we thought we had given them.

A second set of questions asked about the perceived similarity between the computer's interaction style and the subject's own interaction style (e.g., "How similar was the computer's choice of words to your own?"). We wanted to see whether subjects would recognize their respective personalities in the computer. Next, we asked participants to describe the performance of the computer using descriptors such as *helpful, likable,* and *insightful*. And finally, participants rated their interaction with the computer on criteria such as *enjoyable* and *interesting*.

Powerful Results from Minimal Personalities

No one had ever attempted to vary personality with such minimal cues. Was a difference between the two machines apparent? Yes. The dominant computer was rated as significantly more aggressive, assertive, authoritative, confident, controlling, domineering, and forceful—all adjectives associated with dominance. The submissive computer was rated as more submissive, shy, and timid. Statistically, these differences were substantial, yet they had been evoked by minimal differences.

Participants could also recognize themselves in the machines. Participants who had dominant personalities said that the dominant computer was more like them in style of interaction and in phrasing comments. Submissive participants evaluated the submissive computer in the same way.

95

Preference for the computers was also affected by personality similarities. When personalities were the same, the computer received significantly higher ratings for competence than when the personalities were mismatched. Even though the two computers provided *identical* content, dominant participants rated the machine that was like them as more intelligent, knowledgeable, insightful, helpful, and useful. Submissive participants assigned the exact same traits to the submissive computer.

When the personality of the computer matched theirs, participants even thought their *own* work was better. When the personalities were alike, participants were significantly more satisfied with how they had ranked the survival items. The self-evaluation didn't stop at intellectual skill. Participants also said they enjoyed themselves more, had more fun, and thought the whole experience was more interesting.

Personality match-ups matter, person-to-machine as well as person-to-person. And it is important to remember that every participant was an experienced computer user who, after the experiment ended, denied any thoughts of a social relationship with a machine.

Thinking about Personality and Media

A key implication of this study is that personality is easy to create. In this chapter and the preceding one, we've worked backwards on personality in media—from the high end of photo-realistic video representations to the expression of a few words. The conclusion is that the creation of personality does not depend on virtually real representations. Our old brains automatically extrapolate when given a little hint.

A key insight to be gained from this work is that social science research doesn't just *diagnose* the characteristics of media; it can also provide direct guidance on how to *create* media. Although they didn't know it, personality psychologists supplied very specific guidelines for designing dominant and submissive personalities.

Designing Computers with Personality

Older media have many aspects that virtual reality and other fancy devices won't improve, and the words that convey personality are good examples. Sophisticated representations are not necessary to get participants to change evaluations that influence everything from feelings of self-worth to evaluations of a machine. A couple of well-chosen words, reliably communicated, can do the trick.

The creation of personality on a computer is not primarily an issue of artificial intelligence. It's not even an intelligence issue in real life: How we recognize and use personality is quite independent of IQ. Furthermore, when a designer puts personality in a machine, it need not cost much at all, in terms of either money or space on the development calendar. It took the two of us just a couple of days to write enough personality into a desktop computer so that participants thought better of the machines, their work, and themselves.

Virtually *all* interfaces have a personality. This literally applies to anything that presents words to a user, from toaster ovens and televisions to word processors and workstations. Personality can creep in everywhere—the language in error messages, user prompts, methods for navigating options, and even choices of type font and layout. Even if the design domain is a twelve-character LCD panel, personality is relevant.

Personalities in Media Should Be Consistent and Strong

Unfortunately, little thought currently goes into creating consistent personalities in many interfaces, especially those that are not intended to have any explicit social purpose or presence. It's important to remember, however, that even engineers, technicians, and scientists are humans first. Their responses to personality are no less powerful or relevant than anyone else's. They can be as swayed as the rest of us by just a few characters that come after "c:\>."

Rather than consistent personalities, it is more common to see interfaces with many personalities, one for each person who wrote some

copy or specified a graphic image. Hybrid personalities, which inevita-
bly emerge from uncoordinated group efforts, can be unpleasant for users. The result of mixing personalities together is a weak one, like the
proverbial design by committee.

Strong personality should not be confused with dominant personality. Often, when people say that new media should have *more* personality, they are expressing a hunch that the particular personality should be
one that is "in-your-face," emotionally strong, even charismatic. This
personality is often appealing, but the most important definition of personality strength is *identifiability*, not dominance. If people can identify
the personality, generally half will like it. If it's ambiguous, almost no
one will.

Market Segmentation and Personality

Personality may also be an important way to segment the market for
computer interfaces. Traditionally, the primary focus for the marketing
of computers and other highly technical products has been user expertise. But because people are humans first and experts second, perhaps
personality would be a more useful difference among individuals. Another advantage is that personality can be determined by a very short
series of questions; expertise, conversely, applies to a particular technology or to particular applications, and can prove hard to measure.

Which Personality Is the Best?

Which personality should a designer choose when building social iden-
tities into media? A first answer is that there is no personality that everyone will like. This is true because users themselves are pretty evenly
split among the major personality types.

In many interfaces, there is time and space for only one personality.
Which one should it be? The answer depends on the goal of the product.
If it's important that a user think the computer is an active helper, then
the personality should be dominant and friendly. If the focus is on more
aggressive instruction, it should lean more toward dominance than
friendliness. If the help is from a peer, the personality could be more

friendly than dominant. If the computer is supposed to learn from the user, then the personality should be submissive and friendly. There are personalities uniquely suited to different tasks and roles; designers should choose accordingly.

Making one personality fit all cases is hard. One way around this is to offer multiple personalities that can be selected by the user. The content of the interface wouldn't have to be rewritten; all that is needed is to slightly modify the style of interaction, as we did in the study. If each personality is strong and well-defined, users will recognize the ones that are similar to their own. These are the personalities they would enjoy and the ones that would make them think better of a media product and themselves.

8

Imitating Personality

We've had two agreeable responses to our research. One was a nice compliment from a person who said he completely agreed with the findings, and that he had had many of the same thoughts for quite a while. To us, this was a comforting confirmation that we may actually be on the right track, and it felt good.

A second compliment, however, was even better. It was this: "When I first read your stuff, I thought it was completely wrong. But over time, and after some thought, I now think you guys are right." This was a conclusion that could have come only after careful thought—a true intellectual victory. This person had actually *changed* an opinion, and we felt far better than we did when our work merely confirmed someone else's ideas.

What works for intellectual arguments also works for personality. Just as people with similar opinions are naturally attracted, so are people with similar personalities. But for both opinions and personality, the similarity, when it is earned, is better than when it is merely coincidental.

Studies by psychologists show that people who start out different from a person but become similar over time are liked better than people who were always similar. People who change to make others happy are preferred over people who *always* try to make others happy. The idea that people like to gain something rather than always have it has an academic name—"gain theory." In human-human interaction, the theory can be summarized by this simple adage: Imitation is the sincerest form of flattery. If you really want to make people feel good, change for them, and change in their direction.

Changing a personality requires some effort, which is probably the reason why the change is flattering in the first place. But it also suggests a characteristic of personality that is different from the permanence we usually associate with a disposition. Even though people can be *primarily* characterized with personality traits that do not change, such as dominance and friendliness, everyone can *temporarily* change those traits with some effort.

Imitation, Adaptation, and Media

If personality works the same way in media, then a computer that starts out with a personality the opposite of a user but becomes similar over time should be liked better than a computer that had the same personality as the user all along. Interestingly, this change in interaction style, while complicated for humans, is much simpler for a computer. With limited information about the personality of a user, a computer can change its style of interaction in an instant.

Although this attention from a computer sounds desirable, it may also sound foolish. It doesn't *seem* like a computer should be able to flatter a user by changing its personality; after all, even if computers could have personality, they do not struggle to change. As we have already seen, computers *can* have personalities, and they can effectively flatter those who use them.

We made the following predictions:

Rule 1: Dominant people will prefer a computer that starts out submissive but then becomes dominant more than a computer that is consistently dominant.

Rule 2: Submissive people will prefer a computer that starts out dominant but becomes submissive more than a computer that is consistently submissive.

Computer Personalities That Change

The experiment that tested these rules began like the one in the last chapter. We first found eighty-eight people who clearly had dominant or submissive personalities based on their responses to a standard personality questionnaire administered two weeks before the study began.

When participants came to the lab, they were asked to work with one of two computers. One computer was dominant and it communicated in an assertive style, always initiating interactions, and claiming great confidence about its recommendations. Another computer was submissive and it always used tentative language, went second in the interaction, and expressed little confidence.

Each participant was asked to solve the same Desert Survival Problem that was used in the study described in Chapter 7 (Your plane crashed in the desert, several items were recovered, rank the items on usefulness for survival). Participants in the study first ranked the items on their own and then interacted with a computer to discuss the rankings. It was during the interactions that the computer had a chance to show its personality.

Each session had two rounds, with the computer's personality consistent within a given round. In the first round, participants interacted with the computer about eight of sixteen survival items (a flashlight, a jackknife, a sectional air map of the area, a plastic raincoat, a magnetic compass, a compress kit with gauze, a bottle of salt tablets, and a quart of water). In the second round, which came after a break, the interaction was about the rest of the items (a book called *Edible Animals of the Desert*, a parachute, a pair of sunglasses, a quart of vodka, a topcoat, a cosmetic mirror, a two-pound sack of unsalted peanuts, and a ballpoint pen).

For half of the subjects, the personality of the computer changed during the interaction. For one group, the computer started out dominant and then became submissive. For another group, the computer started out submissive and then became dominant. Two additional groups worked with a computer that didn't change at all; it was either dominant or submissive for both of the rounds. Since there were participants in each of the groups that represented each personality, we were able to watch participants when computers changed to imitate them, when computers changed to be different from them, and when the computer was consistently similar or consistently different.

After both rounds were completed, participants moved to a separate room where they answered a paper-and-pencil questionnaire about the computer and the interaction. The answers to these questions were the basis for determining whether participants responded to the imitation of personality in the same way they would respond to a human doing the same thing.

What You Gain Is Better Than What You Had

The first thing to say about this study is that the results of the last chapter's experiment were replicated. When the personalities of the computer and user were matched through both sessions, participants liked the computer better, and they thought it was more socially and intellectually attractive than when the personality of the computer was consistently different. The participants also said that they derived more emotional satisfaction from the machine when it had a personality similar to their own although, as in all of the experiments, no one realized what was at issue.

We are now confident that matched personalities are a good thing, but similarity was even better when it was won. Participants liked the computer more when it *changed* to conform to their respective personalities than when it remained similar. This was true for both social and emotional satisfaction with the interaction. The mere change of a few words in the interface, and a reversal of order of precedence in the interaction, significantly altered perceptions of a machine.

The evaluations of performance were even more remarkable. Recall that in all cases, the computer gave participants the same information, and it made the same suggestions to the user. Nonetheless, when the computer changed to match the participant's personality, participants thought it was more competent, and they thought that the interaction was significantly more satisfying intellectually. They also found the information given by the computer to be more useful than when personality was consistent throughout the interaction.

What happens when a user *loses* something that he or she liked? This happened when the computer initially matched the user's personality, but changed away from the user for the second round. This situation was not as bad as the opposite was good. There were few differences, although participants liked the computer more when the personality changed away from their own than when it remained unlike them for both rounds. Apparently, the computer got some credit for attempting to change, even though it proved to be in the wrong direction, a result also found in human-human interaction.

Thinking about Media and Imitation

It seems unlikely that people would admit to feeling good when a computer changed its personality to match theirs. A computer can't truly care about a user, and it could never gain anything by indulging users with an interaction style constructed just for them. What is unconscious, however, can be influential. Users automatically credited a machine with a change in personality, even though they knew that no credit was due. The effects of the credit were broad, extending beyond liking to evaluations of performance, both of the machine and of themselves.

This study, unlike many of the others, also allowed us to put something back into the social science literature as well as borrow from it. Although an enormous number of studies demonstrate gain theory, it has never been applied to personality, whether in a computer or a human.

This study also suggests a new way to study personality. Typically, the personalities presented in psychology experiments are cursory. An experimental subject is brought into a lab and given information about a fictitious person, often in the form of a list of personality traits. Participants are then asked to report how much they like or dislike the person described. This procedure, however, is artificial. Participants are required to form impressions from descriptions of people rather than from the experience of an interaction.

The reason that psychologists usually manipulate personality with brief written descriptions is no doubt pragmatic. Any attempt to manipulate personality in a face-to-face interaction is hard. The problem can be solved, however, with a *mediated* personality. Using a medium offers several advantages. One is ease. A real person doesn't have to sit with each participant in the experiment. There is also greater experimental control. With media, it's possible to manipulate *only* the personality attributes desired, a difficult task for even the best actor, but a cinch for a machine.

One other advantage is even more substantial: People participate in a real interaction. Experience is not limited to mere descriptions or hypothetical commentary. People actually take turns exchanging information. Even though a mediated personality can be demonstrated with minimal cues, it is experienced over time in a conversation quite close to an actual interpersonal encounter.

Imitating Users' Personalities

One implication of this study is exciting: Media should adapt to the personality of the user. The reason for excitement is that computers should be able to do this extremely well, in spite of long-standing difficulties with other forms of artificial intelligence. Here are some ways for media to adapt to users that we think will work well.

Traditionally, adaptation has been reserved for mundane features of media, for example, offering tips or changing the level of difficulty in error messages. These changes may help, but the language related to *personality* may be far more important than language related to task difficulty. The personality in language may determine whether people think media are useful, and even what people think about themselves.

There is good news about how much personality information is required to *begin* an interaction. It's easy to think that a computer should start out with all the facts about a user. This, however, is rarely practical, short of a formal questionnaire or an interview before a session begins. This certainly isn't what people do in real life, however. In human-human interaction, we get to know people gradually, adapting as we go and using clues about personality that we discover over time.

Asking too many questions at the beginning of an interaction actually is detrimental. It's an uncomfortable start in any relationship. Imagine the negative response if a computer or anyone else said, "Before I'll help you, please answer these questions about yourself." There are also legitimate privacy concerns in an exchange about personality, especially if the interaction deals with personal issues or finance.

When a computer asks questions, it also suggests a fixed relationship. People like and expect that a relationship can change, and if it's new, it should be able to change quickly. If personality is set at the beginning of an interaction, by answering questions that seem unchangeable, people may think that there is no flexibility, no room for reconsideration. When personality appears changeable, a result that can come only from monitoring and learning with each exchange, the interaction could be even better.

What information about people can media use to change personality? There are several possibilities, none of which requires users to answer questions directly. For example, a computer could learn a great deal about personality from the linguistic style of a user, monitoring the use of cautious claims or the propensity to interrupt. It could then slowly adopt new language to become more like the user. This learning could come from almost any exchange, everything from a registration form to a natural language help system.

No Penalties for Mistaken Imitation

How risky is imitation? Could it backfire, inducing *less* favorable responses than would exist if no attempt were made to know the user? Even if designers are uncertain whether a particular adaptation will be successful or not, there is still reason to proceed. Someone who adapts in a desirable direction is clearly liked, but a system that adapts in a negative direction is *not* clearly *dis*liked. Humans and computers both get credit for trying, even when they fail. This is the genius of adaptation—as long as you can go back to the old way, there is tremendous incentive to try something new. Even a poor system for following a user's behavior may be better than no system at all, especially if the decisions are reversible.

Media and Emotion

9

Good versus Bad

Humans have developed wonderful and elaborate language to describe the people, objects, and places they encounter. The ability to effectively use descriptive language has great social advantage. People celebrate those who can provide rich descriptions, discover nuance, and evaluate details. Good poets can capture subtle distinctions in human experience with ease, an intelligent counselor can locate behavior within a complex array of possibilities, and effective travel writers can describe what is unique about every place they visit.

Those people who are less expressive often feel inferior. But what is it exactly that they can't do? Everyone *senses* a reaction to everything, but like the college sophomore struggling with a term paper, many can't find the words to adequately express their feelings.

How different are the experiences of those with and without expressive talent? Perhaps not much at all. There is one critical similarity: Every response that people have, regardless of their talents and training in expression, begins with an extremely simple evaluation of whether the people, places, or objects are *good or bad*, likable or not likable, worthy of approach or something to avoid.

How do we know that this is true? One source is a large literature in psychology about how people assign meaning to things—from other people to jobs to restaurants to television programs. When people are asked to make judgments by using a long list of descriptive adjectives, the most obvious and reliable grouping of the adjectives is related to *valence*—good and bad. The words that describe good and bad, while many, are virtually interchangeable. Words such as pleasant, agreeable, likable, favorable, and enjoyable are understood by all of us as fundamentally black or white, rather than shades of gray.

The psychology literature about "good/bad" evaluations is huge and diverse, encompassing hundreds of studies with similar results. The studies all have one common property, however. Responses to the adjectives require introspection. People have to read questions on a piece of paper, consider their internal feelings, consciously form a response, and then make a mark on a questionnaire.

If valence is indeed fundamental, shouldn't there be a more basic indication of its importance? Fortunately, there is. Our old brains are hard-wired to distinguish good versus bad as naturally and efficiently as possible. The reason is that the distinction will help protect us from harm. A quick decision that a stranger or environment is *bad* is the necessary preparation for the most basic of responses—avoidance. Although there are a hundred words in the thesaurus that amplify or refine this judgment, the route to all of them is through a simple evaluation—good or bad. Once made, this evaluation can influence how we think, how we pay attention, and what we do.

Through time, the human brain (and indeed the whole body) has evolved to do best the things that are most important for survival. Of course, some of the things that were needed to survive in the past are no longer important at the end of the twentieth century. For example, any biological advantages that helped people hunt animals in the wild are now, for most of us, irrelevant. Despite current irrelevancy, however, the advantages are built in and they can influence how people respond to contemporary life. We still, for example, look for facial expressions that signal friend or foe, likely with the same watchfulness that we might have given to a competitor in the wild.

The two hemispheres of the human brain have evolved to be specialized processors of positive and negative information. Positive experiences became associated with the left hemisphere, and negative experiences with the right hemisphere. This basic difference is in addition to other known specialties of the two hemispheres. For example, the left hemisphere generally favors verbal and analytical processing; the right hemisphere, spatial and nonverbal processing.

The evidence that brain structure supports a fundamental distinction between good and bad is compelling. Here are some examples. A drug called amabarbitol sodium can limit communication between neurons in the brain. When this drug is injected into the right hemisphere, that hemisphere goes to sleep. The left hemisphere—the location for positive experience—becomes dominant, and patients report euphoric moods. When the drug is injected into the left hemisphere, the opposite happens. The right hemisphere becomes dominant, and people feel depressed, sometimes catastrophically so. There are similar results when lesions in the brain destroy or limit how one of the hemispheres functions. Lesions in the right hemisphere augment positive (or left hemisphere) experience; lesions in the left hemisphere do the opposite.

The same results occur for people who experience extreme levels of good and bad. When people who suffer from schizophrenia and manic depression experience inappropriate moods, brain activity is lateralized. There is more activity in the left hemisphere when mood is extremely positive, and more activity in the right hemisphere during negative moods. This differentiation also occurs when people are merely asked to imagine positive and negative experiences, and even when the experiences themselves are as simple as tasting a sour lemon or grains of sugar.

Hemispheric differences are not even limited to the *experience* of good and bad; they extend to the *recognition* of good and bad. When people "see" a smiling or frowning face in a single hemisphere (a trick accomplished by quickly flashing a picture to either the left or the right of where a person is looking), they can identify a smiling face more quickly when it is flashed to the left hemisphere than when it is flashed to the right hemisphere. The opposite results occur for pictures of faces that are frowning.

Does the Evaluation of Positive/Negative Apply to Media?

Does the human brain sort media the same way it sorts real life? This would certainly seem irrelevant to survival. Depictions of people, places, and objects on a *screen* are neither physical threats nor significant opportunities, and viewers obviously know this. It seems improbable that viewers would focus on the simple question of whether media are good or bad. Doing so might cause people to miss the subtleties that are the essence of a media experience. Viewers should be able to ignore good and bad, so that they can concentrate on more thoughtful evaluations of what they see and hear.

This argument certainly sounds reasonable, but it does depend significantly on people's ability to keep media and real life separated. This may be much more difficult than it sounds, however. Humans evolved in a world where people, objects, and places were either real threats or real opportunities. Old brains, even though they are far more primitive than the twentieth-century demands of media, may continue to guide responses. We predicted the following:

Rule 1: Good versus bad is a primary evaluation of mediated experience.

Rule 2: There is more activity in the left hemisphere for material that is evaluated as good, and more activity in the right hemisphere for material that is evaluated as bad.

Positive or Negative Media Content and Brain Activity

To test these predictions, we tried to answer a simple question: Can you find the same differences in how the brain processes positive and negative media information that are found when people experience real life? The test of this question, even though it involves a special measure, is straightforward. If good/bad differences are critical for the evaluation of media, then brain activity in the two hemispheres should vary as it does for other experiences—from drugs to moods to tastes that are sweet or sour.

To do the test, we first had to choose media content that was clearly positive and negative. This was relatively easy with material from television. For positive content, we chose situations that are associated with positive experiences (e.g., weddings, holidays, births); segments where people displayed positive responses (e.g., smiles and soothing language); and segments where production techniques emphasized pleasantness (e.g., soft focus and slow pacing). For the negative content, we chose scenes where people frowned or behaved violently and scenes where the production was fast-paced and harsh. We made up five 1-minute scenes for each category.

As participants in our experiment viewed the scenes on television, we used an electroencephalogram, or EEG, to measure electrical activity in the brain. Changes in the EEG while viewing different scenes can be used as evidence that the hemispheres are more or less engaged by the different content. Generally, when one of the hemispheres is activated or more alert, it generates electricity differently than when it is at rest.

Sixteen adult women participated in the study, and each was right-handed (EEG is affected by handedness and gender, so we had to limit the sample to control for these effects). Before each participant viewed television, we attached electrodes to her scalp. Two electrodes were placed on the frontal region of the brain, because the expected hemispheric differences occur most prominently in the frontal cortex. Once the electrodes were attached, participants sat in a comfortable chair and watched television while a computer recorded their brain activity.

Good versus Bad Is Basic

The results confirmed the predictions. In the frontal cortex, we found significantly more brain activity in the left hemisphere for the positive content. When participants saw the negative content, the right hemisphere showed greater arousal than the left, again a significant difference.

These data confirmed that the experience of good and bad media is lateralized the same way that good and bad is for any experience. The human brain, at least at the level of primitive cortical arousal, does not have a switch that activates a different type of processing when media are present. As far as neural activity goes, mediated pictures and sounds produce the same results that would occur if the people, objects, and places were actually present.

What Do Psychologists Think about Media?

Many psychologists wonder why someone would be interested in *television* rather than more general processing capabilities of *people*. When research begins with an interest in media, as it certainly did in this case, psychologists are often suspicious.

Their suspicion is not totally unfounded. Any media message is an example of a hundred different things all rolled up together, and consequently, if you find effects, it's hard to know exactly what feature of a message caused them. It could have been the story, the actors, the setting, the type of program, the network that produced the content, the viewing conditions, or a hundred other things. When psychologists confront this problem, they try to decompose stimuli, breaking things down into small parts. They can then test each one separately.

This is a good strategy, but it has one big disadvantage. Quite often, the strategy yields something that doesn't look anything like real life. There are hundreds of psychological experiments that use very simple pictures, brief textual descriptions, and even crude and arbitrary sounds and shapes that are anything but familiar. The result is often an experiment that may be correct, but one that doesn't connect well with the real world.

We think that the data from this study, on the contrary, are quite relevant. We were able to show that a fundamental psychological response—brain activation associated with good and bad experience—is part of an everyday experience. The apparent complexity of media is less important than the fundamental tendency that people have to assess anything as good or bad. This is an important extension of basic science into the real world.

Valence and Media

Clearly, the difference between good and bad is important. Human survival often depends on quick and accurate assessments of whether experience is positive or negative. Even though that assessment may be less useful now than it was millennia ago, it is unlikely that we can inhibit, forget, or suppress what is primitive. We can add to it by thinking hard, but the primitive response is always a starting point.

The most important implication of this applies to definitions of media. Traditional definitions highlight what is unique about media delivery and media content. Media are television, computers, newspapers, and film. Media content is situation comedies, word processing applications, international business news, and on-line chat rooms. These categories are useful for many discussions, but they miss a critical fact about humans. No matter what criteria we might have for thoughtful evaluations of media (e.g., media increase productivity, they entertain, they give information) or worries about media effects (e.g., media promote violence and aggression, media create political cynicism), we need to be aware that all of these responses begin with a simple judgment: Is it good or bad?

For television and film, and even for computer games, this evaluation seems well understood. A visceral and quick response on the order of "I like it" or "not for me" is a critical reaction for people who work with these media, and they design accordingly. When the function is not entertainment, however, the worry seems to vanish, presumably because loftier purpose means that something as simple as liking is irrelevant. This is a dangerous assumption: Whether a word processor or a word game, all media experience is good or bad first.

The ubiquity of good and bad also says something about differences between people. It is tempting to think that some people think that everything is good, and others think that everything is bad, or that some people are "left-brained" and others are "right-brained." This assumption is wrong. All people use both hemispheres of their brains all of the time, and good and bad experiences (mediated or real) stimulate different hemispheres of everyone's brain. Neural anatomy ensures this, and our environment demands it. The important consequence is that media make everyone feel good *and* bad.

10

Negativity

One of the nicest things about giving a lecture with a colleague is that the two of us can debrief together. You don't have to stew on your own, wondering if everything went OK. If we were to honestly report the content of those conversations, there is a bias in what gets discussed: It's the criticism. Like most people, after quickly assuring ourselves that everyone basically liked the talk, we dissect the negative comments.

While scrutiny of criticism sometimes makes us feel overly self-conscious, psychologists have an explanation that lumps our response in with a number of similar human responses. The explanation is called the law of hedonic asymmetry. It means that evaluations of good and bad are important, but not equally so. The asymmetry refers to the unevenness of good and bad, notably the dominance of negative experience. There is pleasure that we all get used to, but pain is a different story. We dwell on it.

One response to negativity is quite conscious and common—people don't like it. The evaluation of negativity is certain: Negative experiences are subjectively unpleasant. Many of the other consequences of negativity are counterintuitive, because they occur automatically. They are so important to survival that our old brains insure that they don't require a lot of planning or analysis. Responses to negativity are rapid and thoughtless, so much so that they are often denied after they occur.

Painful and negative experiences get attention. Once they have it, all sorts of things happen. People reallocate thinking, store information differently, and experience feelings that change everything from how we feel to how our bodies function.

Negative events grab attention. If traffic planners could get drivers to ignore emergency vehicles on the side of highways during rush hour, millions of people would be home sooner. Why can't we just drive by? And why do our ears perk up when we hear about people's faults rather than their triumphs? Why are we more interested to know that someone has failed rather than succeeded? Why is sickness bigger news than wellness?

Negative information demands more attention because it is consequential. Failures to heed warnings, flee, or prepare a defense are horrible errors, perhaps even fatal ones. Behavioral decisions related to each need consideration, and quickly. A missed opportunity, however, is much less consequential. We'll live another day, and there will be other opportunities.

A comforting piece of advice when confronted with unpleasant experience is to recover quickly, not to dwell on it. While we can't ignore negative experiences when they are new, perhaps people can at least forget them quickly so that their effects won't linger. This is sometimes called the "Pollyanna Effect," and it summarizes a hope that people, with some effort, can remember positive experiences better than negative ones.

Unfortunately, the Pollyanna Effect is limited. When asked to recall important life events, there is a tendency for people to volunteer positive ones: People are more likely to mention their wedding than a public embarrassment. The *intensity* of attention to experience, however, runs in the opposite direction, and because of that intensity, memory *benefits* from negativity, even though the memory itself may be disliked. This certainly doesn't mean that all attempts at teaching or persuasion should include negative material, but it may help explain why we increasingly see negative messages in politics, news, and advertising: They work because they are memorable.

There is one other part to the story about negativity and memory. Negativity not only causes people to remember whatever is happening at the *moment* it is experienced. It also changes the way information is processed *after* the negative experience is over. Experiences that come immediately after negative events are remembered better than experiences that come after positive events. The term that psychologists use to describe this effect is *proactive enhancement*. Negative information wakes up the processing system, focusing attention on whatever follows.

While negativity *enhances* the processing of experiences that come after it, negative experiences *impede* memory for events that come before, a process called *retroactive interference*. This interference occurs because to remember information in the long term, people need to consider it, review it, elaborate it, and mix it with other experiences. When something brutal appears, however, thoughtfulness ceases. We immediately orient to the negative information, and forget what was being considered. The result is something like erasing a tape. Previously recorded information is lost to the immediate demands of compelling negative material.

Mediated Negativity

It is tempting to think that mediated negative experiences are different from their counterparts in real life. After all, negative events in text and pictures can't really hurt people. There are absolutely no physical consequences that could come from ignoring negative media. Perhaps people could even take some perverse pleasure when negativity is mediated, because they could experience it without consequence.

The media equation, however, suggests that negative content works in the same way that the psychological literature says negative experiences do in real life. The fact that the cause of negative experience is textual or pictorial should not diminish natural human responses. Mediated negative material should be as unpleasant, attention-getting, and influential for memory as are negative experiences in real life.

If you substitute mediated forms of negative experience for actual experiences, there are five predictions:

Rule 1: People will not like negative media.

Rule 2: People will pay more attention to negative media than to positive media.

Rule 3: People will remember negative media better than positive media.

Rule 4: People will have better memory for information that comes after negative media than for information that comes after positive media.

Rule 5: People will have worse memory for information that comes before negative media than for information that comes before positive media.

The first rule, that people don't like negative media, is not surprising. People say, often and strongly, that they don't like a variety of negative content, including blood and guts in the news, the harrowing experiences recreated in so-called reality programming, gore in video games, negative political advertising, health messages that threaten physical collapse, people yelling at each other on talk shows, and negative gossip that feeds the tabloid press. For liking, it seems that intuitions and the media equation are the same.

The other predictions, however, seem more unexpected. If the Pollyanna Effect works anywhere, perhaps it should work best with media. Since negative media don't pose the same immediate physical threats as real experiences, there should be plenty of opportunity for people to discount negative media. But can people easily make media into something different from real life?

Negative Experiences on the Screen

We have done several experiments to see if negative media are similar to real-life experiences. Finding negative media to use in research is certainly not hard. We've tried to accumulate several types, from blood and guts in news to harsh commentary in political advertisements.

Study 1: Judging Negative Political Ads

The first question concerned liking. Do people like negative material on the screen any more than they like the same material in real life? Is there any possibility that we all secretly like negative material, especially when we can experience it from the safety of a seat in front of the television? This first study tested negative political advertising.

Before looking at the study, it's important to remember what negative political ads contain. They are not only messages about politics. Actually, their most salient features go well beyond civic information. People yell, doom is forecast, characters are assaulted, and faces cringe and scowl. These are some of the most important cues that humans have to indicate that something bad is happening.

In our study, adults were asked to watch several ads that were divided into three groups: (1) ads that were explicitly negative (negative comments about competitors, and threats about what will happen if a competitor wins); (2) ads that were explicitly positive (no mention of competitors, doom, or societal decay); and (3) ads that mixed negative and positive material, usually in that order.

We showed several ads in each of the three categories to adult viewers. The ads were embedded in regular television programs to simulate a natural viewing situation. We measured how much participants liked the different ads *during* the viewing session. Viewers were asked to turn a dial on a device that they held in their laps as they viewed. The numbers on the dial indicated how much they liked what they were viewing.

There were clear differences in reactions to the ads: The negative ads were liked much less than the other two categories. This difference confirmed that negative messages were unique, which was not a surprise. What was surprising, however, was that dislike of the negative ads occurred within the first ten seconds of the messages. It didn't take participants long to identify negative messages, and to respond accordingly. This means that the psychological consequences of negativity are likely at work early in the experience of these messages.

The same political ads were also used to test memory, in this case recognition memory. Each person was shown thirty pictures for one second per picture. Half of the pictures were from the political ads the participants had just seen, and half were from similar ads that were not shown. After viewing each picture, participants pressed one of two buttons to indicate whether they recognized the picture from the material they had watched, or whether the picture was one they had never seen. The accuracy of identifying the pictures was much better for the negative material.

To confirm the effects of negative media on memory, we did a similar test with information from the audio track of the ads. Participants heard sound clips that lasted for three seconds, half of which were the voices of people and half of which were ambient noises. Similar to the visuals, participants heard half of the sounds from the experiment; the other half were new. The same results occurred for audio as for video; that is, accuracy was better for the sounds in the negative ads than for the positive ones. The conclusion from these tests: Negative information produces better memory for pictures and for sounds.

There is one other way to measure memory that we tried with the ads. Memory can also be defined by the ease with which people can access the information that they have stored. Better or stronger memory is not only the ability to recognize information *accurately*; it is also the ability to do so *quickly*. To test the speed with which participants could make decisions about whether they had seen or heard information, we measured the time it took participants to decide whether information in the memory tests was new or not. The quicker people are at making this decision, the more accessible the information.

The differences between negative and positive messages persisted for recognition latency. Pictures and sounds from the negative commercials were identified more quickly than pictures and sounds from the positive ads or information from the ads that had both. It took 23 percent longer for participants to identify the positive information as compared to the negative information.

In sum, across a wide variety of measures and measurement approaches, negative material was remembered better. The media equation applies to valenced content.

Study 2: Attention to Negative Content

We also predicted that people would pay more attention to negative media. Like memory, attention can be difficult to measure accurately because it is hard for people to know exactly how much attention they are giving when they watch and listen to media. We again used a measure of attention from cognitive psychology called "secondary-task reaction time," the same measure we had used in other studies to look at attention to other features of media.

To review, the measure works like this. While watching television (the primary task), participants in the study hold a computer game paddle in their lap. While viewing, the participants periodically hear a tone in the audio track of the presentation. They are told to press the button on the game paddle as quickly as possible after hearing the tone (the secondary task). The more attention people are paying to the ad, the slower they are at responding to the tone.

In this study, we looked at attention to thirty-second public service announcements about health. There were messages about diet, smoking, and sexually transmitted disease. The positive messages used songs, smiles, and information about health. The negative messages warned of death or severe illness, and they occasionally showed grotesque pictures of the effects of disease.

When we looked at attention to these messages, the results confirmed the primacy of negative material. The negative messages caused longer reaction times to the secondary tones; that is, participants paid more attention to negative messages.

We also concluded that attention to the negative material was automatic. No one in the experiment felt that attention depended on the emotional tone of the message they viewed. If anything, participants thought that they were actually *ignoring* the negative. "It's too hard to watch," one person mentioned. Hard, maybe; compelling, definitely.

Study 3: Negative Media Experiences and Memory

We also thought the negative material would influence the processing of information that came before and after. Using the psychological terms, there should be proactive enhancement and retroactive interference.

The predictions were that information presented after the negative content should be remembered better, and information presented before the negative content should be remembered less.

To test this, we made ten 2-minute news stories, edited from segments of the national evening news, about events that often have dramatic and negative pictures: airplane crashes, malnutrition and disease in children, the Persian Gulf War, natural disasters, sports violence, and urban riots. Each of the stories we made had three parts. The first part was about forty-five seconds long and always showed a newscaster seated at a desk. This was the introduction for the story. The third part of the story always showed the same newscaster in the same studio giving a wrap-up.

For the middle part of each story, we made two versions. One version contained pictures related to the stories, but no pictures that graphically depicted the negative information discussed in the stories. For example, we showed an aid worker preparing medicine or food, but did not show starving children or other disturbing images. For the second version, however, no holds were barred on negativity. We showed the most graphic depictions possible: blood and guts, disease, and violence. In both versions, the exact same voiceover was used for the audio. The only difference in the two versions was the pictures; one version was negative and compelling, one much less so.

After we showed the stories to participants, we made two assessments of memory. First, we wanted to confirm that negative versions of the stories, overall, would be remembered better than the positive ones. To do this, we asked participants to describe what they had seen during the experiment. This time, however, we asked this question two months *after* the participants had seen the stories in the lab. The negative stories won again. Participants could recall more details about the pictures of blood and guts and other negative material than they could about the same stories with tamer pictures.

This is a strong confirmation of the power of negative information, because the memory effects lasted so long after participants first watched the stories. Even though the participants in the experiment each had several weeks to forget or to have other experiences interfere, the original material was not easily forgotten.

We also tested participants' memory for information that appeared before and after the negative material. To do this, we made up a multiple-choice test that covered information presented at the beginning and end of the stories. If the negative material in the middle of each news story had an effect on what came before and after it, this should be reflected in participants's ability to answer these questions.

That's exactly what happened. The participants who saw the extremely unpleasant scenes in the middle of each story could better answer the questions about the last part of the story. The negative information was a wake-up call for attention, and the increased attention made participants better able to process what followed.

The exact opposite happened for information at the beginning of each story. Those participants who saw the highly negative versions actually *forgot* some of what came before the negative parts. Presumably, the jolt that comes with experiencing negative information not only makes you perk up and listen better to what follows, it also makes you less likely to elaborate, rehearse, and consider the information that you previously experienced.

Thinking about Negative Media

What do these three studies have in common? Across a diverse set of negative media, they all demonstrate the equivalence of *mediated* and natural experience. The supposed psychological distance that comes with media does not cause a fundamentally different reaction. Negativity, mediated or not, is powerful, riveting, and memorable. And these effects are *automatic,* so important to survival that they don't require much thought or analysis.

One of the most common divisions in psychology is between thinking and feeling. This dichotomy tempts oversimplification, but it is useful as a way to catalog what we believe is important about media. People most often worry about the effects of media on thinking. How much does television *teach* us about world events, how much do children *learn* about social life, and how much more *productive* are people who use a computer? The present studies suggest that feelings are also important criteria, and they show that the particular feelings that do occur can be caused by the same things that cause them in real life.

If someone feels bad after experiencing media, that may be enough to justify an interest in emotional responses. Feelings, however, are not just important in themselves. Emotions are critically linked to thinking, even when we're trying to minimize their interference. Imagine the worker who goes to an office, sits at a desk, works with sophisticated machines, and then evaluates his or her progress by criteria such as accuracy or the amount of time it takes to complete a task. Despite all the cues that this person is in the most rational, feeling-*less* environment possible, there is no inoculation against the power of emotional response. Everyone has feelings, they are constantly at work, and they have consequences for a broad range of responses that people incorrectly believe are under their control.

The Power of Negative Messages

Is it possible to use negativity to increase the effectiveness of a message? It may seem from these results that it would be useful to put negative material into messages. Attention goes up and memory increases—not bad outcomes if you are trying to convey information. The use of negativity, however, is a double-edged sword. You might increase attention and memory, but often with disastrous secondary effects. For example, negativity may increase memory for the *wrong* parts of a message. When we placed gory visuals in the news stories, people did not learn more about current events. Instead, they remembered the compelling visuals *at the expense* of information about current events. Obviously, this is counter to the goal of fulfilling a civic responsibility, even though it does mean that there is a lot in the news that makes an impression and can attract an audience.

Even though people learn more information (albeit the wrong information), people also don't like the information much. Consider what might happen with products designed for everything *but* emotional effects. Unpleasant textual messages that appear in computer business software, for example, could make the entire experience memorably unpleasant. People might be capable of dissociating isolated experiences from the product, but the dissociation is difficult, so much so that people are not likely to do it continually, especially when they are either tired or distracted by work.

Negativity and Politics

The same double-edged sword (good memory, low liking) is often found in politics, although it is a sword that some strategists might actually strive to create. Why do candidates depend on negative messages to win an election? The answer is that subjective judgments about "liking" for the ad are not the main goal.

Negative advertisements that condemn a rival candidate have two effects. Memory for the negative information increases, and people are turned off to the campaign. No one likes to be around people who are having an argument, and television brings the argument into your living room. The intentional creation of this feeling could be particularly useful to candidates who would benefit from lower voter turnout: Voters would remember the bad stuff, detest the whole exchange, and stay home on Election Day.

Negativity and the Newest Media

If emotions are always present, what are the implications for computers and other technologies that are more purely associated with rationality? Unlike television and film, which explicitly try to influence emotions, computers are ostensibly focused on thinking. They help people order life, make things more efficient, and produce more. Any type of mediated interaction, however, even those that depend on simple text related to topics that are clearly intellectual, can evoke emotional responses.

Emotion is just as relevant to textual presentations on computers as it is to visuals on television. In fact, some of the most powerful creations of emotions in psychological experiments come from having people read words or even just imagine negative experiences based on written instructions.

Media depend on the fact that audience attention can be sold to people who would like to promote products and services. As more different media compete for a finite amount of attention, we can expect to see more negative content across media. If negativity makes people more likely to watch news and movies, it should work as well on the World Wide Web. The bottom line is that negativity is engaging, a fact that already guides professionals in news, politics, and advertising, and a fact we can expect to see applied more broadly in the future.

11

Arousal

The *San Francisco Chronicle* uses little pictures of a man sitting in a theater seat to graphically illustrate movie ratings. The icon appears next to each new review. Instead of a star system (☆ to ☆☆☆☆), a little man sits snoring in his chair, eyes closed and slumped over, if it's a bad film. If the film is great, he claps wildly with wide eyes, erect posture, and a broad smile. The pictures capture the dimension of valence: movies good to bad, and at a glance.

We've always wondered, however, about the little man when he snored. Does sleepiness really mean that he didn't like the film? If he didn't like the movie, wouldn't he express displeasure instead of dozing off? Wouldn't he frown and turn his head away? And if the movie was *really* bad, shouldn't he be jumping up and down with disgust, putting as much effort into his rejection as he put into approval?

A better rating system might have two pictures. One could indicate whether the movie was good or bad, via a smile or a frown. A second picture could show the level of enthusiasm for the judgment: The man could slump in his chair or he could jump up and down, heart pounding and ready for action. The second picture is the key to a second aspect of emotion: arousal. Both positive *and* negative experiences share the potential to arouse. Like valence, arousal has implications for the way people evaluate their experiences, for what people remember, and for whether they pay attention.

Arousal is a volume level on things good and bad. It is the *intensity* of experience, and ranges from feelings of being energized, excited, and alert, to feeling calm, drowsy, and peaceful. If the valence of emotions determines whether people approach or avoid, arousal determines the energy with which they do either. Obviously, people can feel *extremely* good or bad, or just *a little* good or bad. What is the level of motivation? How intense are the feelings? Answers to these questions determine arousal.

Arousal and valence together are the two basic dimensions of emotion. It is possible to assign values on both dimensions to any real-life experience. The values on the two dimensions are independent; a value on one will not predict the value on the other. For example, flowers, a cute baby, and erotica all have positive *valence*, but they have distinctly different levels of *arousal*: Erotica ranks highest and flowers, lowest. Similarly, a funeral procession and mutilated bodies are both negative, but only mutilation will produce significant arousal.

Both dimensions of emotional experience can be observed in a number of ways. Both are expressed in language: Nouns and adjectives describe feelings and adverbs indicate intensity. Emotional cues are also given in facial expressions: Smiles and frowns indicate valence, and the exaggeration of those expressions indicates arousal. People also experience emotion subjectively: They feel good or bad, and they feel tranquil or ready to act. Emotion is also present in physiology: Hearts beat slow or fast, and the amount of moisture in skin changes. Finally, emotion is behavior: People approach and avoid, and they can perform either quickly or not.

In general, there is good agreement among the different expressions of emotion. When a strong negative feeling is present, for example, there is agreement between the words used to express valence (e.g., "I feel very sad"), the facial expressions that accompany the feelings (e.g., downturned mouth, lowered eyebrows), physiology (a slowed heart beat and sweating skin), and physical action (getting up and leaving the room). Although emotion can operate at all of these levels, valence and arousal are essentially biological. Evolution has conspired to ensure that everyone reacts to experience with evaluations of good and bad, and evolution has made us do so with different levels of motivation and urgency.

The *independence* of arousal and valence is critical. Arousal *adds* to what we know about emotions, and it can't be predicted by just knowing valence. This complicates the story of emotion a bit, but the gain is substantial. By keeping arousal and valence separate, psychologists have a better picture of how the intensity of feelings guides attention and memory *independently* of whether the feelings are good or bad. There is something quite similar about feeling good or bad when the experience occurs with equal energy.

How much does arousal affect people? Recent psychological studies suggest that the effect is significant. Arousal is not merely a primitive physical response that can be ignored by the more thoughtful parts of the brain. High states of arousal *increase* the vigilance with which people attend to the world and lead people's processing systems to work at full capacity.

High arousal works like negativity. It's the arousing experiences, as well as the negative ones, that are the best remembered. In fact, there is some controversy about which of these dimensions is *more* important for memory, arousal or valence. A growing literature shows that arousal, whether caused by positive or negative experience, may be equally (and some argue even more) important.

Mediated Arousal

Does the two-dimensional description of emotion also apply to media? If it does, then mediated arousal should have the same effects on feelings and memory as arousal generated by other means. Common sense might predict that mediated experience should *not* be similar to direct experience. Mediation can protect people from actual harm, so one might expect people to experience *representations* of arousal without becoming aroused themselves.

Our prediction, however, was that media are close enough to the real thing to generate a real response. Old brains simply can't make an adjustment for media, keeping our bodies from reacting to what only seems real but isn't. Using the psychological literature, we made these predictions about responses to mediated emotional experience:

Rule 1: People will respond to media content using the same basic dimensions of emotion—valence and arousal—that they use when responding to real-life experiences.

Rule 2: Highly arousing material will be better remembered than less-arousing materials.

Are Pictures Classified by Arousal as Well as Good/Bad?

Our first task was to see if people use arousal, in addition to valence, as a method to classify media. To do this, we selected a range of emotional media content to show in the lab and asked participants to rate the content on arousal and valence. We then compared the distribution of content with previous research.

Our first study used 258 video segments from movies, documentaries, and television programs. The segments were selected to represent a range of emotional experiences typical in media. There were erotic and gory scenes, as well as more benign selections of positive and negative material. Each of the segments was six seconds in duration, and each contained only a single shot.

Eighty-three participants evaluated each of the scenes. Each gave an assessment of how arousing each scene was and judged whether the scene was positive or negative. Viewers made the judgments using two pictorial scales that have been used to measure arousal and valence in several previous psychological studies. Each scale uses cartoon figures to represent nine levels for each dimension. The valence dimension was represented at the extremes by a face that smiled broadly and a face with a big frown. The arousal dimension showed an excited figure at one end (complete with pounding heart), and a calm figure at the other (with no internal excitement). These pictures are actually pretty close to the icons we recommend for the movie reviews.

After each segment, viewers evaluated it by circling the figure that best represented their reactions. Each scene was then given a score for arousal and valence that represented the average across all of the participants.

Pictures Elicit Both Dimensions of Emotion

The distribution of the two dimensions, valence and arousal, was consistent with our prediction. The first thing we noticed about the judgments was that valence and arousal were not related; they were different evaluations that each added something unique. Arousing positive media were a couple making love, and a night-time rocket launch. Arousing negative media were a snake in the grass, and a bloody-faced prison inmate. Calm positive scenes were a leaf floating downstream in a river, and waves breaking on a beach. Calm negative segments were a horse-drawn procession through a cemetery, and a person in a rocking chair on a porch.

Even though the images viewers saw in the study were obviously from popular media, there was no switch in people's brains that caused them to view the segments differently than real life. Viewers did not discount the pictures as merely symbolic, unworthy of serious emotional response, nor did they lump all of the pictures into a single "media" cluster. The media segments were real enough to warrant a complete range of emotional responses.

There was one interesting nuance in the results. The 258 segments were not *evenly* distributed across the two dimensions of emotion. The biggest hole was for material that was extremely arousing but at the midpoint of valence. It turns out that for mediated *and* real-life experiences, as things get arousing, they also are more likely to be either good or bad. Neutrality, it turns out, is not a big part of excitement. It is also difficult to find material that is extremely good or bad and totally *un*-arousing—it's hard to be blasé about highly valenced material.

Arousal and Memory

We then chose a set of sixty pictures, varying in arousal and valence, for further analysis. After presenting the video segments to 125 participants in random order, we asked each participant to write down on a piece of paper a brief description of as many of the pictures as he or she could remember. They were given five minutes for this recall task. Each picture was then given a score based on the percentage of participants who could remember the scene. To see whether results would change over time, we also gave each participant the same memory test two weeks after they saw the video clips.

Both measures of memory (immediate and delayed) showed the same pattern: The more arousing the scene, the better it was remembered. Arousal is important for human memory, whether the experience is mediated or not.

Thinking about Media and Arousal

The most important implication of the research is that media experiences are *emotional* experiences. Part of the emotional experience is valence and part is arousal, but these two dimensions allow for the same distribution of media experiences that are found in real life. There is virtually no type of content and no form of presentation that is *in*capable of causing changes in emotions. This is true even though people may *seem* to approach mediated presentations with the detachment necessary to render pictures and words emotion*less*. Arousal, like valence, works even when it seems wrong that people should take symbols so seriously.

All arousing experiences, whether positive or negative, have important consequences. In the case of negativity, arousal helps people avoid problems: We flee better, fight harder, or act more quickly. In the case of positive experiences, arousal puts us in touch with *opportunity* for pleasure or procreation. Seeking pleasure and avoiding pain, while not a complete motto for the good life, is a reasonable basic strategy for survival. No wonder we are likely to remember things that are arousing. Of course, these findings are hardly news to those who follow the tricks of Madison Avenue. Violence can sell entertainment and even news; sex can sell cars and soap. The data in this study help attach a single explanation to both results—it is the potential to arouse.

This means that negative images aren't the only way to make people remember. There is *some* positive content that has as much chance of enhancing memory as does negative material. This category has a great range of content (from rockets to roller coasters), but the most likely example is sex. We may remember the erotic with the same mastery as the violent and gory.

Arousal and the Design of Media

The relevance of arousal in traditional media cannot be surprising. It's not a shock to learn that the dinosaurs in Jurassic Park can make your palms sweat, or that everyone, regardless of moral position, is aroused by erotic films. But what about media for which arousal seems irrelevant: a computer spreadsheet, the voice of an assistant in a word processing application, or a quick video insert in a reference tool? These products often have purposes that seem at odds with the notion of entertainment or arousal. However, the basis for the success of these products, in addition to their usability and efficiency, is often the potential to arouse. This may require changes in the ways that computing and multimedia products are evaluated.

Although defining products and messages with respect to their arousal potential is a good idea, the same experience will not *always* cause the same level of arousal. Arousal is something that happens within the bodies and minds of *people*, and because of this, there is room for different effects across people or differences for the same person at different times. Here are some ways in which these differences might become apparent.

Excitation Transfers

One cause of individual differences is the unique experience that people have *before* they are exposed to media. Arousal is cumulative. If you have an argument with a friend, and then watch an arousing news story, the level of arousal associated with the news story will be higher than if you were doing something calming before viewing. It's impossible to simply turn off a prior state of arousal and return to a baseline.

137

The transfer of arousal from one event to another has been used successfully by advertisers who want to maximize attention to an ad placed within a pod of several television messages. The commercial will get more attention when it is the first ad in the pod immediately following an arousing program. If you want to get the most bang for your television advertising buck, you shouldn't be too impressed with a Nielsen rating: Those numbers apply to an entire television program or at best a large chunk of a show. A better strategy would be to ask if your ad can be placed first in the commercial break and after an arousing scene.

One might think that arousal builds between experiences with the same valence. It makes sense that two gory segments in a row would result in more arousal than either one by itself. But arousal can carry over from previous experiences that have different valence. Since it is arousal that is transferring, and not valenced arousal, it is quite possible that a positive arousing segment could increase the excitement associated with a negative arousing scene that follows. This is counterintuitive, but important. Watching a rocket launch could intensify one's response to subsequent violence.

Arousal Management

Arousal is not wholly outside of our control. People do *manage* excitement. People instinctively make corrections when life gets too boring or too intense. Everyone has a natural inclination to moderate arousal over time to maintain an optimal level of excitement. The media equation suggests that arousal management is no different for mediated and unmediated experience. If you become too aroused at work, you can just as easily watch a calming television program as sit in the park.

This begs a question: Do people use media to unwind or to excite? The answer is both. We often select mediated experiences because they can change our current state of arousal. If the late-night horror movie gets too scary, we change the channel to a documentary. If writing a paper gets too boring, we click on a computer game. There is a hopeless confusion between mediated and real experiences in the cadence of arousal. Mediated experiences are different only because they are available and controllable.

The personal management of arousal may be particularly interesting when people are allowed more control over their use of media. Not long ago, active management required getting up to turn the channel or an effort to switch to a different medium. Interactive media, however, allow for arousal to be fine-tuned in short order. For example, this is an easy possibility while browsing the World Wide Web. You can move from site to site, and even within sites, according to the need for excitement or calm. The same will be true for interactive television, and computers that run several programs simultaneously, especially if one is a game.

Arousal and Daily Life

What about the link between arousal and the rest of life? Arousal is intimately linked to rational thought. The separation of thinking and feeling is an illusion. It is not the case that the older portion of the brain somehow keeps arousal locked away, never to influence other parts of mental life. We can't keep arousal at bay just by thinking.

Nor is thinking without arousal possible or even desirable. Good teachers know that enthusiasm is as good a predictor of attention and learning as any other part of their presentation. Advertisers, preachers, authors, newscasters, and politicians know the same thing. Without some allowance for the link between emotional response and cognitive response, the world would be a boring place indeed. Attention, if relegated to a purely thoughtful and rational choice, might deny a fundamental joy—the pleasure of relying on an automatic and effortless way to satisfy an important human need.

A downside lurks, however. Overreliance on arousal may encourage its management to the *exclusion* of thinking. We only have so much effort to give, and arousal and thoughtfulness drain the same reservoir. Thinking could easily suffer when the balance favors excitement. The challenge is to ensure that no single method of attention wins.

Media and Social Roles

12

Specialists

Consumers are often influenced by testimonials. We were certainly counting on this when we chose quotations for the jacket of this book. We thought that expert opinions about the ideas in the book might persuade readers to spend time and money on it. Readers would know that at least a few people had responded strongly and positively to the ideas.

All reviews, however, even if positive, are not created equal. A sophomore in one of our classes said that we had told him amazing things about media. But we left his name off the book jacket in favor of a prominent person who had said exactly the same thing. What's the difference between a sophomore and a CEO? And what do the people quoted on the jacket have, even if you don't recognize their names, that others don't?

One answer, among many, is that the people quoted are specialists. Their titles suggest expertise, even if you know nothing about their specific accomplishments. When people need help with something complicated or important, they seek the advice of a specialist rather than a generalist. This is the essence of our respect for professionals. Not only do we anoint specialists in the professions—doctors, lawyers, and engineers—we will settle for nothing less, when the circumstances warrant, than a neurosurgeon (not just a doctor), a patent attorney (not just a lawyer) or an integrated circuit specialist (not just an engineer). Specialists know more.

Psychologists who study specialization have shown that respect for experts is basic. Experiments have shown that the products of specialists are perceived as better than those of generalists, even when identical. Consequently, the right labels attached to the right people can mean the difference between a positive and a negative evaluation.

A more surprising finding, however, concerns the truth behind the labels. One might assume that specialization needs to be demonstrated, not just proclaimed. On the contrary, a great deal of research shows that simply being labeled a "specialist," independent of any verification that the label is warranted, is enough to do the trick. Like the Scarecrow in *The Wizard of Oz*, you can become a genius simply because someone labels you one. It doesn't even matter if everyone knows that it isn't true.

Why are labels, even random ones, so powerful? Psychologists have two answers, both based on the idea that deep thinking is hard, and can't be sustained constantly. First, categorization simplifies interactions. If you know that someone is an expert, you can make assumptions about how he or she will talk, think, and behave, and how you should respond. The predictability gained by applying a label makes people reluctant to scrutinize the label's accuracy.

The second explanation is that people are biased toward acceptance. People take labels at face value, at least until they have time to think carefully about their validity, because doubt requires greater thought. To reject the label of "expert" means marshaling evidence that the label is wrong. Acceptance, however, takes no work at all.

Can Media Have "Specialties"?

The role of specialist, like any other social role, seems profoundly human. This observation, in the spirit of our attempt to apply what is human to media, was good reason to see if roles could work with media. Could the role of specialist be applied to a communication technology? And if so, would people respond the same way they would if the role were occupied by a real person?

While the role of specialist might seem natural for a computer, we wanted to see if it could be applied to a form of media where there is clearly no tradition of expertise. We chose television, and at first, just the television *set*. In particular, we wanted to find out whether labeling a television set as a specialist in one type of content would encourage people to perceive the programs shown on that set as superior. Despite some hilarity as we planned the experiment, we were anxious to see if a social role could define a box of wires and glass.

We summarized our thoughts about media and specialization with this prediction:

> Rule 1: Content on a television set that is labeled a "specialist" in that type of content will be perceived as superior to identical content on a television that is labeled a "generalist."

Labeling Media

When participants came to our lab to participate in the experiment, we randomly assigned them to watch a "generalist" television or "specialist" television. Those who watched the "generalist" set were told they were watching an ordinary TV that we used to show both news and entertainment shows. On top of the 20-inch set was a sign that read "News and Entertainment Television."

Those participants assigned to the "specialist" were told that they would watch programs on two *different* televisions. They would watch news on a television set that we happened to use only to show news programs. This was emphasized with a sign that said "News Television." Sitting next to the news TV was a second, identical set that was used only to show entertainment; it bore a sign reading "Entertainment Television."

No one thought that the labels were absurd. In fact, no one said a thing about the labels during or after the experiment. All of the participants were quite willing to watch the programs and then tell us what they thought about them.

Each participant watched both news and entertainment segments. We chose these categories because they were familiar and different genres of content and because it was plausible to specialize in each. There were four "hard" news stories: a wounded police officer, a fraudulent business, a recent book about suicide, and the closing of a military medical center. The four entertainment segments came from network situation comedies: *Cheers*, *The Cosby Show*, *Roseanne*, and *Who's the Boss?* All of the segments were between two and three minutes long.

After viewing, we asked participants to evaluate what they had seen. To determine whether the news was perceived as better on the "specialist" television, we asked participants to make the following ratings: overall quality of the news, liking, and how important, informative, interesting, and serious each segment was. To determine whether the entertainment was better on the "specialist" television, we asked participants to judge overall quality and liking, and to indicate how entertaining and relaxing each segment was.

Perceptions of Specialist Televisions

If we had to make a list of what makes television news good or bad, the last thing we'd consider important, if intuition were the sole guide, would be a simple label on top of the set. The results of the experiment, however, suggest that this feature belongs on the list. Participants clearly thought that identical news segments were of significantly higher quality, and participants liked the news more when it was viewed on a news-only ("specialist") television than when it was viewed on the news-and-entertainment ("generalist") television.

Participants also thought that the news was significantly more important, informative, interesting, and serious when it was shown on the specialist set. The effect was so strong and consistent that out of twenty-eight assessments (seven questions for each of the four segments), twenty-six of them showed a preference for the content on the specialist television—a remarkable pattern.

The same preference for programs from a "specialist" occurred with entertainment. Participants thought that the situation comedies were significantly better entertainment when shown by the specialist set than when they were shown on the news-and-entertainment television, and they liked the segments better. Also, the segments were rated as significantly funnier and more relaxing on the specialist television. In fact, all sixteen assessments of the entertainment segments showed a preference for programs on the specialist television, again a remarkably significant pattern.

What makes these results extraordinary is that not one of the participants thought that the TVs had produced or were responsible for their content, and everyone said that it made absolutely no difference whether they saw the content on a single generalist TV or on two specialist TVs. Whatever responses occurred were unconscious and automatic.

Are "Specialist" Television Networks Better?

Although it seems silly to talk about television sets with specialist and generalist roles, these distinctions *are* made in many homes, albeit informally. The TV in the den, for example, might be used only for watching sports, the TV in the kitchen for game shows and talk shows, and the TV in the living room for news and prime-time programming. The same could be said for different computers, especially as they make their way from the study to the living room. The study is for words and numbers; the living room, for games.

A more familiar cue for specialization, however, is the network or channel that provides the content. Traditionally, "generalist" networks (ABC, CBS, NBC, Fox) show a variety of content. Viewers can see news, situation comedies, advertising, talk shows, soap operas, sports, and feature-length films on the same channel. More recently, however, a number of "specialist" networks have appeared, each with a considerably narrower range of content. These networks include the Cable News Network (CNN), sports on ESPN, Court TV, the Cartoon Channel, and the Weather Channel.

If the idea of "specialist" applies to television *networks* as well as to television sets, then the same content should be perceived as superior when it ostensibly comes from a "specialist" network than when it comes from one with no single talent. Our second study tested this prediction.

The best-known specialist network (CNN) shows news, so we chose that type of content. First, we recorded twelve news stories from local news programs. We recorded both hard news and news features. The stories were about one minute long, and they used a variety of traditional formats, including an on-camera anchorperson, voiceover video, and a reporter desk-shot. We avoided stories that could easily be identified with past events so that participants would think that they were watching "live" news during the experiment.

When participants came to the lab, those in the specialist condition were told they would watch news stories from several "news-only" networks: CNN, HNN (Headline News Network), SNC (Satellite News Channel), and RNN (Regional News Network). Participants in the generalist condition were told that they would see news stories from "information/entertainment networks": ABC, CBS, Fox, and NBC. To reinforce the source of the stories, we superimposed the name of the network at the bottom left of the screen. We even added the words "a news network" or "an information/entertainment network" to the logos. After viewing, participants evaluated the stories.

Specialist Networks Are Better

The network labels worked just like the ones for the television sets. There was a clear tendency for participants to evaluate identical content more favorably when they thought it came from a news-only (specialist) network than when it came from an information/entertainment (generalist) network. Participants in the specialist condition (i.e., those who thought the stories were done by CNN and other news networks) rated the news as more important, interesting, informative, and serious than those who watched the identical stories on a generalist network.

We also found something new in this study, something that we had not imagined could be true. Participants who watched stories ostensibly produced by specialists evaluated the clarity and color of the television picture as significantly better than did participants who watched the same stories supposedly produced by the generalist network. This result was so remarkable that we immediately examined the technical quality of our videotapes to see if we'd accidentally produced a bad copy. We hadn't. The tapes used in the study were identical copies from the same master. The label "specialist" was powerful enough to influence assessments not only of content but also of visual quality!

Thinking about Labels for Media

These studies provide perhaps the most compelling evidence yet that social responses to media are not dictated by "common sense." No viewer thinks that television sets have an ability to influence the content that they display. Nonetheless, people are influenced by labels, and the influence goes beyond their ability to analyze their own responses. No participant in the experiments, all reasonable people with extensive media experience, thought that these responses were possible.

These social orientations to media indicate that it is *natural* for people to treat media socially, perhaps easier than treating media in any other way, including as a tool. That media should have a social role is quite reasonable, especially if there is an explicit claim to support the label.

Assigning social roles is one more way that human beings instinctively reduce uncertainty about their world. When people or media have a particular role, just as when they have a strong personality, we feel that we know more about them. This simplification is often seen as pernicious, nothing more than a stereotype that causes people to miss nuance. But it is also a reasonable psychological strategy that helps people make complex things simple. People can think their way beyond simplifications, but old brains ensure that simplicity is there if we need it.

Using the Label "Specialist"

One obvious implication of these studies is that claims to specialization are effective. Specialization influences feelings about media as well as objective judgments about the information that media present. If media claim specialization, they'll be better liked and appear more competent as well. Ethical questions aside, there is little doubt that claims to specialization work.

Specialization and Media Organizations

If it's good to be an expert, what should media organizations claim expertise in? There are certainly reasons for media companies to have broad interests, and perhaps even interests unrelated to media, but one argument against breadth is that it diminishes a claim to a coherent expertise. This is especially true when companies with different specialties combine efforts to offer general services or to create some different specialization unrelated to the talents for which they are known.

When different media organizations converge, their specialties converge as well. Entertainment mixes with information, business mixes with home, productivity with fun. The claims to specialization, and any resulting expertise that comes from specialization, could be lost, even if the quality of content remains the same. Most Americans turned to CNN during the Gulf War. It was the specialist in what people cared about: news. Would the same have been true if CNN also showed movies?

Other media combinations may also create role confusion. What will it mean, for example, when a cable television company offers phone service? The specialties that are associated with a particular channel on the television or a particular appliance in the home will now be switched or combined. While consumers may be able to understand that the cable company merely owns wires that connect houses to a central switch, they might question the quality of service when they use a cable box to make a phone call. Television sets are not specialized to make phone calls, regardless of the technical possibilities.

How Are Labels Assigned to Media?

Roles were defined unrealistically in our study—we put signs on top of a TV set, and a note on the screen. These markers wouldn't be of much use in communicating roles to people who use media outside of a university lab. How will people know what media can do? How will people define media specialties?

One obvious cue will be past experiences with content. If the Comedy Channel always makes you laugh, and if CNN always has news, that's enough to assign a role. The role assignment isn't complicated. The consistency in programming is enough.

What about media that are not as clearly defined? Are there cues other than content that would work? One cue likely to be increasingly important is the context in which media are used. By context we mean simply the room or place where media are experienced. Traditionally, there has not been much variance in context—the television was in the living room, the computer in the office. But what happens when the computer moves to the living room, or when the television cable is connected to a computer in the study?

We think that context might have the same effects that our signs had in the experiments; that is, context can suggest a role. The living room may suggest family and fun. The study may be for productivity and business. Both of these roles could influence what people make of the content they experience there even when the content is identical. Imagine a computer encyclopedia running on a living room computer. Would it be as comprehensive and intelligent as the same software running in the study? Maybe not. Might it also be more fun than its counterpart in the study? Likely yes.

Nowhere are roles better understood than in advertising. Persuasive messages are often crafted to establish quickly the expertise of the spokesperson, often with great success. Consumers like the same reassurance in persuasive messages that they like from doctors, lawyers, and teachers. Advertisers also effectively use roles that are associated with well-known people to influence how a message should be interpreted. Even if an actor only *plays* a doctor on television, he or she is perceived to know more about medicine than an actor who plays a lawyer.

In newer media, the construction of different roles is as new as the technologies themselves, but it should be as consequential as it was for the TV sets in the experiments. In designing characters or agents for computer software, for example, assigning the label "specialist" is relatively easy. If the software performs a range of tasks, a designer could simply assign different characters to the tasks that are best performed by specialists. Specialty tasks might include financial calculations, statistical analyses, or medical advice, tasks that require specialization in humans as well.

Integration versus Specialization

One problem with the use of specialization is that it appears to conflict with the need to integrate. When a *single* media appliance can do more and more different things, it will be desirable, in terms of both usability and marketing, to create a sense of commonality across the different functions. A cable television connection, for example, can potentially provide entertainment, information, and even phone calls, shopping, financial services, and a network hookup for the computer. A computer can crunch numbers in the checkbook, process video signals for the home theater, and turn on and off the heat and lights.

Integration is a clear goal for computer software that is bundled in "suites." Different applications are given identical interfaces, which makes everything simpler and easier to use. Other desirable characteristics of suites, such as the seamless transfer of data between applications, should not undermine the notion of specialization. But how can you have both integration and specialization?

One way to integrate *and* specialize is to use a "master of ceremonies," an MC. The role of MC would serve to mark integration, and then different specialists could appear only when their expertise is required. Most obviously, the roles of MC and specialists could be played by characters or video images that appear on a screen. Using distinct representations would prevent confusion about which role is currently "on stage." The roles need not be visually explicit, however. They could just as easily be different voices or even a special place in the interface for text. Most of the benefits of social responses to media will accrue even when roles appear as sounds, words, or places.

13

Teammates

All of the research in this book was conducted in teams. The number and names have changed over the years, but there have always been several people involved at any given time. The concept of a team, we have always thought, has great scientific merit. We can check each other's work, we benefit from a variety of specialties, and we can intelligently debate ideas. To foster the team concept, we have offices close together, we share an e-mail alias and a World Wide Web site, we use a common room where our computers are located, and we try to meet formally once a week.

As scientifically valid as the team concept is, however, we have to admit there is a nonscientific benefit as well. It's just plain comforting to be part of a group. There is mutual admiration, the feeling of being with like-minded friends, and cooperation beyond what could be expected from more distant colleagues. Interestingly, the benefits of team membership seem to accrue even to newcomers. The new people on the team are often the ones who benefit the most, a clue that the team concept has value beyond science.

Plenty of good evidence shows that our team experience is typical of *all* groups. Psychologists have shown that being part of a group has an enormous effect on the attitudes and behaviors of the people in them. Group effects are so powerful, in fact, that the way in which people join a group makes little difference. Count off by 2s, form two teams, give each a name, and magical things happen.

One thing that happens on teams, even when the assignment is arbitrary, is that members think that they're more similar to each other than to those on the outside. For example, people tend to think they are more similar to others born in the same community than to the general populace, as do "team players" assigned by a company to work on a business project. The tendency to find similarity in groups may even explain a belief in astrology: People who share a birthday *must* share other things as well.

People admire and respect others in their group. We've done no poll of our own research team, but we all likely think that those on the team are smarter than most. We could certainly point to scholarly achievements to bolster the claim, but truth be told, there is simply a basic motivation to acknowledge teammates.

Research also shows that people cooperate more with team members, and they agree more with their positions. Even in cases when this isn't true, teammates are likely to yield more often and more quickly. A tendency toward agreement helps explain the phenomenon of "group-think." This can occur when a group of people, even very intelligent people, makes bad decisions just because the group members don't want to challenge one another.

What about collaboration with media? Could people be affected by the same team designation when the team includes media instead of people? This is what we set out to show. If people experience a communication technology as a teammate, they may exhibit the same changes in attitudes and behaviors toward media that they show toward one another.

Making a Computer a Teammate

How can media, in this case a computer, seem like a "teammate"? The answer comes from social psychology experiments with actual people. Researchers generally agree that two factors are key: *group identity* and *group interdependence*. Group identity simply means that a team must have a marker, often just a name. The name doesn't have to describe the team (the San Francisco 49ers don't actually pan for gold), but the name must distinguish the team from all others. Group identity, of course, is not restricted to a name. Teams can also have a color, a mascot, or a uniform. Our research team has a name (Social Responses to Communication Technologies, or SRCT), a logo, and a letterhead.

The requirement of interdependence means that the behavior of each team member can affect all of the other members. For our research team, this characteristic is most apparent at academic conferences. If one member of the research team gives a brilliant presentation or loses a debate, we know that the audience may draw conclusions about the entire team. And we'd do the same.

The teams we created in our experiment comprised a person and a computer. Group identity turned out to be the easy part. Half of the experimental subjects, the "team" participants, were told they were on the "Blue Team." To reinforce this, Blue Team members wore a blue wristband, and they used a computer with a blue border. The "team" computer also had a label that said "Blue Team" on top of the machine. To ensure that participants in the team condition felt dependent on the computer, we told them that we would grade their performance, and that the final evaluation would depend on both their work *and* the work of the computer.

We wanted the other half of our experimental subjects to think that they were on their own, and not teamed with the computer. We asked each "Blue Individual" to wear a blue wristband. For these participants, however, the computer was labeled the "Green Computer," and the computer had a green border. Also, there was no mention of "team" in the preparation for the task, and we told them that they would be evaluated *solely* on the basis of their own work—the computer was simply there to help.

If the role of teammate is applicable to media, these simple steps should generate changes in the attitudes and behaviors of those who use the different computers. We predicted the following:

Rule 1: People teamed with a computer will feel more similar to the computer than people who are not teamed.

Rule 2: People teamed with a computer will think better of the computer than people who are not teamed.

Rule 3: People teamed with a computer will cooperate more with the computer than people who are not teamed.

Rule 4: People who are teamed with a computer will agree more with the computer than people who are not teamed.

Operating as a Team with a Computer

We wanted participants to work on a collaborative task that would make them feel as if they were on an equal footing with the computer. We returned to the Desert Survival Problem, an exercise used in other experiments. To summarize briefly, participants imagine that their plane has just crashed in the desert, and they must rank, in order of importance, twelve items that have been salvaged from the wreckage.

When participants came to the lab, they first tried to solve the Desert Survival Problem on their own. After ranking the items, they went into another room, one at a time, to work with a computer. Before the interaction with the computer began, they were told either that they were on the same team with the computer and would be evaluated together, or that they were working on their own and would be evaluated accordingly. Everyone then exchanged information about each of the twelve survival items with the computer. After this interaction, participants were told that they could change their initial ranking.

When the interaction was complete, participants went into another room where they made their final rankings. Everyone also filled out a questionnaire that asked for evaluations of the computer and evaluations of the interaction itself. The questions included "How similar was the computer's approach to your approach in evaluating the items?," "How helpful were the computer's suggestions?," and "How much did you try to cooperate with the computer?"

Similarity of Teammates

When participants thought they were on the same team with a computer, several things happened. First, they thought that the computer was more like them than did participants who worked on their own. They also thought that the computer solved problems in a style more similar to their own. They even thought that the computer agreed more completely with their own ranking of the survival items.

The effects of being a teammate were not limited, however, to the perceived similarity between users and the computer. Teammates also thought that the information given by the computer was more relevant, helpful, and insightful, even though it was in fact identical in all cases. Participants even found the method of presenting the information to be friendlier when it came from a teammate. Feelings of cooperation were also enhanced by team membership. Teammates tried harder to reach agreement with the computer, and they were more open to attempts by the computer to influence them.

What about behavior? Could the status of teammate also change what participants *did*? Yes, it could. Teammates actually changed their answers more to conform with the ranking given by the computer. Those participants who thought that they were operating on their own were less likely to change their responses after they wrote them down at the beginning of the experiment.

Identification versus Interdependence

The definition of "teammate" used in the experiment had two parts: identification and interdependence. One required a team name, the other knowledge that people would be judged as a group. Since *both* of these factors were used at the same time, however, we couldn't know which was more important. Since their combination proved powerful, we now wondered whether one was more important than the other and whether both were needed to create the team effect.

To answer this question, we invited two additional groups of participants to the lab. Each person in these groups was given one reason to think they were part of a team, and one reason to think that they were on their own. For one group, we made them feel part of a team with a shared name and wristband color, but told them they were on their own for the evaluation. We did not give the other group a team identity, but we told them their evaluation depended on a team effort with the computer.

What happened? Interdependence had an enormous effect, and identification had no effect at all. Participants who depended on the computer for their evaluation, regardless of whether they were identified as part of a team or not, showed all of the team effects. Teammates thought that they were more similar to the computer, they thought that the computer performed better, they cooperated more with the computer, and they changed their answers more to conform to the computer. In contrast, withholding a team name changed nothing.

This result left us thinking that group identification might not be as important as the literature suggested. We made one last attempt to see if it could work by itself. We invited two more groups to the lab, and this time, we varied *only* identification; we said nothing about group or individual evaluations. One group got a name and matching wristband, the other didn't.

This time, identification did work. Participants who were labeled as teammates felt more a part of a team and thought they were more similar to the computer than did participants who weren't identified. They also felt that the computer was friendlier. This led to the conclusion that identification and independence are both important, but identification is less powerful, especially when the two are combined.

What Should We Now Think about Teams?

Psychologists have long been excited by how little it takes to make people feel part of a team, and by how much is gained when they do. Our studies extend this research by showing that feelings of "team" are powerful enough to affect people's interactions with media. A team is simple to create—a name will do—but it's even more powerful when people are asked to rely on media for their own success.

We thought that one of the effects in these studies was more important than the others, especially in relation to all of the other research about the media equation: People were willing to change their *behavior* as a result of social experiences with media. Not only do people think and feel differently about themselves and the machines they work with, people actually performed differently as well.

Another important conclusion concerns differences between identity and interdependence. These have never been isolated, even in the literature on human-human relationships. We now have evidence that dependence is critical for generating team membership. This doesn't mean that team names are *un*necessary, but it does suggest that identification works best by fostering interdependence.

The Human-Computer Relationship: One-up vs. One-down vs. One-across

There is a lot of debate about the relationships that should be encouraged between people and computers. One view argues that computers should be *tools*; they should be "one-down" in relation to the user. To foster user dominance, designers should encourage people to think that the *user* is in charge. Computers should do what users tell them to do, nothing more, nothing less.

An opposing view is one of computer as *master*, "one-up" in status relative to the user. The computer should take charge and absorb as much of the work as possible. The user consumes information, and isn't much interested in how it is managed. Under this view, computers are "wizards," "autonomous agents," or "guides."

These views are similar in one important way—they both suggest asymmetry in the human-computer relationship. The teammate research, however, suggests the relationship should be more equal, more like "one-across." Computers and users should be peers, and people should be made to feel dependent on computers without feeling inferior or superior. Being on the same team encourages people to think that the computer is more likable and effective, and it also promotes cooperation and better performance.

What needs to be done to create this equality? Not a great deal. Much of the relationship can be defined with language. Merely saying that tasks are team efforts will do. A team label could substitute for other labels that define asymmetry, such as "wizard" and "tool." The computer could also tell people that it needs help to complete its tasks. This is quite simple, and is always true, at least to some degree. The fanciest of computers, lacking cooperation from the humans who use them, will never be able to give people exactly what they want. There are too many questions, too many conditions that require sorting.

This advice is occasionally met with cynicism. Why should we advocate linguistic tricks that may fool people into responses that they should be ashamed of? Computers are merely machines, and they shouldn't encourage people to think otherwise.

We think that this view is unnecessarily severe. People and machines *really do* depend on each other. Machines can't succeed without people, and while the opposite is certainly possible, modern society is conspiring to limit the number of times when this is true. Why should it be *in*appropriate for computers to say and do the things that humans say in order to make life better? The idea that because a computer is a machine it must refrain from niceties or social competence seems harsh. People are not foolish because they like to work on teams; people are *human* because they like to work on teams.

We suspect that the encouragement of team interactions may take time to creep into the design of new media, in spite of our prediction of immediate payoff. One reason for the pessimistic timetable is the insistence on the part of some who guard the high-tech gates that machines should be *in*human. The argument is that since computers don't think like people, they shouldn't conform to human social standards either. However, if it's a good idea to add "please" to "Wait for this file to be copied," then why shouldn't the computer also say, "This task can best be accomplished if we work as a team."

14

Gender

Our research team is led by two men—Byron and Cliff. We are often quite aware of our gender during presentations of research. There are two different topics that pique awareness. One is technical. Many of the implications of our research are for complicated technologies, and we often speak about technical details. At these moments, it seems good to be male (as well as for one of us to have worked at Intel). Our industry audience is predominantly male, and regrettably, the same advice might be a tougher sell for two women.

But consider another part of our presentation. We tell the same audience that computers should be polite and nice, and that the relationship between people and machines would be more amiable if their personalities matched. At those moments, we have occasionally felt betrayed by gender. What could a man, especially one with a math and engineering background, know about social relationships? We sympathize with one of the male engineers who responded to our research by saying, "I got into engineering because I didn't *know* any social rules."

Both responses, those that overestimate and those that underestimate our capabilities, are the product of stereotypes. The two of us know nothing more or less about computer architecture or interpersonal relationships just because we are male. But to many people, and perhaps to everyone on occasion, stereotypes *seem* true. This is the subject of an extensive literature in psychology.

What Is a Female and What Is a Male?

Psychologists know that stereotypes are one of the most pervasive aspects of human thinking. Some stereotypes supposedly mark differences in the way men and women appear physically, and differences in their behaviors and attitudes. We use the word "supposedly" because many of the distinctions have limited or no basis in reality.

In the United States, research has shown that praise from males is taken more seriously than praise from females. Also, women are thought to know more about love and relationships than men, and men are thought to know more about technical subjects than women. What we noticed about our own responses during industry lectures apparently was not unique. We experienced stereotypes that were part of our culture, and so common that everyone, including us, agreed what they were and when they applied.

Stereotypes can also dictate what men and women are *supposed* to do. These distinctions are also products of culture, and often they are unfavorable to women. For example, research shows that women who engage in dominant or forceful behavior are generally regarded less favorably than women whose behavior is more submissive, while the opposite is true for men.

There are debates about the extent to which stereotypes are culturally or biologically determined, but there is no debate that they are powerful and pervasive in every society. Generally, their power is true for both men and women. Indeed, research has shown there are few differences in the degree to which men and women ascribe to gender stereotypes.

None of these results is comforting, to say the least. This fact alone justifies the substantial effort in psychology to describe and explain how stereotypes work. Most of these discussions, however, relate to gender in its most obvious form—the presence of actual people. When researchers study men and women, they most often refer to actual bodies that are obviously one gender or the other.

The most minimal of cues, however, can determine what is male and female. With an eye toward gendered *media*, we note that even when real people are absent, gender is embodied in words and voices, and even in small changes in the frequency characteristics of a voice. These gender markings can encourage the same stereotypes that people apply to real people.

Voice is one of the most powerful indicators of gender, absent an actual person. Female voices are clearly different from male ones, and the differences are quickly and reliably recognized. When listening to a voice, a determination of gender can be made in seconds. Even if the two of us had been heard on tape, everyone in the audience would have immediately detected two males, and as a consequence, all the stereotypes associated with our gender would have been immediately relevant.

The need to classify voices by gender is so compelling that people make distinctions even beyond the simple dichotomy. Not only are voices male or female, but they are also masculine or feminine. Masculine voices are deeper and louder; feminine ones, higher and softer. There is evidence that even when we know a person's actual gender, gender stereotypes still apply based solely on the masculinity or femininity of the voice.

Gendered Media

Gender can apply to media in two ways, only one of which is new. There is a long tradition of research that considers portrayals of gender in media *content*. All types of content have been studied, including entertainment, news, and advertising. We assume that CD-ROM titles and computer agents will be added to the list in the near future. In all of these areas, studies typically count portrayals (e.g., there are more men than women on television in a ratio of about 2:1), and several studies have shown that biased gender portrayals can create and sustain stereotypes with the same power as real-life experiences.

All of these studies, however, focus on presentations of actual people. We wanted to see if subtler gender cues would cause similar stereotyped responses. What might happen if a *computer* had "gender"? We thought that this was particularly interesting because it seemed so unlikely that a metal box with a CPU could be male or female. But computers can have voices, and that may be enough.

Based on the work of psychologists, we predicted the following, all of which we thought would be true for both male and female computer users:

Rule 1: Evaluations from male-voiced computers will be taken more seriously than evaluations from female-voiced computers.

Rule 2: A female-voiced computer that evaluates will be liked less than a male-voiced computer that evaluates.

Rule 3: Female-voiced computers will be seen as more knowledgeable about love and relationships than will male-voiced computers.

Rule 4: Male-voiced computers will be seen as more knowledgeable about technical subjects than will female-voiced computers.

Study 1: Male and Female Computers

Bestowing gender on a computer is not as difficult as accepting the idea that it might be influential once accomplished. Almost all computers have audio output, which means that they can talk. We simply made the computers talk with male or female voices. Actually, we used three voices of each gender to ensure that any differences wouldn't be attributable to the quality of any particular voice.

In the first experiment, we invited participants to the lab and told them that they would be working with a computer to learn about various topics. We also told them that we were interested in how well the computer performed, and that we'd like to know how they felt about the computer after they were finished.

One at a time, participants sat down in front of a computer and participated in an interactive tutoring session. They were tutored on three topics: love and relationships (a stereotypically female topic), mass media (a stereotypically neutral topic), and computers (a stereotypically male topic). Everyone received identical information, except that some heard a male voice and some heard a female voice give the information.

After participants finished the tutoring session, they moved to a second computer that used only text. They used this computer to complete a multiple-choice test that covered the three topics. After the test, participants moved to a third computer, which did two things. First it told participants which questions they had gotten right and wrong. Then it praised the teaching job done by the first computer. For half of the participants, this third computer had a female voice, and for the others, it had a male voice. After participants finished the session, they were asked to evaluate the computers that tutored and evaluated them.

The results showed that users deemed a computer good or bad for reasons other than clock speed and RAM. Both men and women were more influenced by praise from the male-voice computer than they were by the identical praise from the female-voice computer. Participants were so influenced by male praise that they even thought that the original computer that tutored them, a separate machine in a different part of the room, had done a better job of teaching when it was praised by a male-voice computer than when it was praised by a female-voice computer.

Participants also thought that the evaluation from the male-voice computer was more friendly than the female one, even though the comments were identical. Finally, we found that participants responded to the computers very much like our own observations about our lectures. The female-voice computer was rated as a better teacher of love and relationships, and a somewhat worse teacher about computers. All that was needed to activate gender stereotypes, for both men and women, was a computer voice.

It's important to remember reasons that *won't* account for these results. All of the content on the computers was identical for all participants; everyone denied that they harbored gender stereotypes; no one thought that the gender of media voices would influence them; and everyone was an experienced computer user. Participants also thought that the three computers were programmed by the same person, and that the person was male which, although true, is ironic since they also said they harbored no gender stereotypes.

Study 2: Male/Female versus Masculine/Feminine

We also studied voices that were masculine or feminine, not just male or female. If gender stereotyping is powerful, a masculine-sounding voice should elicit male stereotypes, and a feminine-sounding voice should elicit female ones, and this should be true regardless of the actual gender of the speaker.

We made the following predictions, each based on studies in psychology that have found the same results in human-human interactions.

Rule 5: People will assign higher levels of drive to people depicted with masculine voices than to those with feminine voices.

Rule 6: People will assign higher levels of extroversion to people depicted with masculine voices than to those with feminine voices.

Rule 7: People will assign higher levels of intelligence to people depicted with masculine voices than to those with feminine voices.

Rule 8: Evaluations from media people depicted with masculine voices will be taken more seriously than evaluations from people depicted with feminine voices.

In the study that tested these predictions, participants viewed screen depictions of six women who had voices that were electronically altered to be "feminine" or "masculine." We created the presentations by first videotaping the women as they spoke about things they had done earlier in the day. Next, we electronically manipulated their voices so that each woman would speak with either a "masculine" or a "feminine" voice. "Feminine" voices were amplified in the higher frequencies and reduced in the low frequencies, and the voices were played at softer than average volume. To create "masculine" voices, we amplified the lower frequencies, dampened the higher ones, and made the voices louder than average.

Participants individually viewed a videotape of the six women on a large-screen projection television. Each participant saw three women with feminine voices, and three with masculine voices; which faces had voices altered to be feminine, and which masculine, was decided randomly for each subject. After viewing and listening to each presentation, participants evaluated them.

The results were that masculine-sounding women were perceived as having significantly more drive, willpower, reasoning skills, persuasive ability, and learning capability than the feminine-sounding women. Women on the screen with feminine voices were also perceived as more introverted than those with masculine voices. The conclusion: Viewers applied stereotypes simply on the basis of a subtle gender cue in voice, even though all of the voices came from female faces and audio speakers sitting beside a television screen.

Thinking about Gendered Media

Gender is powerful enough that it is apparent in media even when it seems wholly irrelevant. Think about all of the features of the computers in the first experiment that should have led participants to ignore stereotypes. Computers are inanimate objects, computers have no biological features that mark them as male or female, there were no pictorial representations linked to the voices, and the words "he" or "she" were never used. All that appeared on the screen was plain white text on a black background.

Gender is also not simple. There is information that cues stereotypes even in the tonal characteristics of voices with identical gender. Merely counting the number of male and female voices on computers or any other medium will not reveal all. There are enough gender cues, even in the corners of media, to activate radically different ways of thinking about what is presented.

Stereotypes make a complex world simpler, even if they also cause us to miss critical individual differences. People try to know the gender of those they interact with because it cues them about how to behave, what to say, and how to say it. A tendency to simplify may have had some value as humans evolved, and the tendency may therefore have some basis in biology as well as culture. In human-computer interaction, however, *none* of the stereotypes have *any* basis, but they are still applied.

Designing Media That Have Gender

In our experience, people who design new media try to opt out of gender issues. Some treat male voices as gender neutral. They are not, however. A male voice, even on products that usually have a male voice, elicits responses that are not neutral but instead carry a host of expectations.

Media designers seem to share a quiet hope that gender can be disguised with voices that are synthesized and therefore apparently ambiguous with respect to gender. This is unlikely. Everyone assigns gender to voices—even computer-synthesized voices—and they do it quickly. Everyone might not agree on the gender of a particular voice, but each person will attribute one, will feel certain that the attribution is correct, and will behave accordingly.

Other Stereotyped Voice Characteristics

Stereotypes, and the voices that encourage them, involve more than gender. There are other indicators of gender besides voice, and voice indicates more than just gender. All people automatically assign an age to a voice, bringing to bear another set of stereotypes. Very often, people assign a social class and a geographic location, which leads them to have even more expectations about how a person (or computer) will behave, and about how behaviors should be interpreted. In sum, no matter what choice a designer makes to represent the computer or a computer-based agent, it will come with a range of expectations.

Because of stereotyping, designing a character or agent involves tough decisions. Imagine you were a designer who wanted to encourage senior citizens to use a computer. You might think the solution is obvious: Give the computer a voice that sounds like a senior citizen. You might expect this to encourage seniors to identify with the computer and thereby feel more comfortable with it. However, what we know about stereotyping suggests that users might instead think the computers are relatively incompetent—after all, senior citizens stereotypically know little about computers.

Societal Implications of the Use of Gender

Producers of new media will have to answer the hard questions about the distribution of gender in their products that have been part of media discussions for decades. For television, the questions have come from a variety of places. Gender portrayals have been investigated by Congress, the Civil Rights Commission, the Federal Communication Commission, and several public interest groups. Hundreds of academic studies have examined gender portrayals, many of them done with policy in mind. To answer the questions, the television networks have each established broadcast standards departments that monitor their own products, conduct research about the portrayals, and formally respond to critics. This same level of concern is not true of new media.

There are certainly valid concerns about the gender distribution of the practitioners of new media, but little about the machines and interfaces that they make and study. The questions asked about gender and computing, if they follow those asked of the older media, will be of two kinds. One sort of question is generally asked within the groups that produce media. If there are gender stereotypes in the real world, stereotypes created by culture over long time periods, why shouldn't they be used? Why shouldn't media meet the expectations of the people who use the products? When productions vary from established norms, the content can be confusing. It's easier to process what is expected than what is new or *counter*-stereotypical.

A second sort of question turns the responsibility for stereotypes around. Why should media perpetuate them? Why shouldn't media be proactive? Why shouldn't gender portrayals be absolutely equitable, even if that is not the case in real life? This way, those things that we don't value can be changed, and reasonably, media have a responsibility to be active in that change.

Our studies certainly do not provide all the answers to these questions, nor will any single research effort that we can imagine. Not only do the answers depend on input from radically different places (e.g., law, economics, public policy), but they also require judgments that transcend social science. The experiments do, however, signal a critical similarity between media, regardless of their technical sophistication, and regardless of the various communities that make them. Computers and television are similar not only because their technology is converging, but also because they afford the same problems and opportunities of stereotyping.

15

Voices

If this book were an oral presentation, the fact that it was *co*-authored would be more apparent. For any collaboration, but maybe even more so for ours, you could not help but be aware that there were *two* people speaking—same gender, but substantially different appearances, personalities, voices, accents, language, gestures, and even fashion. If movie critics Siskel and Ebert are successful because they are different, then we're on the right track.

Readers, however, are forced to listen to a single voice, never really knowing when one person is speaking and the other is silent. Our graduate students delight in bets about which of us writes different parts of co-authored papers, but for most readers (and even for the two us after a month has passed), it's impossible to tell who is speaking when you read the words: Co-authorship melds into a single voice.

This means that reading and hearing about this research could be different. The ideas are the same, and the data don't change, but a missing element in these pages is the intensity of multiple voices. Part of the success of Siskel and Ebert must be that when both thumbs are up or down, it is a more forceful judgment because there are *two* of them. Even when they disagree, the debates are at least easy to follow (there is one body for each side in the argument) and, perhaps because of that, entertaining as well. Imagine if there were only Siskel, and for movies that deserved one thumb in each direction, he would assert "some people might say…," and then comment, "but on the other hand…".

For some people, two presenters are a distraction. Two sets of facial expressions, nonverbal gestures, and other personal idiosyncrasies interfere with the transmission of ideas. But regardless of whether you think that two voices are better or worse, it *is* something that's noticed. People like to count and keep track of how many other people are around.

One obvious way to monitor the environment is visual—count the people that you can see. Often, however, there is little or no visual information to enable a good count, and people rely instead on voices. This gives people the advantage of being able to monitor a much larger area (people can hear in directions that they cannot see), and it is possible to do so without regard for visual problems like darkness, weather, or occlusions. It makes sense, then, that a big fraction of the brain is devoted to the recognition and processing of voices. As a result, people rapidly distinguish human voices from all other sounds.

When there are multiple voices, they usually occupy different locations in space, and they have different physical embodiments as well. What happens when all the voices come from the same place? As the telephone demonstrates, especially during a conference call with several people, it makes little difference for voice discrimination. People can easily parse different voices coming out of the same device, and it doesn't matter at all that the voices have no bodies. Also, when we hear the *same* voice over two *different* telephones, we know that it was the same person who spoke both times.

These are solid comments from psychology, and their accuracy is verified in the customs of stage performance. A good impressionist, simply by changing voice and intonation, can make an audience feel as if they hear different people. The same body in the same location can be different people simply because of different voices. When the voices are different, there are independent social actors with unique points of view.

Voice Discrimination and New Media

Many forms of media, particularly computers when they display text, seem more like "voices" from a book than ones that are live. When people are actually present, each body counts as a separate social actor, but when the voices are mediated by a machine, they seem like they're bunched into a *single* social presence—the computer itself. Even though most software has multiple authors whose words are presented by several speakers, we seem to lump them together into one "voice."

Why do people think a computer speaks with a single "voice"? A computer is one thing, a *single* entity that receives input and alters its behavior accordingly. Even though one computer *can* produce multiple voices, it seems hard to imagine a single machine as a group of people, one person for each of its separate voices.

Voices, however, are powerful indicators of social presence. The psychological research suggests that people might have a hard time combining several of them into a single entity. Consequently, computers may be as many social actors as there are voices, because different voices mean different actors. The same voice, on the other hand, should count as a single presence, even when it is played on different machines that are in different places. In short, one presence per voice, not one presence per machine.

Our predictions about multiple voices on computers were the following:

Rule 1: Users will respond to different voices on the same computer as if they were different social actors.

Rule 2: Users will respond to the same voice on different computers as if it were the same social actor.

Matching Social Actors and Voices

We created situations that varied the number of voices that a computer used in an interaction. We started by simply comparing a computer that used a single male voice with a computer that used two different male voices. If one computer equals one social actor, then the different voices should meld into one. But if each voice is a different actor, which was our prediction, then the fact that they were on a single machine shouldn't matter.

Study 1: One Computer versus Two Voices

We started with the finding (from Chapter 2) that people give more positive responses when a computer asked about itself as compared to when a different computer asked about the first. In this study about voices, we wanted to find out whether people would give more positive responses to a *voice* that asked about itself rather than to a *different voice* that asked. In this experiment, participants were tutored by a computer and then took a test. Then the computer bragged: It told each user that it had done a very good job tutoring. The computer used a single male voice throughout.

In the last part of the experiment, participants assessed the computer's performance by indicating how well adjectives it presented described the computer. For half of the participants, the adjectives were presented in the same voice as the tutoring. For the other half, a *different* male voice asked. Everything else in the interaction was the same.

When participants answered the questions that the computer asked, we thought they would do one of two things. When the evaluation was done using the same computer *and* the same voice, we thought that participants would be polite and answer the question positively. After all, we essentially had one "social actor" asking how well it had done as a teacher. Participants wouldn't want to make it feel bad by criticizing.

As expected, participants who answered the questions on the same computer with the same voice were significantly more positive about the job the computer had done than were the participants who were questioned on the same machine but by a different voice. Participants were also more honest when answering to a different voice, as reflected in significantly greater variance in their responses. In other words, people were polite to *voices* on the computer, not the computer itself.

Study 2: A Replication Using the Gender of Voices

The first study showed that people respond to different voices as different social actors, even if they are on the same machine. The next study tested the strength of this discrimination by applying it to gender stereotyping. Specifically, we examined the finding that males praised by other males are perceived more positively than males praised by themselves, but females praised by other females are perceived *less* positively than females praised by themselves. Although this finding is never greeted with cheers, it does provide a good opportunity to study the separateness of social actors. This is a particularly strong test because we predicted *opposite* effects for female as compared to male voices.

In this experiment, subjects were tutored by a computer with a male or female voice, and then they took a test. The performance of the computer was then praised, and participants answered a paper-and-pencil questionnaire about how well the computer performed. For half of the participants, the evaluation was in the same voice as the instruction; for the other half, the evaluation was in a different voice. When two voices were used, both were male or both were female.

The results for male and female voices were in the directions we predicted. The male-voice tutor that was praised by a different male voice was perceived as better than the male-voice tutor that praised itself. The female-voice tutor that was praised by a different female, however, was perceived as *worse* than the female-voice tutor that praised itself. Again, the social actor was a voice, not a machine.

Study 3: Same Voices, Different Boxes

The first two experiments answered the question about different voices on the same machine—they were perceived as separate social actors. Next we wanted to know what would happen with the same voice on two different machines. If the same voice comes from two different machines, is it one or two social actors?

To test this, we created a variant of Study 1. Although all subjects heard only one voice, half of the participants in the experiment heard a *separate* computer praise the performance of the teaching computer. If two machines mean two social actors, then we would find differences when we compared the two groups of subjects.

We found no differences, however. The same voice produced the same evaluation, regardless of which machine played it. Moving a voice from one machine to another does not change the identification of the actor making the comments.

Thinking about Voices versus the Machines That Produce Them

Voices are powerful cues about presence. Two voices mean two distinct social actors even when the voices are associated with a *single* box. Different voices can overshadow features of computers that otherwise point to similarity, including identical interfaces, text, and pictures, and even the knowledge that the different sessions were programmed by the same person. The number of social actors in the exchange equals the number of voices that enter the conversation, not the number of machines or the visual similarity between them.

It was certainly possible that the presence of a single computer might have been powerful enough to mesh voices into a single persona. However, in this respect, computers are similar to other media. Consider a radio news broadcast. It's obvious that listeners think that the voices of two anchors indicate the presence of two people. In these studies, like the radio, the computer itself was *invisible*.

Designing with Voices

Interface designers have traditionally assumed that voices are a wonderful addition to computing. They bemoan the disk space needed to store them, but their value is unquestioned. The present chapter suggests a more balanced view.

Voices and Casting

For some applications, inclusion of voices may be a mistake. Voices carry baggage. They activate stereotypes associated with gender, age, personality, and a hundred other things. Users will expect voices to provide information that is consistent with the stereotypes, and if the voices do not, they'll want to know why not. Incorporating voices might necessitate a redesign of the entire interface so that style, behavior, and language are consistent.

It's a big deal to separate a voice from the person who owns it. In animated films, for example, actors sometimes specify that their voices should *not* be used in advertising for the film, because they fear that they would lose control of their public presentation. Audiences might associate the behavior of their *animated* character with their real voice, and consequently, with their real-life persona. The opposite of this, of course, is exactly what the studios hope for when they cast a voice. They look for one that *already* has a personality so they can use it to enrich the animation.

This suggests two conclusions. First, designers should cast voices based on more than clarity and tonal quality. They should also attend to the consistency of voices with the behaviors, attitudes, and language of the character or agent to which it will be attached. This will likely require more than instinct. Voices need to be evaluated by users so that consistency can be coordinated and verified.

Also, a badly cast voice is likely much worse than no voice at all. Voices will have social meaning, whether it is wanted or not. This is an important reminder that social responses to media do not always mean *positive* responses to media. Negative social responses to inconsistencies between voice and other features result in confusion, distraction, and dislike.

The Disadvantages of Multiple Voices

How many voices should an interface have? More may not equal better. Multiple voices can complicate an interface, making the human-computer relationship more like a small group than a dyad. Too many voices, like too many people in the room, can cause social overload. People might forget who's who or forget where they left off the last time they met.

Multiple voices also mean multiple relationships *among* the voices. Each voice will have a relationship with the user, but also with the other voices. It doesn't really matter if the voices talk with each other; people will still relate to them as a group. When people join a new group, an important question is whether those already in the group know each other, and if so, how well. Who is one-up to whom? Are there subgroups or coalitions among the voices? In the absence of good answers, people may assume the worst.

The more voices, the more relationships, and the more necessary it is to have explanations for them. Constantly updating the social map in the interface could easily interfere with task performance. Further, the relationships multiply quickly. With one voice, a user needs to keep track of only one dyad (the user and the voice); with two voices, three relationships; with three voices, six relationships, and so on.

The designer must also assign each voice a "place." It would not be appropriate for a voice to come out of the left speaker one minute and the right speaker the next, without an explanation of why and how the voice moved around.

The Advantages of Multiple Voices

When might it be useful to have many voices? One instance is when specialists are needed. A generalist voice, perhaps the moderator in a software application, could act as a master of ceremonies, introducing voices that have particular expertise. Specialist voices could take advantage of stereotypes (a French accent for a cook) or suggest a particular person (the famous cook Julia Child). Conversely, a reputation could be manufactured through repetition.

Multiple voices could also integrate or differentiate functions within media that have many uses. For example, computer programs are often sold together as one product, called a "suite." For suites, integration is paramount. People like to feel that they're not starting all over again every time they change applications within the suite. This could be accomplished by having the same voice introduce each of the programs or by having a single voice for the help system. That voice would be one social actor, and by appearing in all parts of the product, it would tie things together.

This may also work for new kinds of televisions. Consider the relationship between a television, a set-top box (used to control an interactive television), and a remote control. Assume that all three could emit sound, a likely scenario. Voices could be used to integrate or differentiate the devices. If it is desirable to link them, the same voice could be used for all of them. If it is desirable that the set-top box be invisible, no voice should come from that box, nor should a voice refer to it.

One of the best uses of multiple voices is to play them against each other, for example, in a "good cop/bad cop" routine. Consider the following voice-mail system: One voice pleasantly answers the phone, announces the company name, and attempts to put the call through to the desired person. A second voice then says that the caller must wait because the connection cannot be made. After a bit, the first voice (at this point, clearly the "good cop") returns to apologize for the delay, and the voice attempts the connection again. If still no luck, of course, that announcement is left to the "bad cop." As long as only the "good cop" associates itself with the company, positive feelings should result.

At the most basic level, these studies raise the question of "What is *one*?" What is the minimum set of cues necessary to encourage people to count *one* social presence? The two of us have the same answer. To be more persuasive, we'll deliver them in two different voices.

"My answer is: Much less than is traditionally thought."

"And I agree: Less than one might think."

16

Source Orientation

In the prefaces of books about research, it is common to acknowledge a large group of collaborators and then add that none of them should be held responsible for mistakes in the pages that follow. This certainly applies to us: We've had many collaborators, yet no one should think that any of them is the source of our errors.

What's interesting about this disclaimer, however, is that it is fatuous. What if we omitted it? Is it possible that people would read something foolish, and then start wondering which of our colleagues was responsible? Hardly. Most probably, *we* would be considered the ultimate source of everything written, whether it originated with us or not.

The association between sources and their content is powerful, and hard to counter. If we attempted to pin errors on other people, readers wouldn't buy it: We are the source. Our voices are on the pages, and we are responsible for the mistakes. There are ways to profit from the association, however. Even if we politely acknowledged borrowing something *good* from someone, we would benefit for the same reason we'd be blamed for the errors.

Whether messengers are killed or kissed, of course, depends on what they have to say, but their identification with the information is assured. Psychological research shows that people automatically assign responsibility for messages to those who deliver them, even when the receiver knows the link is dubious. What is most *proximate* is the messenger, not someone in some other place.

Why do humans focus on what is proximate? Psychologists have found that keeping track of people who are present is hard enough. Adding others who live in other places or lived at other times is often too demanding. The most immediate threats and opportunities are those in front of us, and we assign attention and responsibility accordingly. This is particularly true if the content of a message is difficult or if it's the end of a tiring day.

In one classic experiment about sources, several people heard speeches about a controversial issue. Each participant was told that the speakers had nothing to do with the content of the speeches; they were merely reading what was written. Half of the participants heard speeches on one side of an issue; the other half heard the *same* speakers defending the opposite sides. When participants were later asked about the speaker's opinions on the issues, everyone thought the speakers agreed with the speeches, regardless of which views had been presented. The speaker was the source, not the person who wrote the words.

This principle appears often in literature. When asked, "Who said, 'To be or not to be, that is the question'?" most people would answer, "Hamlet." But he is a mythical character who never said anything. William Shakespeare said, "To be or not to be ... ". When people answer the question, they don't picture William Shakespeare sitting down and writing the line; they picture Hamlet. We think of Shakespeare only if we *can't* think of the character.

Celebrity endorsements conform nicely with these examples. Few people think that a famous person in a commercial is the real source of the comments he or she makes about a product. Yet the endorsements work, as numerous studies show, a reminder that what people think is true is often at odds with what actually works.

Because it is difficult to keep distant sources in mind, people tend to become fatigued and frustrated when they do have to think about them. This leads people to feel less positively toward the content. For example, constantly thinking about the author while watching a play changes entertainment into work.

Mediated Sources

The issue of source orientation is a natural one for media. Even when the medium is not the message, it's at least a messenger. As messengers, are all media equal? We think not. One of the most important distinctions between media is modality, especially the difference between pictures and words. These two modalities, and the different media that depend on them, can substantially alter the ability to represent a source that is not present.

One of our recent studies demonstrated this difference. When participants were asked to assess the credibility of news on television, they were influenced most by the credibility of the news anchor, even though they knew that his stories were written and researched by several other people. The people behind the news, as well as the news organization they belonged to, had no impact on the perceived credibility of the news itself. Print was different, however. For newspapers, participants were more influenced by the credibility of the organization that produced the news than by the writer of the story.

Why this difference? In television, the news anchor is the proximate source. It *seems* like the anchors are responsible for the entire presentation, even if they are not. They get the blame and the credit, and it's their credit that may actually explain why they are media stars. In the case of newspapers, however, individuals are invisible. Many stories don't even have bylines, and when they do, they are easily ignored. The most present and visible source in print is the news organization.

We were interested in the breadth of this bias to favor proximate sources. One of the most often mentioned *absent* sources in new media is the computer programmer. Programmers are never proximate, yet they are often cited as the ultimate source of all computing. Among those who think about media, they get much credit and blame. Do computer users agree? Or are the programmers no more apparent to people than print journalists?

Source Orientation in Human-Computer Interaction

Many people have offered the following comment: "Of course I treat computers socially—when I use a computer, I'm thinking about the *programmer.*" They then add that it seems more reasonable to be social because of this thought. This view holds that computing machines are merely appliances interposed between users and programmers. If a computer says, "Please wait, file being copied," it's merely the programmer making a request.

Our major arguments against this, so far, have been people's comments. People tell us that this isn't true. They consistently deny thinking about the programmer or any other distant source during interactions. There is a problem with this rebuttal, however. We've shown many times that people have trouble giving accurate self-reports about experiences with media. Maybe people *believe* they're not thinking about a programmer, but maybe they really are. However, if people orient to proximate sources, as the psychological literature says they do, the following should be true:

Rule 1: The computer will be considered the source of information, not the programmer.

Rule 2: People working with computers will not think about programmers during an interaction.

Rule 3: Interactions with computers are more desirable for users when they don't think about a programmer.

Psychological Relevance of Programmers

How can you show that someone isn't thinking about someone who isn't present? We thought of an answer when we remembered how to calm down at a horror movie: Chant, "It's only a movie, it's only a movie." This trick helps to override the natural response to take the film literally. In other words, attention gets directed past the content of the film to scriptwriters, producers, and directors. These people are generally not as scary as the content they create.

This gave us the idea to tell participants in an experiment that they would be working only with a computer, but that they should think about the person who programmed the computer while they are working. We didn't tell the other group what to think about. If people always think about a programmer, regardless of whether they're instructed to do so, then there should be no difference between these groups. If people orient to what is proximate, however, then there would be differences: Thinking about a programmer should change responses to the programs.

We asked participants to work with two computers that would teach them different things. After each tutoring session, participants were given a test and they were evaluated by the same computer. We had two sessions (and two computers) so that we could tell the participants that they did extremely well in the first round, and poorly in the second. We wanted to see if the results changed depending on whether participants had succeeded or failed.

After each lesson, participants filled out a questionnaire that evaluated the computer. They were asked to indicate how well certain adjectives described their session. Some of the adjectives addressed the quality of performance (e.g., *helpful, clever*); others measured social responses (e.g., *friendly, likable*). The perceived similarity between the user and the computer was also measured.

The important difference in the experiment was whether we referred to the programmer or to the computer. Half of the participants were told that they were working with programmers, and that the programmers had different ways of tutoring. They were also told that they would be evaluated by the programmers after the session. The other half were told the exact same things, but the word "computer" was substituted for "programmer." When participants worked without a programmer, the computer referred to itself as "this computer." When a programmer was mentioned, the computer referred to itself as "I."

Programmers Are *Not* Psychologically Relevant

We found clear differences between participants who were instructed to think about the programmer, and participants who were free to think about any source. Those participants who did not have to think of the programmer thought that the computer was significantly more friendly, more effective, more playful, more computer-like, and more similar to themselves than did those participants who were asked to think about the programmer. The valence of the evaluation (positive or negative) did not affect how people responded to the programmer/computer distinction.

Moreover, participants felt more positively toward the computer when they were not asked to think about the programmer. Of the thirty adjectives that were either positive or negative, participants who heard nothing about a programmer had more positive feelings for all but two.

From this we concluded that people could think about a distant source, but only if they were so instructed and only with a significant cost. The default was to think about the computer as the immediate source, and not to think about the programmer, who was out of sight and therefore out of mind.

Thinking about Sources

People do not respond socially to computers because they imagine an interaction with a programmer. Computers are no different from traditional media: Presence is relevance. We had been forced to rely on people's comments to know that this was true, but now we have verification that doesn't depend on the introspection of users.

Do People Willingly Suspend Disbelief?

This study suggests there is no "willing suspension of disbelief." Translated a bit, this is the idea that people can *willingly* decide what is proximate. The claim is that people can intentionally forget about the fact that media are artificial and produced elsewhere and can *pretend* that what's in front of them is real. People supposedly suspend disbelief because it's enjoyable to pretend.

Our studies, however, question how willing this suspension really is. The next time you see a play, try to suspend *belief*. Try to ignore the characters and sets on the stage and simply think about the author who enabled it all. Two things might happen. First, you might not be able to follow the plot—it's hard enough without this distraction. You also might leave the theater exhausted. The burden of adding thoughts about a distant source to thoughts about the ones in front of you will burn mental energy.

The traditional notion of "suspension of disbelief," however, suggests that it is work to accept the reality of what is present. If suspending *disbelief* is work, then why is it that we get more confused and tired when we think about the author? The reason is we're suspending what comes naturally for old brains—a belief that the actors are real people in real places. Accepting what is present—that mediated life is real life—is no work at all.

Media versus People as Sources

Inferences based on hidden information are hard, and therefore unlikely. However, most research on source orientation concentrates on what is hidden. For example, there is extensive discussion of the *real* similarities between thinking machines and thinking people, at the expense of qualities that are much more present and obvious.

Consider Searle's Chinese Room problem. Imagine that you are standing in front of a room with a closed door. There is a small opening in the door. Into this opening you put a piece of paper with a Chinese character written on it. The "room" then pushes out a Chinese character that is a logical response to the one you pushed in. How would you respond? Searle argued that your response would depend on whether you thought that there was a real person with real intelligence in the other room or just a machine in there that was producing characters.

The media equation suggests that people will ignore the question of objective intelligence in media (and in the Chinese Room) because people do not focus on "real" intelligence, like IQ, when they judge other people. Instead, people form impressions of intelligence, and they rely on cues like language ability and even appearance. These criteria, however, are not accurate predictors of things like IQ. The same faulty criteria will likely be applied to media as well.

A similar confusion of the real and perceived intelligence of a source appears in the Turing Test. In this test, a person sits in front of a teletype and has a typewritten conversation with something in another room. In the other room is either a person or a computer. After five minutes, if the person can't tell whether there's a computer or a person in the other room, then the computer passes the test: It's intelligent.

Determining whether the computer/person in the Turing Test is *really* intelligent is too hard. If people considered it at all, they'd probably just determine whether the source *seemed* intelligent; if it did, it would seem a full-fledged source. Researchers could profit from adopting the same approach that people interacting do—assessing a source by deemphasizing questions about objective intelligence in favor of psychological questions about *perceived* intelligence.

Designing with Sources in Mind

Sometimes users do think about the programmer or the company that produces content. For example, when experienced computer users are stumped by a problem, they often think: "Maybe if I think like the person who programmed this thing, I'll be able to fix it." The point is that users think about the programmer or producer of the product when things go *wrong*; users don't think about them when things go right. And this negative feeling will likely generalize to the programmer or producer. This may be one reason why people often have relatively negative feelings about the companies that produce high-technology products.

The key to solving this problem is to provide a scapegoat that is a separate and identifiable source. The scapegoat should be a special representation, dissociated from the company, that the user is expected to turn to when all else fails. This representation could deliver the bad news that although there are a few more things to try, it is likely a lost cause. This would deflect negative feelings away from the creator (and hopefully the product).

Programmers and machines are not the only possible sources in human-computer interaction. There can actually be several layers of sources, and even many within the computer itself. For example, when a character in computer software presents information, either via a word balloon or speech, that character becomes the proximate source. Relative to the character, the machine itself is distant. Although users may "know" that characters are all driven by a single computer, a user's natural response is to orient to the most present social actor. Characters are certainly close enough to the real things to count as sources. The added layer of characters likely makes the machine a more distant, and hence more invisible, source.

Media and Form

17

Image Size

Try answering these questions about media: What movie did you last see? What are you doing with your new computer? What do you think about how your local newspaper covers politics? What's wrong with television for children? What do you think will be the important new multimedia products?

Answers to these questions, while different in a hundred important ways, share one thing—they are all about media *content*. They are about the people, stories, and settings in movies, the names of applications on your computer, what was said about politicians in the newspaper, violence on children's television, or the potential for new media to take us to places we've never been.

No doubt, content is important, and that is the part of the media equation that we've emphasized so far. Our research shows, however, that content is not the only characteristic that conforms to the equation. Also important are the *forms* of media—their size, shape, fidelity, synchrony, and many other features created by people who operate cameras, edit visuals, draw pictures, make graphics, and design the boxes that display the results. Each of these can change how people respond to content.

The Case of Size

Imagine that a favorite movie is recorded on a new data card that fits in a pocket. You could decide to use the card in any number of places and

193

devices. You could play the movie on a standard television. You could take it to the study and play it on the computer. You could play the movie on a hand-held personal communication device. And you could play it on the home theater, complete with high-definition display and surround-sound audio. Digitalization enables *any* content to be played wherever and whenever desired.

An important question about the different playbacks is whether they are really the *same* movie in each case. Obviously it's the same story, same actors, and same scenes, so the author or director might say it's the same experience. A computer scientist would have to say that it's the same content because the bits in the data file don't change just because the displays do. But what about *psychologically*? Are big pictures psychologically the same as small ones?

The answer, if media are anything like real life, is no. They are *not* the same experience. Size is one of the most primitive cues we have about what's happening in the environment. Size can determine whether the objects and people around us are safe or dangerous, something to approach or reason to flee.

The list of scientific findings that verify the influence of size is impressive. People generally like big things. Infants show a preference for larger objects over smaller ones. Height in men is positively related to physical attractiveness, income, and occupational status. Since the 1860s, in all but two presidential elections, the taller candidate has won.

Size also influences arousal, presumably because large things need attention. Large things are consequential, both as problems and opportunities, and consequently, they encourage a preparation for action. And because arousal enhances memory, we could expect anything large to be more easily recalled as well.

Media and Size

Is size relevant to media? Size at least describes an obvious difference. Media now come in a lot of *different* sizes from the laptop, to the desktop, to the countertop, to the home theater, to the movie theater. We could lengthen this list by adding new technologies at the extremes—everything from wristwatch televisions to IMAX theaters.

If the findings from psychology apply straightforwardly to media, then larger displays could be different experiences than small ones—even if the content is identical. One important response that might change is arousal. Big pictures should be more arousing, and with that response, more demanding and memorable as well.

This rule might sound improbable. Unlike real life, large media are no more likely to do harm than small media. The size of an *image* is simply a function of the size of a screen, the position of a chair, or the framing of a picture. A big picture of a face doesn't mean that a person has grown. Pictures have nothing to do with the actual sizes of the things depicted in them. Consequently, size should have no bearing on the meaning of a picture or whether it can arouse.

It may not work that way, however. The human brain did not evolve in a world where images could be made arbitrarily large or small. Human responses were shaped more by literal significance. If an object, especially one that moved, appeared large, it *was* large or close, either of which was cause for concern. Even now, when something *seems* large, it *is* large, psychologically at least.

What exactly makes something *seem* large? An easy answer is absolute size, measured by feet and inches. There is another answer, however, accounted for by a characteristic of human vision. When displays are large, more of the picture is in peripheral vision. This means that the boundary between the screen and the rest of the environment is farther in the corners of vision. This makes the boundary less noticeable, a feature with important implications for arousal.

Imagine a picture of two people in a conversation, one person on the left of the picture, and the other on the right. You are sitting three feet away from a tiny screen just four inches by three inches. When you stare at the center of the picture, it is possible to focus on a large portion of the image. Even the parts of the picture that are in peripheral vision are not far away from the exact point where your eyes are focused. It's easier to keep track of the person you're *not* looking at while you focus on the other.

Now imagine the exact same picture on the home theater. The screen is four feet by three feet and you are now sitting seven feet from the screen. In this case, you are able to focus on only a small part of the screen. The point on the picture where your eyes are focused (called foveal vision) makes up a much smaller part of the screen. You would need to move your eyes several times just to take in a single face.

The face you *aren't* looking at is now quite a bit to the side. Any action by that person is likely to be much more of a surprise, because the action is farther away from where attention is focused. Since action outside of direct attention could be more consequential than action right in front of us, the response to motion in peripheral vision is greater arousal. The preparation for response is more urgent.

Heightened arousal will also mean better memory, so we could expect better memory for information on the big screen. The arousal and the memory that result, however, do not depend on content in this case. It is a response to *form*. Regardless of content, if the picture is big, it has our attention.

We made the following predictions about what might happen when identical media content is displayed in different sizes:

Rule 1: Larger pictures will be more arousing than smaller ones.

Rule 2: Larger pictures will be better remembered than smaller ones.

Rule 3: Larger images will be better liked than smaller ones.

Viewing Big and Little Pictures

These predictions are straightforward with one catch: Exactly what *is* big and little? Most of the literature that talks about the effects of size refers only to *relative* differences. There are some industry standards, however, that might constitute important sizes to study first.

Study 1: Effect of Picture Size on Arousal and Memory

In our first study about size and arousal, we used a 22-inch picture diagonal, the U.S. average of home television screens, as well as a 90-inch diagonal, the largest screen that could reasonably be expected in a home theater. The total area of the bigger screen was over 16 times that of the small screen. We wanted to *maximize* the differences between the two screens, but keep the differences within expectations for what could be found in the home.

In this study, 125 adults viewed 60 video segments that showed a variety of scenes. Half of the participants saw all of the scenes on the average screen, and half saw them on the large one. The pictures in the test were selected to elicit different emotions. There were depictions of violence and blood, exciting and pleasurable activities, erotic sexual scenes, as well as positive and negative scenes with little excitement, such as funeral processions, flowers, and children playing.

We measured arousal by having participants circle pictures that showed a person experiencing different levels of arousal. The pictures ranged from high arousal (a picture of a person with an excited face and racing heart) to low arousal (a calm look and no internal agitation). There were five pictures between these extremes. After each video segment, participants were asked to circle the picture that best represented how they felt at that moment.

The larger screen significantly influenced the subjective experience of arousal. Bigger pictures equaled more arousal.

Picture size also affected memory. One week after participants watched the video segments, we invited them back to the lab. They were asked to recall and write down a brief description of all the segments that they could remember seeing one week earlier. Those participants who saw the pictures on the large screen could remember significantly more scenes than those who watched on the smaller one. Technically, everyone saw the same content. Psychologically, the experiences were different.

Study 2: Effect of Picture Size on Liking of Images

What do people think about big screens? Do they like them? Do they seem more lifelike? Does the action appear faster? We tried to answer these questions in a second study. In this case, participants viewed segments from entertainment movies. Each segment lasted between two and three minutes.

The scenes were chosen to maximize the chance for the large screen versions to knock the socks off viewers. There was fast action and high-fidelity surround-sound audio. The scenes were from movies like *Days of Thunder, Apocalypse Now,* and *Top Gun.*

The results are good news for companies manufacturing big screens. Movie scenes on the larger displays were liked considerably more. The scenes were more exciting, the action faster, the pictures more realistic, and viewers reported feeling more a part of the action.

Larger screens mean more arousal, stronger memories, and more positive evaluations of the content they displayed. And all of these results are pretty much the same in the real world. Size matters, real or reel.

Thinking about Size

One implication of the studies is that big pictures are better, at least if you're trying to arouse or excite people. Others have suspected this throughout the century, however. Ever since the transition from Kinescope and Mutoscope "peepshows" to projected images, the power of the film experience has been attributed, at least in part, to the size of the screen. The early film industry recognized this and promoted their new technology as superior even to a live stage performance. The major rationale? Film was "*larger* than life," in a literal, rather than literary, sense.

The most *un*expected use of these results, however, may be in the design of new media in the areas of computing and multimedia. We consider the unexpected first, and then return to television and film.

Big Screens and Computers

Computers are special machines. When looking to buy one, you're advised to consider things like clock speed and memory capacity. Among some technologists, monitors are interchangeable and common, much less interesting than CPUs and software.

The separation between computing and displays, however, is psychologically difficult. People who aren't technologists must keep in mind two separate functions: computation and display. What happens, however, when people are too preoccupied or just don't care enough or know enough to think about this difference? In time, many of us may succumb to what is true for more familiar media—the screen is where the action is.

This progression has already occurred for television. A television set also has several components, such as tuners, filters, and an electron gun. Most people, however, think of a television as *one* thing—a place where people and places are displayed. But this was not always the case. When television was new, every set required a champion to keep it going, someone to wade through a manual, coax reception, and understand the components. Now the set itself is considerably less significant. It can't really be repaired and it's easy to operate. All of this easily encourages a more social and natural orientation to the display, because there is no constant reminder that it's a machine.

Displays are important. Already, manufacturers of laptops and multimedia monitors compete fiercely with information about screen size. What if one computer came with a VGA projector capable of lighting up a wall, but was a bit slow and had limited RAM, while another offered a 17-inch diagonal image, but had a little more RAM and disk space? Which wins in the marketplace? Don't underestimate the power of size and the accompanying arousal.

Big Screens and Movies

When you make a movie, there's not a whole lot to be done about display size, unless the film will play *only* on TV or *only* in an IMAX theater. Otherwise, it's necessary to produce pictures with the knowledge that they will be displayed in *different* sizes. When this is necessary, what should be considered?

One important consideration is image size relative to actual size. What happens when a picture of a car is considerably larger or smaller than a real car? Or when a person is several heads shorter or taller than a real person? It's possible to combat such distortions with framing tricks. With very large screens, the camera should not zoom in too close to people's faces. On the other hand, if a shot is framed for display in the video window of a desktop computer, get as close as possible. The picture will be small, and the larger size will help create presence.

Big Screens and Education

Are big screens always good? Perhaps not. There are some good arguments *against* big pictures. One is that too much arousal can be *counter-productive* in learning. It is quite possible for emotional experience to distract. The consequence is that little mental energy is left to contemplate, rehearse, or integrate information with prior experience.

The problem concerns *what* is remembered. It is clear that arousal predicts memory; when arousal is high, the brain marks the event that precipitated the arousal, and we are more likely to remember it. What is it, however, that is marked and remembered? Most likely, it's information specifically related to arousal, and *not* the information that most people would think of as educational.

Imagine that you've made a film that uses a roller coaster to illustrate the principles of gravity and centrifugal force in physics. The pictures in the film are point-of-view shots of a rider on the roller coaster. The physics lesson is in the audio that goes with the pictures. On a small screen, the video may not be overly compelling, and the audio will have a chance to sink in. On the big screen, however, the viewer is ducking and diving with the people in the lead car, with little mental energy left over to listen to the physics lesson. On the big screen, the response to the film could be this: I had a great time and I'll certainly remember how it felt to be in the roller coaster, but I can't tell you much about the *physics* of bodies in motion.

The physics film is also a reminder that we shouldn't associate arousal with content that is bad. Arousal is easily generated by prosocial media experiences. If a child watches an educational program on the big screen, arousal will increase and so will a heightened *readiness for action*. It's not necessary that the content be violence and gore.

Action readiness does not dissipate when the set is turned off. Arousal is easily transferred to the next activity. If this is another positive activity, no problem; we'll be excited and ready to go. If the next activity is negative, however, the excitement that is transferred could energize antisocial behavior. Most often, bad media effects are thought to be the result of bad content. The research on screen size is a reminder that valence is not the only issue.

Presenting multimedia on large displays may yield some pleasant surprises. Based on our research, we believe that multimedia (and maybe even the spreadsheet as well) will look quite good on the home theater. There might be problems making input devices convenient, but the larger screens should heighten arousal as well as liking. Some people think that computing on a big screen will too thoroughly mix work with arousal and fun. Once again, however, we shouldn't underestimate the value many of us place on a confusion between them.

Life with Multiple Screens

There is an interesting caveat to the proliferation of screen sizes in film, television, and computing. Not only is *absolute* size of screens growing, but the *variance* in sizes is growing as well. Screens are becoming both bigger *and* smaller. The number of different choices about where to experience media is huge.

This variance may offer a substantially different way to pick media. Instead of choosing different content, people might choose based on size. The home theater could be the place to get aroused, maybe even so much so that we'd have to keep a smaller set around to relax.

18

Fidelity

Try this visual exercise. Focus on a single letter in a word from this sentence. Then, without changing your focus, try to be aware of something to the left or right of the page. You can likely *identify* an object to the side, but you'd be hard-pressed to provide an accurate description of its edges, surfaces, shading, reflections, or even its exact shape. It would be impossible to read words located there or to describe the content of a picture you had never seen before.

The reason is that acuity is not the same throughout the visual field. The only area of vision where resolution is good is foveal vision, and that is a very small area centered at the exact point where your eyes are focused. One word to the left or right of that point, and things begin to blur. This is why visual experience is a progression of separate glances, all tied together to serve some goal, but none capable of providing the big picture.

Most of the visual field is in peripheral vision, and peripheral vision has a special deficiency—image fidelity. When vision is fixed on any particular word, facial feature, or object, most of what we see is rendered quite poorly. Since most of what we see is in peripheral vision, we could say that people have enormous experience with images that are poorly defined.

Experience with low visual fidelity, however, is not limited to peripheral vision. We also spend a lot of time in compromised visual environments. Everyone regularly confronts darkness, twilight, fog, glare, and obstructions. Occasionally, we even *intentionally* introduce visual compromise, as when we choose candlelight instead of overhead light.

Few visual experiences *absolutely* depend on perfect visual fidelity. Each time we confront a compromised visual environment, we are capable of using a substantial ability to extrapolate from less-than-perfect visuals. What is curious about these experiences is that they don't seem to be much of a problem at all.

Mediated Visual Fidelity

These psychological comments contrast sharply with the answer to this question: What is an important deficiency in present-day television? Communication industries throughout the world, in collaboration with governments, and with the apparent approval of investors, are depending on one particular answer: the fidelity of the pictures. It is argued that with better pictures, we will forget the boundaries between screen and reality, and become truly immersed in the picture. And, of course, we'll be willing to pay a lot for the experience.

The prediction of a reality revolution based on image resolution begs an important psychological question: What *un*reality problem does enhanced visual fidelity solve? The psychology of human vision suggests that sharper pictures solve no important visual problems, as low visual fidelity is familiar and not particularly troublesome. Shoppers at the appliance store might *like* as sharp a picture as possible, but as a *psychological* criterion for believability or immersion, visual fidelity may be overrated.

This led us to the following prediction, based on common visual experiences in the real world:

Rule 1: Lower-fidelity visual images on the screen will be evaluated no differently than higher-fidelity images.

Does Visual Fidelity Affect Viewers?

We predicted that poor visual fidelity is a *natural* phenomenon and therefore would not influence how viewers make sense of the information they view. It is unusual in the social sciences to predict that *nothing* will happen. In the case of visual fidelity, however, a lot is riding on the affirmative, which may be justification enough for testing whether the affirmative is right.

A thorny question in studies about fidelity is how to alter the picture. What should a great picture and a crummy picture look like? In our first study, high-fidelity pictures approximated the best video that could be expected in the home. We used the best equipment possible and we digitized the pictures and enhanced them with a computer. The video was displayed with a bright video projector on a six-foot rear-projection screen. The result looked extremely good, much closer to a future high-definition television image than to the current broadcast signal.

Our version of poor image fidelity was an engineer's worst nightmare. First, we copied the original material through five generations, and on bad tape. Then we used a less bright projector, and no computer enhancement of the pictures. Viewers saw fuzzy pictures that had poor contrast, few distinct edges, and visible scan lines.

Our test used sixteen scenes from action/adventure movies, two each from movies like *Days of Thunder, Indiana Jones, Total Recall,* and *Casualties of War.* We chose a high-action scene and a calmer scene from each film. Participants watched by themselves, and they sat seven feet from the screen.

Visual Fidelity Had No Effect

We measured three responses to the video: attention, memory, and evaluation of the experience. Attention was measured with a reaction-time task that recorded response times to tones placed at random points in the presentation. We measured recognition memory by showing participants a series of pictures after they were done viewing and asking whether they had seen them previously or not. Evaluation of the content was based on questionnaires.

Despite the variety of tests, there were *no* differences in responses to the two levels of fidelity. Even more damaging to the case for enhanced visual fidelity was that participants couldn't even tell the difference between the conditions. A question that specifically asked participants to rate visual fidelity showed that the two fidelity versions were perceived as identical. A strong manipulation of image quality didn't much matter across a broad range of sensitive measures.

Whatever imperfections constitute poor video fidelity, they are not sufficiently *un*familiar or *un*natural to be psychologically intrusive. Low visual fidelity may be tolerated much like similar imperfections in the real world. Even though new technology can make visuals look almost identical to real life, people might not even *notice*.

A conclusion that there are no psychological advantages for image fidelity seemed reasonable, although risky given this single test. We have even more confidence in this conclusion, however, because two studies at other universities drew the same conclusion.

Should Visual Fidelity Influence Design?

Consider a trip to the appliance store to buy a new television. Many people have the same script for this purchase. Go to the store, walk down the rows of sets in your price range, and then pick the one with the *best picture*. This may seem at odds with the results of our study, but there are problems with this script.

One problem is that people are notoriously bad at comparative judgments of image quality. Judgments can easily be influenced by clever manipulation of displays, tweaking that has more to do with the controls on the set than image fidelity. For example, high contrast is probably more important than small differences in screen resolution.

Another problem is the difference between an *ability* to notice a difference and the psychological *importance* of what is noticed. Some people may be able to see differences in the screens, most easily when they are placed side-by-side, but the difference may not determine how information is processed.

Visual Fidelity versus Screen Size and Shape

What if you could change only one feature of media pictures? How does visual fidelity stack up against other features, notably image size and image shape? Our research suggests it might lose to both.

New television sets are larger, in part because they have to be to show off the increased image fidelity. People like big pictures, as long as there are no highly visible scan lines.

People also like horizontal shapes. This is true in architecture, and even in preferences for common objects and drawings. Screens that are more horizontal approximate more closely the aspect ratio of human vision, as people can see farther to the sides than they can above or below the point of focus. Also, horizontal screens are likely more arousing because more action occurs in peripheral vision, that is, to the left and right of visual focus. This is the same for real life: Most information arrives laterally.

Because film is presented in more horizontal formats than television, movies don't fit on traditional televisions. One way to change the shape of a television set is "letter-boxing," the procedure that blacks out the top and bottom of video pictures to ensure that the sides of the film can be seen. In an informal study we did, we found that people hated the technique at first. But when we showed them what they missed when the images were cut to fit the shape of the television, they changed their opinions significantly. When the television sets themselves are more horizontal, we think the attraction may be even greater.

The venue where all of these features compete is high-definition television. This new form of television is anticipated mostly as a standard that will enhance image fidelity, but the new sets will probably be popular because they are larger and have a more horizontal aspect ratio (16:9 instead of the 4:3 for current television and computer screens).

We give size and shape an advantage over image fidelity on one other score. New TV screens may be well liked even when nothing is on them.

Big and wide screens are *always* big and wide, regardless of the picture that appears and even regardless of whether any picture appears at all. You can show off your new purchase without even turning the set on.

Relevance of Audio Fidelity

What about audio fidelity? Unlike video, poor audio fidelity is psychologically unfamiliar, even weird. The typical background hiss or reduced frequency range on taped audio, for example, has no real-world counterpart. And the fact that all the sound in media usually comes from the exact same direction is also unfamiliar, especially when the picture suggests it should be all around us.

Media artists have long noted the power of lifelike sounds and voices, even when they seemed to emanate from pictures of lesser quality. For many designers, the formula for immersion *begins* with audio. They go to great lengths to eliminate background noise, to preserve the familiar highs and lows, and to make sure that the sounds come from the right places, just as they would if the listener were experiencing them in real life.

If the professionals are right, the fidelity of sounds should be important. We predicted, based mostly on the idea that poor audio has no real-world counterpart, that audio fidelity would have an effect on the same responses that showed *no* differences for visual fidelity. The next three predictions were about audio:

Rule 2: Audio fidelity will affect attention to media.

Rule 3: Audio fidelity will affect people's memory for audio information.

Rule 4: People will evaluate better audio fidelity differently than poorer audio fidelity.

Strong Effects of Audio Fidelity

The test of these predictions was part of the study about visual fidelity, and it included the same sixteen movie clips. In addition to versions that had high and low visual fidelity, we also created two audio presentations that represented extremely good and extremely bad sound.

The high audio-fidelity condition was easy. We used the CD-quality audio recorded from the original material. We played this audio through a high-quality surround-sound stereo system, and the result was great sound.

For low fidelity, we added three audio glitches to the original tracks. First we copied the audio several times. Then we cut the frequency response by limiting the lowest and highest sounds, and we even added some noise in the form of hiss from a bargain tape recorder. The end result was a decidedly poor recording, but still intelligible and synched with the visuals.

The results showed that audio fidelity was much more powerful than video fidelity. There were significant differences between high and low audio fidelity for each of the three measures: attention, memory, and evaluation. First, the high-fidelity audio produced faster reaction times to secondary-task tones that were periodically sounded during the movie segments. This indicated that participants were actually giving *less* thought to the audio in the high-fidelity condition, likely because the audio was more familiar.

Participants also remembered less about what they heard in the high audio-fidelity movie clips and they were less able to identify accurately sounds taken from the movies. This was probably because poor audio fidelity led the participants to orient to the unusual sounds rather than become immersed in the movie. Immersion also led participants hearing the high-fidelity audio to have somewhat poorer memory for the *visual* sequences.

Subjective evaluations of the movie segments differed as well. Participants felt that with high-fidelity audio, the video segments were more likable and realistic and took more effort to process.

Our conclusion was that audio fidelity matters. When it is poor, presentations sound *un*natural, and people consciously monitor the content. When it's good, people are immersed.

Thinking about Audio and Video Fidelity

This research has implications concerning how to evaluate the theoretical status of seeing and hearing in media. It may not be advisable to elevate either sense to *the* dominant consideration in discussions about how media work. The important question is not which is more important, but rather how either one works. The answer to this question will have to depend on three *different* areas in psychology: one for vision, one for hearing, and one for how people differentially respond to the familiar and the unfamiliar.

Designers Should Focus on Audio

For designers of *multi*media, audio is a good place to invest. It appears to deliver more psychological bang for the buck. In part, this may be true because the necessary investment is less. There are easier audio-fidelity solutions, and they are generally cheaper than those for video. But even if the costs of improving vision and sound were the same, these results suggest starting with audio.

Audio fidelity can also help the visuals, quite apart from the technical quality of the pictures, because good audio can even make people think that the visuals look better. This is a good argument against waiting to upgrade audio fidelity until there is a level of video fidelity that matches. With media, objective descriptions of resolution are much less important than how the content is *perceived*.

19

Synchrony

Consider this friendly exchange:

"How did you like the draft of the last chapter?"

"I thought it was fine."

Clearly, a positive response. What would you think, however, if there were a three-second pause between the end of the question and the beginning of the answer? A certain response becomes a questionable one. After three seconds, you know there's more to the answer than "fine."

Timing means a lot. Humans interpret behaviors that occur in tiny units of time. From studies in psychology and communication, we know that timing is a key in *all* interpersonal exchanges. A slight pause, a quick hint of a smile, or a momentary look of puzzlement all tell a lot about the people we encounter and how we should respond to them. A few milliseconds either way, and things change.

Media and Timing

Timing slips occasionally occur in traditional media, such as television or film, but they are rare. Generally, problems with timing are attributable to those in the actual conversations, and not to the technologies per se.

Newer media, however, quite often present timing problems that *cannot* exist in the real world. In video-conferencing systems, for example, the eye can detect transitions between the frames when too few frames are used. The result is a bizarre jerkiness when people move. The same thing happens, and is often even more exaggerated, on new video-phones and some computer applications that play video.

One of the most noticeable errors occurs when lips fail to move in synch with the words coming from them. Viewers stare at the moving lips, focused on the mismatch of sound and mouth, instead of concentrating on what is being said.

Asynchrony between lips and speech detracts from the plausibility of mediated presentations. Even if the speakers presented are themselves unbelievable, we expect lips and voice to be synchronized. Even if the speaker is a bird, we at least demand beak-synch. People depend a lot on naturalness in media, even when presenters are characters we couldn't otherwise imagine.

What happens if one or more basic timing features are compromised? What if the pictures and sounds that constitute media are altered so that they depict people in a way that viewers never experience? We think that there are two possibilities.

A common assumption among some media designers is that people are sufficiently focused on media *content* that they can forgive slight imperfections in the timing of its delivery. Consider a video-conferencing system that shows images at frame rates slower than needed to render natural motion. Under this view, imperfections are not a problem. Users are expected to mindfully ignore the imperfection in exchange for the convenience of communicating with distant colleagues.

There is another quite different view, however. While people may be able to *consciously* discount problems in the delivery of media, the technical difficulties are still unusual psychological experiences. Unnatural timing cannot be ignored or forgiven with an apology for the delivery system. This may be true even if it seems obvious why the weirdness occurred, and even if it seems unreasonable that a technically sophisticated person would let such a problem influence a judgment.

A person in a video conference who appears to have jerky movements is not just someone compromised by technology. It is also a picture of a person who doesn't move well, a clumsy and uncoordinated person. Judgments about the speaker's competence, however irrelevant the technology problem may seem, could change accordingly.

The hypothesis for this study of unnatural experiences was that if small time units are important in the real world, then they will be equally important in the world of media. Just as we can't constantly remind ourselves that a scary movie is artificial, we can't constantly remind ourselves that unnaturally timed motion or speech is merely a function of technology.

We chose to study the synchronization of speech and lip movement because people have extensive experience with voices that are synchronized with the movement of lips. This easily allows people to recognize irregularity in lip synchrony, even if they can ultimately discount it. Another reason we started with this problem is that synchrony between video and audio is frequently compromised in new media, especially in the use of computers that show video, and in video-conferencing, particularly over the Internet. In many cases, it is often hard to find enough bandwidth or computational speed for a completely natural presentation. Something has to give, and what does often involves audio-video synchrony.

One of the effects we studied was the evaluation of a speaker's abilities. When the lips and voice don't match, it is cause for puzzlement. Instead of viewers asking, "What's wrong with the technology?," we thought they might ask, "What's wrong with the speaker?" This last question has *social* consequences, since it may cause viewers to make a negative evaluation of the person talking.

The prediction about audio-video asynchrony was this:

Rule 1: Audio-video asynchrony will result in negative evaluations of the speaker.

Creating Asynchrony in the Lab

We had participants in an experiment see and hear two levels of audio-video asynchrony. One level was perfect synchrony, or as perfect as

213

we could get with standard video. In this condition, there was no appearance of mismatch between the pictures of people speaking and the words coming from their mouths. In the other condition, we set the asynchrony at a level that we thought would be quite noticeable: five video frames or one-sixth of a second.

There were eight video clips shown in the test. They were each two to three minutes long, and each one showed people talking: newscasters delivering news, narrators in advertisements, and characters in entertainment drama. All of the segments were close-ups of faces shown on a 40-inch screen. For each participant, half of the clips were randomly selected to be shown with asynchrony. In each case of asynchrony, the audio preceded the video, because this never happens in real life.

Effects of Unnoticeable Asynchrony

The first thing we looked at was participants' ability to detect synchrony problems. The recognition of asynchrony turned out to be even more difficult than we expected. We asked three questions to see if participants in the experiment noticed problems. The first one asked viewers if they noticed anything strange about the presentations. If they didn't mention a problem with synchrony, we then asked if they noticed anything unusual about the audio. If they said nothing about synchrony again, we asked them specifically if they noticed that the video and audio channels were not synchronized. Only half of the participants in the asynchrony condition said "yes" to *any* of these questions.

In spite of the difficulty in noticing them, the problems did have an effect. When the audio preceded the video, the speakers in the presentation were evaluated more negatively. They were judged less interesting, less pleasant, less influential, more agitated, and less successful in their delivery. And importantly, this effect held for viewers who could not even identify the problem. Thus, there is no psychological discount for broken or underdeveloped technology. Rather, technical problems have social consequences.

Thinking about Asynchrony as Unnatural

Most applications of the media equation assume that real life and media life are equal. This study, however, adds a twist. Certain alterations to reality can be accomplished *only* in media, and this manufactured reality is, like poor audio fidelity, something for recipients of media presentations to reckon with. The new reality, rather than being attributed to technology, is instead taken as something natural but wrong. And in media, as in real life, strange occurrences are evaluated negatively.

Design and the Asynchrony Problem

The problem of unnatural presentations seems critical, especially since media may compromise basic perceptual cues for some time to come. Even if solutions are known, they are often too expensive to implement. Audio-video synchrony, for example, is not a mystery; engineers know how to make it perfect. It's just that not all of us can pay for their services or afford the machines that will render the problem obsolete.

These problems need psychological as well as technical attention. Without it, the consequence may be this: Designers produce incredible technology, but the wonder of their products is significantly diminished because they break a few simple but fundamental rules about how people work in the real world. Technical marvels become social failures, perhaps like the genius who, because of problems saying hello and good-bye, is relegated to obscurity.

Asynchrony Is Widespread

Several new technologies compromise perceptual basics. Telephones that also show video are feasible and interesting, but so far they can show video only at extremely slow frame rates. This ensures that the voice and the pictures of the person who is supposedly attached to the voice are significantly out of synch. In fact, synchrony is compromised on many videophones so much that viewers may not even be able to determine who is in the picture: It couldn't be the person talking, because the lips aren't moving with the voice.

Video-conferencing systems are also plagued by problems that seem technically trivial but are psychologically critical, all of which relate to timing. Consider this scenario. A speaker is explaining a concept. The listener, watching in a different city, is desperate to interrupt with feedback, but the system can't deliver the response at the correct moment. The speaker, not hearing or seeing any feedback, just keeps talking. Meanwhile, the listener gets frustrated because there is no reciprocity, no *joint* action in the conversation. The listener has no ability to affect what is being said. A dialogue turns into a monologue. Everyone becomes frustrated.

This type of problem may occur frequently in the absence of "back channel" responses. In face-to-face conversations, these are utterances or gestures by which a listener lets speakers know how they are coming across: sounds like "uh-huh" or "um," a nod of agreement, or a knowing smile. Back channel responses are extremely useful, and they are precisely timed. Without them, frustrations may build, all because of an *un*reality imposed by technology, an unreality that is taken as socially significant by the people experiencing it.

All timing problems are aggravated by the fact that people often are unaware that they occur. Small timing errors, in spite of their social significance, are often not discussed because effects *seem* unlikely. If those people who actually purchase the products aren't aware of them, they might not even appreciate a remedy.

Fixing Asynchrony

What should designers do about timing problems? Obviously, keep improving the technology. In the meantime, however, users have solutions of their own. In video-conferencing, people have substituted gestures for language, even though they can't be timed as precisely. A hand in the air tells the speaker that feedback is coming, even if the technology can't deliver it on time. The visual signal is akin to saying "Over" on a walkie-talkie before the other person can begin talking.

Designers who recognize the importance of well-timed responses can build other functional equivalents of real-world exchanges. A light or audio cue could be used to interrupt a conversation, for example. It may be much more important to have *some* way of substituting for perceptual fundamentals than to depend on people's ability to ignore them. We should not hope that people will forgive and forget.

The sophistication of solutions might not matter much, and it is even possible that a slightly *less* sophisticated one could work better. We know from the synchrony study, for example, that a small timing error is a problem. But what about asynchrony that is even more exaggerated, for example, a single video frame that changed every couple of seconds? In this case, you have something more akin to a slide show with a voiceover. Granted, even slide shows are a bit unnatural, but the effect might be considerably more aesthetic and personable. A soft dissolve between the single frames might even make the slow pace of visuals pleasing. In any case, making media do *less* than they can, rather than do all they can, may sometimes work better.

A more drastic strategy is to *delay* the introduction of technology and the products that depend on it until the problem is fixed. This may not seem necessary in the case of audio-video synchrony, but at times this might be right. Consider the example of talking computers.

Computer-generated speech may be the epitome of *un*naturalness. As sophisticated as speech technology is, the computer's voice still sounds strange. Even if people can readily understand what the computer is saying, the voices do not sound like any possible example of human speech. What are the effects of listening to a voice that is different from every other voice experienced in the real world? We guess that the effects might be rather like the evaluations of speakers in the asynchrony experiment. People may not be aware of why, but the speaker just doesn't sound smart or likable.

Who worries about unnaturalness the most? The answer is another example of differences between Silicon Valley and Hollywood. Video and film artists are critically focused on *all* aspects of quality. Any compromise is considered costly. Perhaps these artists can more easily afford to be picky because they deal with more developed, and in some senses easier, technology. But perhaps they are picky also because they know that message form and content are hopelessly confused.

Meanwhile, the technologists of multimedia and computing are often quick to forgive imperfections. They expect that people will approach technology with sophistication. Part of that sophistication, so the expectation goes, is the ability to keep straight what is the *real* content and what is merely a technical glitch awaiting a fix in the next revision. This conception of users, however optimistic, ignores the fact that all people are humans first, a species that viscerally dislikes unnaturalness.

20

Motion

For animals in the wild, and no less for humans, moving objects are often threats or opportunities. Motion alerts people to pay attention. This is especially true for movement that might harm us. Consequently, objects that move toward us or loom in front of our faces will get the most attention—and quickly.

When people are exposed to motion, particularly motion that is a visual surprise, they focus on the source of the motion and stop all other unnecessary activities. This reaction is called a visual orienting response, and it is more than just a mental reaction. Visual orientations can also produce physical changes in the body, like increased blood flow to the brain and constriction of blood flow to the limbs. These physical reactions prepare the body to process the *consequences* of motion.

Motion on the Screen

If motion is a fundamental natural response in the real world, what happens when it occurs in media? On screen, there are counterparts to most natural forms of movement. Objects and people move as we view (e.g., they move stage or screen left and right, front and back, and enter and exit) or the camera moves (e.g., it pans to the left and right, tilts up and down, or dollies near, far, and around). There is even motion imposed after the pictures are taken: cuts, dissolves, and other special effects.

Motion on the screen, however, seems quite different from motion in real life. Screen motion occurs in only two dimensions, and it is projected with dots and lines of fluorescent light. Screen motion merely *represents* real things by using visual tricks. Televisions and computer monitors are not *actual* physical threats; nothing leaps from them into our laps. When confronted with a threatening picture, the viewer doesn't physically strike back or leave the room. Nothing, in fact, *really* moves.

Movement in media is most often discussed with regard to its *interpretive significance*. In other words, motion has meaning, but it does not demand response. Film techniques that depict motion are traditionally viewed as forms of media that serve the content of media.

If pictures are natural environments, however, then there might be visual orientations to motion even though the places in which it occurs are mediated. We predicted the following:

Rule 1: When a picture presents a visual surprise, viewers will orient to the surprise.

Rule 2: When objects or people in pictures move, attention will be higher than during segments with no motion.

Looking for Orienting Responses

What is there to observe as evidence that orientations to screen motion are a natural response? Visual orientations are generally not part of conscious experience, so it's difficult to ask people about their reactions, even if they're eager to help. Hence, we borrowed directly from psychological research a covert technique for measuring visual orientations.

Orienting responses are indicated by changes in brain electrical activity as measured by the electroencephalogram, or EEG. Psychophysiologists have shown that when people are alert, their brains generate a different amount of electricity than when they are mentally resting. Our plan was to collect EEG responses from people while they watched television to see if those responses reflected the presence and absence of motion on the screen.

The EEG data were collected one person at a time. Six electrodes were attached to each participant's scalp before viewing began. The electrodes picked up the faint electrical signals given off by the brain as it processed the television pictures.

We measured EEG reactions during a half-hour viewing session. Participants watched a situation comedy program, and they also saw several commercials during breaks in the program. We collected EEG information every half second during viewing, which resulted in a huge set of data. The responses to one particular advertisement, however, nicely illustrate the major findings of the study.

The ad was for sausage, and the message was structured as follows. The ad opened with a still picture of a sausage package. Pictures of sausage sizzling in a frying pan, then being served on a plate, followed. The ad ended with the picture of the package. We were trying to see which features of this ad made people pay attention.

Brain Activity Changes While You Watch Television

Does attention come and go in relation to movement, as we predicted? It does. Here is a more detailed story of the ad.

When the sausage package first appears in the upper portion of the screen, it is still. Following some background music, an announcer says, "It's coming…". Three seconds into the ad, the sausage starts rolling, apparently down a table. It continues to roll for about five seconds, and then it stops. At that point, the sausage appears to be about ten times the size that it was at the beginning, and the sides of the package actually protrude outside the left and right borders of the monitor frame. The sausage is then still for a couple of seconds while the announcer continues talking.

Attention, as measured by the EEG, closely parallels the movement of the sausage. For the first two seconds, attention is low—nothing is moving. Then the sausage roll starts moving—surprise—and attention increases at exactly that moment. This is not just because the sausage is moving; it is also moving right toward the viewer's face. After the sausage comes to a halt, there is a slow decrease in attention while the announcer talks: The threat has been removed.

At this point in the ad, something happens that is familiar yet dramatic: There is a cut. The picture on the screen totally changes. One moment it's a sausage package, and the next moment a hand appears from off-screen to crack eggs into a frying pan. The egg spills into the pan, and then the picture cuts to a different image, this time a still shot of sausage patties frying in the same pan. The frying patties are shown for about two seconds, before a third cut introduces a new scene, the first frame of which shows a fork thrusting into view from the upper left side of the display.

The EEG data continue to be synchronized with the parade of movement/no movement in the ad. When the eggs are cracked in the pan (movement), attention is quite high. When the still patties are cooking in the pan (no movement), attention decreases. When the fork pokes in from the side (movement), attention is high again, and so on throughout the ad. Overall, attention is strongly associated with the presence and absence of motion. In fact, the biggest and quickest increases in attention occur within one second after the onset of dramatic movement.

Are these changes in EEG meaningful? The increased attention to movement also had a more familiar effect. Pictures that occurred one second after each motion began were remembered better than pictures that appeared at the exact moment of motion onset.

At What Level Do Media Influence People?

We have a confession about the two predictions that appeared before this study was discussed. They mistakenly suggested that we wrote them down and *then* tried to see whether they applied to media, a decidedly deductive process. Actually, the discovery was substantially more inductive, which is to say that we went fishing. We had some idea that EEG might tell us how people were thinking while they watched the screen, but we had not yet focused on motion as an important factor in the media equation.

When we sat at the video player with a record of the EEG in front of us, we were quite surprised to see that every time attention increased quickly, something had moved on the screen. This was a level of primitive response that we hadn't anticipated. We were thinking more about obvious features of the message like the quality of the writing, the appropriateness of the pictures, and the way that the food was displayed. No one thought about or commented on the presence of looming motion.

We had missed something important. Mental engagement in pictures was determined by primitive responses to motion—the exact same responses to motion in the real world. When something in a picture moves toward us, we *do* duck, at least mentally. Human responses to movement, ingrained into every old brain, are working to protect us from harm, even though, through a miracle of the twentieth century, we are merely watching television. By watching people's *brains* watch television, we found good evidence for the media equation.

Putting Motion into Media

There is an excellent lesson in the last five seconds of the sausage commercial about making an effective message. At about twenty-five seconds into the ad, the sausage rolls *away* from the viewer and then it is still. A logo is then superimposed while the announcer gives the most important product claim in the ad.

At this point, however, attention is at the *lowest* point in the entire message. Things have been still for too long. The result? The audio information is out of synch with a visual cue that alerts viewers. Important thinking occurs in short periods of time. Information that people need to think about, like a brand claim, should be strategically linked with visual demands like movement.

Motion and Rest

In the sausage study, we looked for motion to enhance learning. There are plenty of examples, however, where the presence of motion could easily *detract*. This is true because attention constantly varies around an optimal level. When attention becomes too much effort, people try to

223

decrease it. Some media content—music videos are a good example—are packed with so many visual and auditory surprises that they offer no time to rest. When motion is overwhelming, thinking shuts down. If there is no rest afforded by the stimulus, it will be initiated by the viewer.

The cadence of motion and rest is a critical part of a successful presentation. Is there a natural or best cadence that designers should emulate? We know of no attempt to define this cadence empirically. There are plenty of artistic intuitions, and most suggest that constant motion is bad. The people who made the sausage ad, for example, created a message that *alternated* segments of motion with segments that had no motion. This allowed for periods of rest, and it made the pictures more stimulating because there were more times when motion began. Unfortunately for the designers, however, they placed the key audio information where there was no motion.

Several studies in psychology show that learning improves when there are visual rests. For example, students learn more when there are large windows in a classroom because they can take visual breaks. Memory is enhanced when people have a chance to stop and think about information instead of being forced to continually orient to new stimuli.

The cadence of motion and rest can be varied, depending on the goals of a presentation. Motion can prepare a person to attend and learn, but conversely, motion can interfere if it interrupts a critical segment. Thinking, however, may not always be the important goal. We might play games and watch entertainment precisely to *avoid* thinking. At those times, we willingly allow someone else to control our attention. Motion would be a good bet to do just that.

Motion and Different Blocks of Time

Rules about the use of motion within very short time intervals may not work when larger message segments are considered. In the sausage study, attention varied significantly within seconds and there were even effects that took place in milliseconds. We could easily imagine, however, that if the same motion segments were placed in a different context, the effects might change.

What might happen if new motion segments were introduced constantly? In this case, orienting responses would habituate, which means that they would diminish with each successive orientation. There is evidence in psychology that the effects of motion on attention and memory could even reverse: If the message becomes *too* complicated, people may tune out. In any case, however, the *whole* message is greater than the sum of its parts, the smaller segments that make up the message.

Peripheral Motion

The surprise value of new motion (and consequently the strength of mental orientation to motion) is also not the same everywhere in a visual display. In the sausage ad, we learned lessons from responses to the hand cracking an egg, and the fork thrusting in from the side to jab at cooking sausage patties. The onset of motion in both cases began at one *side* of the screen, and this makes it special. Motion in peripheral vision (the area of vision that surrounds the point of visual focus) is more arousing than motion at exactly the point of visual focus. The evolutionary significance of this is easy to see. Motion that we aren't directly looking at (motion to our sides) is potentially more harmful than motion that we stare at.

In computing, unnecessary peripheral motion might include clocks and displays with changing numbers, progress bars or pie charts that constantly update, or even eyes in the tool bar that follow the cursor. When these motions occur, eye gaze is diverted, the interruption is evaluated, and some portion of the central message is likely ignored. Each of these features requires, as a property of the stimulus rather than a choice of the viewer, constant visual orientation.

How Much Motion Is Enough?

How much motion does it take to cause an orientation? So far, the implication has been that motion needs to be explicit and big. Small movements, however, can also be important. Think about a flag slowly waving in a breeze, a body heaving slightly while breathing, clouds forming, and tree branches waving. The perceived reality of a natural setting may depend on these movements, and since they are not psychologically competitive with thinking, they may heighten naturalness without being a diversion.

Although these small movements are inherent in film or video of a natural scene, they could easily enhance artificial scenes as well. On a computer, for example, light shadows could advance over time, room perspective could change as people navigate an interface, and objects that continually move in real life, like flags and trees, could do the same on the screen. Characters on the screen could idle with a breathing motion or occasional head movements rather than wait frozen in the corner of the screen. Motion doesn't have to be dramatic to indicate life.

21

Scene Changes

One of the most common features of media may be the most psychologically odd. It is the ability, possible *only* in mediated communication, to instantly cut between radically different visual experiences. Where in the real world could you see twilight in the Kalahari Desert at one moment, and in a few milliseconds be whisked to a sunny beach in Hawaii? How do people respond to these transitions? Are visual cuts natural acts or bizarre intrusions?

The "cut," a discontinuity between segments of visual material, is a fundamental aesthetic and cognitive unit in media. Cuts are basic to art and perception. While the term "cut" has historically been reserved for motion pictures, the technique is also no stranger to computing and multimedia: Windows pop open, material disappears, and of course, computers play video.

Aesthetically, cuts bring together segments from different visual compositions. They have artistic value, and film editors specialize in their placement and meaning. In computing, less creative attention is paid to cuts on the screen, but that is changing. Production values will eventually drive software as much as they now guide the products of Hollywood.

Cognitively, cuts can provide structural cues that direct attention, and they can serve as markers for the visual units in memory. The most likely visual memories we retain are the moments associated with the end of one unit of behavior and the beginning of another. In media, those moments are often punctuated with a cut. Based on psychology and aesthetics, the possible effects of cuts are broad: They may determine the media experiences we will like and what we will remember about them.

We have conducted five studies about cuts that try to determine how they are processed. Our goal in all of the research has been to look for similarities between visual cuts on the screen and similar experiences in real life.

Study 1: Physical Responses to Scene Changes

Our first question concerned the most primitive response to cuts that we could imagine. Do cuts, like the beginning of motion, trigger visual orientations?

Cuts not only change the content and meaning of pictures; they change the physical properties of information, everything from lines and edges to color and luminance. It is hard to imagine the potential for a more complete change in sensory experience. A replication in real life would have to be as rare as quickly closing your eyes and wheeling around to look in a different direction. When anything like this happens, people experience a visual orientation, a jump in attention, and an acute psychological focus on what is new.

We thought that cuts in media might also cause visual orientations. Our first prediction was that visual cuts would have a physiological effect every bit as apparent as orienting responses to novelty in the real world. The prediction was this:

Rule 1: Visual cuts in media will cause a visual orienting response in viewers.

The physical changes we used to identify visual orientations were the same as for the motion study—changes in brain-wave response.

During a thirty-minute video program, we looked at 720 points where cuts occurred. We examined the EEG record at the moment of the cut and for several seconds afterward. The changes in EEG at these points were obvious; cuts demanded attention. The most pronounced effects didn't occur immediately, however. The greatest effects were one second after the cut; they dissipated quickly thereafter.

These places in the EEG record were surely the marks of orienting responses, and because of this, we concluded that cuts in visual media, like visual novelty in the real world, cause visual orientations. When the visual field (mediated or not) changes, our bodies respond.

Study 2: All Cuts Are Not Equal

One film editor, after hearing this result, responded coolly, "I was trying to do that." The same film editor, however, also expressed a worry: Extraneous cuts might seriously detract from a message. If cuts are an intrusion at the level of a *physical* response, it would be an error to have one more cut than is necessary or to place a cut in such a way that it competed with other goals of a message.

This comment suggests that all cuts are not equal. Some might be good and useful; others, distracting. What might constitute a bad cut?

Editors have several informal rules about how cuts should be used, and many of the rules map pretty well onto findings about how people respond to novelty. One important category of editing rules has to do with the relationship between the *content* in the segments that are joined by a cut. The general rule is this: Make sure that the segments being joined are meaningfully related.

If this rule is broken, you might have one scene with a person walking from left to right, followed by one where the person is walking right to left. If you really got it wrong, the second appearance might be a totally different person, and one not suggested at all by the scene itself or the unfolding story. In either case, you'd be guilty of a "jump cut," an unnatural progression of action, and your work could be fodder for a film-school demonstration of what *not* to do on a shoot or in editing.

To test the psychological validity of this editing rule, we looked at the effects of cuts that joined related versus unrelated segments. By related, we mean that the segments are part of the same story, even if they are visually unique. That is, they are semantically related. Unrelated segments violate expectations; they join two distinct stories. Unrelated cuts should therefore be the ones that attract attention.

The specific prediction was this:

Rule 2: Cuts between segments that are semantically related will be less intrusive than cuts between segments that are semantically unrelated.

We created six segments of related and unrelated scenes for an experiment. The versions where the cuts were between related material followed this formula: The first segment was the first scene in a story, each additional segment was the next logical scene in the story, and all of the action in all of the segments occurred in the same physical place.

The unrelated versions were a mess. The cuts joined segments from six program genres: animation, news, commercials, action, drama, and comedy. Each segment was a different scene, and no story was apparent. It was like channel surfing on a cable system.

Responses to cuts happen quickly, as the EEG data showed, so we returned to secondary-task reaction time because this technique could measure quick responses. This task requires participants to listen for an audio tone while they watch television, and to press a reaction-time button as quickly as possible. If participants are paying a lot of attention to the primary task—watching television—then their responses will take longer.

For each type of cut, related and unrelated, we placed the tones in one of three locations: at the exact same time as the cut, one second after the cut, or two seconds after the cut. We could now compare how much attention it took to process the cuts at three points in time.

We found that unrelated cuts *are* harder to process. But the differences between the unrelated and related versions were not manifest at all of the three time points. For the tones that were placed exactly where the cut happened, there were no differences in reaction times. This was expected because the cut was just starting, so it couldn't intrude.

At the one-second mark, however, the differences were large, at least for reaction-time experiments—almost twenty milliseconds. The joining of unrelated segments boosted demand on mental effort. In the version with related segments, however, we found *no* extra mental demand. At the two-second mark, the responses were again equivalent, so the demands of a cut, as in the first experiment, dissipate quickly.

This analysis of related and unrelated cuts came from responses that occurred at several places in the video presentation. There were no differences between cuts at the beginning or between cuts at the end of the viewing session. Since each of the segments lasted over a minute, however, we had a chance to see how cuts worked within each of the segments. Does it get easier or harder to mentally process cuts as the sequence progresses?

The answer is that ease of processing depends on the relationship between the segments that are joined. When the segments joined by cuts were related, it required less attention to process each successive cut. By the third cut in a sequence of seven, considerably less attention was needed to process it, and the trend continued for the entire sequence.

When the cuts joined *un*related segments, however, no such decline in effort occurred over time. Each segment in the series was sufficiently different that the same amount of attention was required at all points in the presentation. Our conclusion was that all cuts are not the same. Cuts are not important merely because they join two different pictures. It matters whether the pictures form a plausible sequence—a story.

Study 3: Stringing Cuts Together

We wanted to pursue the question of cuts in a sequence and see what would happen when several were strung closely together within the same story. What happens when cuts occur every couple of seconds? We thought of this as the MTV question, because the namesake cable channel is well known for video with an enormous number of cuts per unit of time.

People might process visuals that have lots of cuts in either of two ways. If we generalize from the results for *single* cuts, their greater frequency could cause constant orienting. Another possibility, however, is that when several are rushed together, cuts work differently than in any single instance. The message may become too hard to process, and people may tune out. The cause is information overload, and the consequence is that attention declines.

Our next prediction allows for both possibilities:

Rule 3: The number of cuts and the level of attention are related.

We arranged a competition between messages with different numbers of cuts. We began with more than 400 television commercials. We counted the number of cuts in each, and then selected the eight messages that were the most visually complex (most cuts), and the eight that were the least visually complex (no cuts). For example, one ad showed thirty seconds of rapid-fire pictures, about one every second, of different products. Conversely, another ad showed a couple walking slowly down a beach: no cuts and very little motion at all.

The messages that had many cuts were given *less* attention than those that had none. The important conclusion is that media can easily exceed processing capabilities. When this happens, people tune out.

Another interesting result came from comparing the complex and simple ads with the picture turned off. This resulted in an odd test of the effect of *visual* complexity on people who could only *hear* the messages.

To our surprise, multiple cuts *still* had the same effect when the picture was turned off. The simple messages were given *more* attention than the complex ones even when the picture *couldn't* be seen. But why? The likely answer is a useful comment about how complex media really are.

In any piece of media, pictures *and* sounds cannot be easily separated. In a television message, as in real life, not many things can *only* be seen, and few can *only* be heard. Most likely, what is seen and what is heard are different indications of the *same* thing. If media don't provide the visuals, people will imagine them on their own.

We think that the participants who couldn't see the ads imagined visuals that went with the audio. And while they were doing this, the breaks in the audio, breaks that were actually caused by the *visual* edits, told them where to make their *mental* cuts. We called this result the "absent-channel effect": Visual complexity can produce effects even when no visuals are shown! This may not be news to folks who produce radio drama, but it is a reminder, especially relevant to multimedia, that what *isn't* shown, but is otherwise suggested, can be an important part of a media message.

Study 4: Cuts and Evaluation of Content

We have also tried to broaden the list of psychological effects that cuts might cause by studying political advertising. It's easy to find political ads that have either many or no cuts, and the candidates advertised are good targets for viewer evaluations. Our question was this: Do viewers think differently about politicians when a bit of dynamism is added to the message?

We selected eight ads from congressional campaigns that were visually static (no cuts, no camera movement, and all pictures taken in the same location), and eight that were visually dynamic (candidates presented in a number of different settings with segments joined by multiple cuts).

We expected that the increase in visual dynamism would produce more positive evaluations. The cuts would create movement, interest, and through generalization to the people portrayed, more favorable judgments of the candidates. Our prediction:

Rule 4: Visually dynamic messages will create more favorable evaluations of the people in them than visually static messages.

In the experiment, we gave participants a chance to evaluate the personal qualities of each politician shown in the ads. The result was that candidates were rated better when they appeared in ads with lots of cuts than when they appeared in ads with none. More cuts equaled more honesty, trust, intelligence, open-mindedness, and sincerity.

This may be depressing news to those who wish politicians could be evaluated exclusively on issues. In fact, the news is even worse. Cuts worked especially well when they were placed in messages that emphasized *images* (human qualities of the candidates) rather than *issues* (policies advocated by the candidates).

The most influential combination was image information combined with dynamic visual style. If candidates talked about themselves and did so in a lot of different locations and from a lot of different camera angles, then viewers thought they were darn good politicians. If candidates talked about the issues, and did so standing still, viewers perceived them as weak.

Study 5: Cutting Back and Forth

A final study looked at cuts as interruptions. Cuts are the points where we go back and forth between different types of media content. For traditional media, especially television, a common interruption is a commercial. If you're the person without the remote, you'd probably also add channel surfing to the list.

With computing, back-and-forth is even more common. We find everything from e-mail interrupting word processing, to the use of a help file to figure out how to use the word processor. On newer machines, the very concept of "multitasking" makes the notion of interruption intentional, commonplace, and desirable.

We had two questions about cuts that signal an interruption. First, when a cut introduces an interruption, what characteristics of the *prior* media experience will make the interruption more or less intrusive? Second, once the interruption is finished, and there is a cut that refers *back* to the original material, what makes that *re*orientation difficult or easy?

Most of the available help from psychology on these questions comes from research about reading. That research shows that the integration of related information is far easier than the integration of unrelated information. The duration of the interruption is also important, with longer interruptions resulting in more difficulty for the reader.

The explanation for these conclusions relies on an idea about how thinking progresses. Thinking spreads along established pathways that exist between *related* thoughts. If you hear the word "table," you are far more likely to think of "chair" than "boat." Once a word is heard or read, activation spreads to similar words along mental pathways established through experience.

If information in a message is presented in an order that mimics the established links between information in memory, then processing is relatively effortless. However, the moment that something *un*expected is introduced, something that has no link to currently activated thoughts, then the interruption makes thinking more difficult. A new network of information is activated, and the one that was active starts to decay. Essentially, one way of thinking has to be put away to make room for something new.

This also explains why the amount of time that passes during the interruption is important. When the initial segment is relatively long, it should be easier to return after an interruption because the mental network associated with it was used for a longer time and it will take more time to decay. When the original segment was of shorter duration, activation would be less complete and more sensitive to decay. Based on the same logic, if the interruption *itself* is long, then there should also be more chance for decay, and a return to the original segment would be more difficult.

Two predictions follow:

Rule 5: After long periods of exposure to a media segment, interruptions will require more attention than when exposure to the original material is shorter.

Rule 6: Long interruptions, regardless of the length of exposure to the original media segment, will require more attention to the original material after the interruption.

We tested these predictions by presenting participants in an experiment with three segments of television. The first and third segments were part of the same story. The middle segment, the interruption, was from a different program. We varied the amount of time that the initial segment was shown (ten seconds or thirty seconds) and the length of the interruption (ten seconds or thirty seconds).

The results: First, if you spent a longer time on the original segment, then the interruption required more attention; that is, it was *more* of an interruption. Second, it was harder to reorient to the original segment when the interruptions themselves lasted thirty rather than ten seconds. When thoughts were allowed to decay over time, reconnecting was more difficult.

Perhaps these results could be predicted by anyone who has tried to write in an office where people and other problems cause frequent interruptions. What might not be obvious, however, is that cutting to irrelevancies depends on such small differences in time. When we think, we activate memories. The ways that we use those memories in turn activate other thoughts. The entire system is sensitive and delicate. Seconds matter.

Thinking about Cuts

One of the most natural things to do with media, the joining of two different pieces of visual material with a cut, is a significant visual manipulation. Cuts mimic the most dramatic attention-getting devices in the real world, cues that have shaped human response throughout evolution. Cuts compress these responses into a single simple and quick visual trick.

It's important to note that people don't have to *learn* to assign significance to cuts. Even though cuts exist only in the domain of media, they are close enough to salient features of the real world to be critically important psychologically. Consequently, they are processed without special discount or consideration. Cuts are visual orientations to novelty, no less significant than any other real-life cue that elicits the same response. Cuts impose motion, they transport us across space and time, they combat boredom, and the novelty is quick and certain.

Cuts are likely one of the greatest attractions of visual media. Cuts allow a visual presentation to simulate real-world experiences that would otherwise take *considerably* longer to unfold and therefore would take considerably longer to benefit from. Cuts allow viewers to fly between different perspectives, gain a bird's-eye view, and easily monitor several places at once.

Cuts and Other Forms of Movement in Films

The history of making media can easily be described in periods, each of which ups the visual ante with techniques that prey on instincts. Cuts have certainly increased in films to a peak in the last decade. Quick cuts have increased at the expense of *slower* transition techniques. Fades were popular in the thirties and forties, but were replaced in the fifties with faster dissolves (fades gradually decrease the intensity of frames in one scene before starting another scene; dissolves overlap scenes as one fades in and the other fades out). Even dissolves were too slow, however. Now straight cuts predominate.

Trends in cinematography are usually discussed in terms of aesthetics. Fades, for example, are seen as a mere fad, eventually replaced with a new one. We think this analysis is wrong, however. The increased use of cuts may be a sign of a larger movement toward "souped-up" media. What constitutes "souped-up" may say more about how *humans* are built than about fashion. People respond well to techniques like cuts because they take advantage (for better or worse) of how people navigate the real world. Some artists already understand the media equation quite well.

Using Cuts Effectively

Occasionally it is desirable to minimize intrusions from message form. If the goal of a message is *not* to sneak up on a viewer with a visual surprise (and titillate in the process), there are ways to minimize disruption. First, ensure that cuts join related and expected material. For example, first have a long shot that shows an entire scene. This simulates what people naturally do when they first arrive in a place: They look around. Then cut to the central object or person of interest. The resulting disruption is minimal because the cut joins expected segments, yet the sequence compresses a lot of different looks into a package that can be quickly processed.

Cuts can also be used effectively for chunking visual segments into meaningful pieces. Here again, surprise is not the goal, but rather memorability. People look to break information into a few meaningful pieces and then remember only a representative bit of each piece.

Cuts can help memory by defining the important breaks, the equivalent of placing periods and commas in text. The placement of a cut is a strong signal that one unit is finished and another will begin. The information that surrounds the cut, just like information that surrounds any unit of actual behavior, will be the most memorable. If learning and memory are goals, the most useful pieces of a presentation should end with a visual break.

Cuts and Computers

Many of these implications describe common practice in the film arts, but more often they describe common problems in newer media. In film and television, edits usually occur on purpose. But new media are different. The operative style with respect to cuts in multimedia is anarchy.

Cuts on a computer do not conjure images of someone taping together pieces of celluloid, but they could benefit from the same considerations. For example, long establishing shots preceding close-ups should work on the desktop as well as in film. The relationship between cuts in an application can be emphasized with similar visuals. This is true for the switch from a word processor to a help screen as well as the switch between two people talking in the same room. Major steps during the completion of a task can be usefully marked with cuts. This is true for the steps in producing, filing, and printing a document as well as for markers in an educational film. And several quick cuts in a row can encourage viewers to tune out. This is true for a bunch of windows that close one right after the next as well as for quick segments in a music video.

Technically, cuts on the computer are produced in totally different ways. Windows pop open at the press of buttons, and sometimes on their own; icons turn into new screens; applications switch places; and screens disappear, again sometimes on their own. But even though these "cuts" appear to be distant cousins to those in motion pictures, they are psychologically more like brother or sister.

22

Subliminal Images

It's important that the first few minutes of a research presentation go well. In our own presentations, we usually have an introduction that is well planned and well rehearsed. During this introduction, we make eye contact with people in the audience, but we're mostly occupied with what to say next. If asked to report about how the audience was responding, we'd have a difficult time reporting accurately about whether there were smiles or frowns.

Or would we? Psychologists have accumulated a lot of evidence to suggest that we had indeed processed the faces in the audience, but unconsciously. While we couldn't report *in words* what the faces looked like, if forced to guess how the talk was going, we would be able to describe, with better-than-chance accuracy, whether the presentation was a boom or a bust.

Psychologists call this research area "semantic activation without subjective awareness." This means that people can think about things without knowing why. There are several kinds of experiments in this area, but the same basic idea cuts across them all: Things that we're not aware of can influence how we think and what we think about.

One type of experiment in this area uses the *dichotic listening* task. Dichotic listening occurs when a person hears two conversations at once. This is sometimes referred to as the "cocktail party" task, because it simulates what many people do when several conversations are going on at once—they converse with a partner but eavesdrop on everyone else.

Psychologists have studied dichotic listening by asking people to listen to conversations through stereophonic headphones. The voice of the main speaker is presented in only one ear. People are then asked to speak aloud (or "shadow") the speech coming to that ear. While people shadow the main speaker, a separate voice is routed to the other ear. Shadowing requires a great deal of focus, and because of this, people *report* not being able to understand anything that the second speaker says.

Subjective experience, however, is often wrong. Even though people don't *think* that they hear anything that the second speaker says, when they are asked to make guesses, they are correct at a rate better than chance. Something gets through, though not consciously.

Another experimental task used to study unconscious processing looks at the effects of quickly flashed words that appear next to, and usually slightly before, other words. People are asked to concentrate on the center of a display. They are told that a word will appear there, and when it does, they will have to identify it as quickly as possible. Just before the display is shown, a different word is flashed in another area of the display. Since viewers are asked to focus on the center, the other word is seen only in parafoveal vision.

Visual acuity is not good in parafoveal vision, and quickly flashed information there usually cannot be identified. Nonetheless, evidence shows that information in parafoveal vision has an effect. If the word in peripheral vision is "boat," for example, people can more quickly identify the word "water" than unrelated words.

Unconscious Processing of Media

Our question was whether unconscious processing works any differently when it unfolds in media. The possibility that media influence the unconscious has certainly been a popular one, and the addition of computing to the media mix has only heightened interest in what has come to be known as subliminal persuasion. Given the computer's ability to manipulate content quickly, might it be even better at subliminal seduction?

The literature about subliminal persuasion already includes some of the most popular books about media this century. The possibility that dastardly media folks are hiding pictures in magazine ads or quickly flashing commercial messages in movies is captivating. When reading about this topic, you'll find claims that pictures of genitalia are hidden among ice cubes in magazine liquor ads, and you'll read about pictures of popcorn boxes inserted into feature films to bolster sales at intermission. The books discuss fantastic theories but they lack good evidence to bolster the claims. We tried to remedy this problem with an experiment that tested whether or not people would use media information without being consciously aware that it had influenced their judgments.

From the psychology literature that showed how this process works in the real world, we made the following prediction about how it might work with television:

Rule 1: Images in television messages that people cannot consciously identify will influence how people make judgments about media.

Creating Subliminal Content

For this experiment, we used one other technique from the psychology literature. It is called "backward pattern masking." Psychologists quickly flash images and then measure the influence of the images on how people evaluate material presented after the images appear. In these experiments, researchers first determine how long a picture must be shown for people to be able to identify it. Once this threshold is known, they then test what happens when the picture is presented for *less* time than it takes to consciously identify.

In these experiments, an image is first presented too fast to be consciously seen. Then, a different picture is presented, and participants are asked to identify the second picture as quickly as possible. The result? Even pictures that people cannot see can affect how quickly they identify the second picture.

243

We wanted to see whether evidence of unconscious processing could be found using the pattern masking technique with standard television equipment and typical television content. Does evidence from psychology, based on rules about how perception works, generalize to media?

Inserting Subliminal Messages in Traditional Media

For the experiment, we chose television segments that showed people talking in news shows, advertisements, and dramatic programs. After participants watched each one, we asked them to evaluate the emotional state of the person on the screen: Was the person happy or sad?

Before viewers made the evaluations, we quickly flashed one of two pictures on the screen. One was a happy face, the other a sad one. The quickly flashed pictures were our best approximation of backward pattern masking—but on television.

The sequence for each segment began with an orange circle shown in the middle of the screen accompanied by a voice that said, "Please look at the orange dot now." We did this because we wanted to ensure that attention was directed at the screen and not elsewhere in the room.

The next image was the subliminal part. We quickly flashed either the happy or the sad face. The idea was that the emotion of the face would influence the evaluation of the video segment that followed. After the picture of the smiling or frowning face was shown, we showed a patterned mask, which is a black-and-white picture of geometric shapes. Without the mask, the image of the face would linger on the retina, and viewers would have more time to identify and consider the initial face.

The critical feature of the flashed pictures was their duration. Each of the two faces was shown for either one video frame or two video frames, and there is something very important about the difference. If you show a smiling face for one video frame (33 milliseconds), and then follow it immediately with one frame of a patterned mask, it is *impossible* for people to tell what was in the picture. Everyone is aware that *something* happened (it looks like a flashbulb went off), but no one can tell that they saw a picture of a face.

If the picture of the face is on the screen for two video frames, however, no one has a problem identifying the contents of the picture. This difference represents the two levels of awareness used in the psychology experiments. One frame equals no subjective awareness; two frames equals definite subjective awareness.

After the face and patterned mask, we showed a longer television segment. Viewers held a joystick that they used to evaluate the person in each segment. Pushing the stick to the right meant that they thought the person in the segment was happy; pushing to the left meant the person in the segment was sad.

Effectiveness of Subliminal Messages

One result was that when viewers could clearly identify the happy face, they thought that the people in the segments that followed were themselves happier. And the opposite was true for the sad face. In other words, *priming* works. What you see at one moment activates a way of thinking that influences subsequent evaluations. People just can't switch gears that quickly.

Strikingly, the same priming effect occurred when viewers had no conscious knowledge about the picture that was flashed at them. When the flash was a happy face, the people that followed seemed more happy. When the flash was a sad face, the people that followed seemed more sad. Quickly flashed pictures that conveyed emotion became active in viewers' minds, even though the viewers had no subjective awareness of their presence.

What Subliminal Effects Are—and Aren't

What we don't see or notice can have an effect in media just as in real life. The media delivering the information need not be complicated: The effect works with a standard VCR and television set. This result is one more indication that media are not special with regard to how information is processed psychologically.

It is important to note, however, that these results are not like most of the popular notions about subliminal persuasion. Subliminal effects in the popular literature are mostly about ambiguous forms or at least ones that are hard to see; for example, body parts or words hidden in pictures. This study, and the other psychological research as well, used pictures and words that were explicit and obvious. We doubt that the experiment would have worked if the pictures were fuzzy or otherwise disguised.

The popular notions of subliminal persuasion also assume a process of unconscious influence that is considerably more complex. The popular argument is that subliminal experience is generalized to something that is apparently *un*related to the initial information. For example, the letters S E and X, rendered imprecisely in ice cubes, are said to generalize to a product in the same picture. The argument is that the letters will bring to mind the word "sex," which will then make people think about sexual images, which will then make people feel good and aroused, which will then influence what they think of a particular brand of vodka poured over the cubes. This is a complex series of generalizations, much more complex than is demonstrated in our study, and a sequence that we think is unlikely.

Subliminal Content in New Media

The specific design implications of this discussion are pretty simple, and different for television as compared to newer media. For broadcast television, subliminal persuasion, at least in the form of quickly flashed pictures and words, is banned by the Federal Communication Commission. This has been true since the 1970s, when controversy erupted over a TV ad for a memory game called Husker Du that displayed the words, "Get it," on the screen for a fraction of a second.

Computers and software, however, are *un*regulated. There are no official prohibitions of these techniques anywhere in the world of multimedia. Consequently, the issue of subliminal persuasion has gained new life. Designers and the public now discuss subliminal effects in *multi*media—everything from advertisements embedded in screen savers to attempts to bolster employee morale with hidden messages flashed on networked computers. One of the more interesting aspects of these discussions is that it might be easier to accomplish subliminal intrusions with a computer than with a television, because software can respond to the particular input of individual users and timing is more precise. Of course, ethical and legal issues abound.

Final Words

Conclusions about the Media Equation

Our strategy for learning about media was to go to the social science section of the library, find theories and experiments about human-*human* interaction—and then borrow. We did the same for information about how people respond to the natural environment, borrowing freely. Take out a pen, cross out "human" or "environment," and substitute *media*. When we did this, all of the predictions and experiments led to the media equation: People's responses to media are fundamentally social and natural.

Summarizing the Media Equation

Media experiences equal human experiences, a conclusion that we elaborated across a variety of concepts—from politeness to personality to emotion—and across several of the social sciences—from neuroscience to social psychology and sociology. There are few discounts for media, few special ways of thinking or feeling that are unique to media, and there is no switch in the brain that is activated when media are present.

People's responses show that media are more than just tools. Media are treated politely, they can invade our body space, they can have personalities that match our own, they can be a teammate, and they can elicit gender stereotypes. Media can evoke emotional responses, demand attention, threaten us, influence memories, and change ideas of what is natural. Media are full participants in our social and natural world.

The Media Equation

Everyone Responds Socially and Naturally to Media

A focus on individual differences is tempting, but all people, those from different cultures, ages, educational levels, and levels of technology experience, respond to media similarly. Our studies included children, adolescents, college sophomores, homemakers, business executives, and computer scientists. All of them exhibited the media equation when using communication technologies.

There may be individual differences in some social and natural experiences, but the need and desire to understand the world as other people and places is basic. New terms in discussions about individualizing media, from microcasting to customizable content, should not encourage the wrong conclusion that each of us is substantially different from everyone else. The media equation applies to everyone.

Media Are More Similar Than Different

Just as people are more similar to one another than different, so too are communication technologies. Psychologically, the PC is not terribly different from the TV. New technologies share important features with old ones, and fancy technologies often aren't. We found support for the media equation using text on a computer, a computer-controlled home theater, small and large televisions, voices in a multimedia tutorial, and motion in political advertising.

The similarity between simple and sophisticated media is particularly impressive. Claims about amplified responses to new media are often exaggerated. Our research is a reminder that we can cry when we read, and we can be bored in a virtual world. Social and natural responses come from people, not from media themselves. Ultimately, it's the pictures in our heads that matter, not the ones on the screen.

The Media Equation Is Automatic

Social and natural responses do not require strategic thinking; rather, they are unconscious. The responses are not at the discretion of those who give them; rather, they are applied always and quickly. And they signal no human deficiency; rather, they are useful and reasonable.

People automatically assume reality because throughout evolution there was no reason to do otherwise.

The automatic responses defined by the media equation can be initiated with minimal cues. We saw the equation work with personality expressed in a couple of words or with a simple line drawing. The equation worked with physical responses to motion in a picture and emotional responses to the size of a display. It worked with a slight variation in the pitch of voices and with a slight imperfection in the synchronization of voices and accompanying visuals. The breadth of these responses, if a lot of thinking were required, would be impossible.

Many Different Responses Characterize the Media Equation

The media equation does not just apply to the rare occasions when people yell at a television or plead with a computer. Even the most passive uses of media lead people to allocate attention, assign personality, manage arousal, assess competence, organize information in memory, determine likes and dislikes, and experience physical changes in the body and brain. For example, it would be tempting to think that responses to computers are only concerned with efficiency, and responses to television and film are only concerned with entertainment. Responses to all media, however, are broad and deep, and all are part of the media equation.

What Seems True Is More Important Than What Is True

Analysts of media often are preoccupied with what is true and false about the information experienced. Are computers *really* intelligent? Can a television *really* have a social role? These questions, however, miss an important fact: What *seems* to be true is often more influential that what really is true.

Our studies show that *perceptions* are far more influential than reality defined more objectively. When perceptions are considered, it doesn't matter whether a computer can really have a personality or not. People perceive that it can, and they'll respond socially on the basis of perception alone. The same is true for emotional responses to pictures or feeling better when teamed with a computer. These responses are unfairly labeled as irrational. They are merely human, and part of any communication experience.

People Respond to What Is Present

Media are celebrated for their ability to represent things that are not actually present, a recognition that media provide symbols for the real world. People are certainly capable of understanding media this way, but it is a difficult understanding to sustain. More often, people respond to what is immediately present, often with little consideration for who sent a message and little consideration for a source's motives or intentions about what the message should mean.

We found several cases where prominent features were more important than hidden ones. People did not think about programmers when they interacted with computers, they didn't concentrate on persuasive intent when they processed television commercials, and they didn't judge the aesthetics of pictures that were arousing. People responded to what was immediately present, not to more complicated stories about who sent the information and the senders' intentions.

People Like Simplicity

The research showed that people are more *simple* than we often imagine. Humans are built to reduce complexity, not only to create it. The need for simplicity suggests what might make people comfortable when interacting with media. Rather than empowering through endless choices, media can empower through ease of use, and that often means freedom *from* choice. Money aside, almost everyone would rather go to a restaurant, where the ingredients are prepared for us, than to the grocery store, where both choice and complexity abound.

"Simple" also means predictable—everything from personalities to specialties to information joined by cuts in a film. When people know what to expect, they can process media with a greater sense of accomplishment and enjoyment. The desire for simplicity can be pernicious, however—people stereotyped media by gender with little encouragement.

Social and Natural Is Easy

A prediction without controversy is that media need to be easy to use or they will fail. Often, people assume that ease of use can come only with instruction. To work with most media, arbitrary rules must be learned and relearned, and most sophisticated media require constant reference to a manual. Our research suggests an alternative: People should be able to use what comes naturally—rules for social relationships and rules for navigating the physical world.

Designers of media can profit from reliance on what people do best. Machines will be more approachable, content more understandable, and interfaces more sensible if they follow the rules of the social and natural world. People already know how to be polite, they know about personalities and emotion, and they are aware of how objects work in natural environments. People will use these responses whether media encourage them or not. A lack of concern for social and natural rules by designers does not mean that the rules will be irrelevant; instead, users will simply be frustrated and unhappy.

Empirical Methods Show What Otherwise Would Not Be Known

All of the conclusions about the media equation were made possible by methods in the social sciences. The methods are part of the same library sources that contain the theories. These methods do not rely on people's ability to be introspective, and they provide objective data. If we had asked people to comment on whether they were polite to computers, whether line drawings have personality, or whether they pay more attention to low-fidelity audio, we would have had nothing to report. And without statistics, we could not have tested our ideas. Social science methods are a critical complement to techniques such as focus groups that rely on introspection and impressions, because social science methods allow for the discovery of objective human responses to media that could not otherwise be known.

What Should We Now Think about Media?

There are a lot of ideas about media. How important is the media equation?

We think this question is critical. Research is not merely a dispassionate comment about how things work. The conclusions also affect what people do: What they study and how, what they think are important problems, how they think the problems should be solved, and even whether the problems should be considered at all. So the stakes are high.

Our most concise answer to the question about importance is this: It is difficult to think of a product design meeting, an academic seminar, or debates about policy, parenting, or ethics that would not be changed, at least a bit, if the media equation were considered. Many of the discussions would need to be turned upside down.

The media equation suggests a new perspective on media. Media, if the interest is in *people*, are defined by concepts like the ones that organize this book, from politeness to personality to arousal to specialization to motion. Knowledge of how media work with people is knowledge of things social and natural.

References

Chapter References

Chapter 1: The Media Equation

page 3. For a demonstration that some children think that televised popcorn will fall out when a TV set is turned over, see: Flavell, J.H., Flavell, E.R., Green, F.L., & Korfmacher, J.E. (1990), Do young children think of television images as pictures or real objects? *Journal of Broadcasting and Electronic Media*, *34*(4), 399–419. Flavell, J.H., Green, F.L., & Flavell, E.R. (1986), Development of knowledge about the appearance-reality distinction, *Monographs of the Society for Research in Child Development*, *51*(1), 1–68.

page 3. For a discussion of differences between novice and expert users, see: Turkle, S. (1984), *The second self: Computers and the human spirit* (New York: Simon & Schuster).

page 4. We use the term "media" in its broadest sense, including communication technologies, content, and services. For detailed discussions of various conceptualizations of media, see: McQuail, D. (1994), *Mass communication theory: An introduction*, 3rd ed. (London: Sage). Nass, C. & Mason, L. (1990), On the study of technology and task: A variable-based approach, in: J. Fulk & C. Steinfeld (Eds.), *Organizations and communication technology* (pp. 46-67) (Newbury Park: Sage). Reeves, B. (1989), Theories about news and theories about cognition, *American Behavioral Scientist*, *33*(2), 191-198. Reeves, B. (1996), Hemispheres of scholarship: Psychological and other approaches to studying media audiences, in: J.Hay, L. Grossberg, & E. Wartella (Eds.), *The audience and its landscape* (Boulder, CO: Westview Press).

page 5. Evidence that people who ask questions relevant to themselves get more positive answers than people who ask questions about others can be found in: Finkel, S.E., Guterbock, T.M., & Borg, M.J. (1991), Race-of-interviewer effects in a pre-election poll: Virginia 1989, *Public Opinion Quarterly,* 55, 313–330. Kane, E.W. (1993), Interviewer gender and gender attitudes, *Public Opinion Quarterly,* 57, 1–28.

page 5. For demonstrations that people are polite to computers, see: Nass, C., Moon, Y., Morkes, J., Kim, E-Y., & Fogg, B.J. (in press), Computers are social actors: A review of current research, in: B. Friedman (Ed.), *Moral and ethical issues in human-computer interaction* (Stanford, CA: CSLI Press). Nass, C., Steuer, J.S., & Tauber, E. (1994), Computers are social actors, *Proceedings of the CHI Conference* (Boston, MA). This study is also described in Chapter 2 of the present book.

page 5. For discussions about the importance of movement in visual processing, see: Bolivar, V.J., & Barresi, J. (1995), Giving meaning to movement: A developmental study, *Ecological Psychology,* 7(2), 71–97. Brown, E.L., & Defenbacher, K. (1979), *Perception and the senses* (New York: Oxford University Press). Haber, R.N., & Hershenson, M. (1973), *The psychology of visual perception* (New York: Holt, Rinehart, & Winston). Kolers, P.A. (1972), *Aspects of motion perception* (Elmsford, NY: Pergamon Press).

page 6. For a demonstration of the effects of orienting to motion on a screen, see: Reeves, B., Thorson, E., Rothschild, M., McDonald, D., Hirsch, J., & Goldstein, B. (1985), Attention to television: Intrastimulus effects of movement and scene changes on alpha variation over time, *International Journal of Neuroscience,* 27, 241–255. This study is also described in Chapter 20 of the present book.

page 6. For a discussion of technology as tools, see Heidegger, M. (1977), *The question concerning technology, and other essays* (New York: Harper & Row).

page 7. For a discussion of the confusion of real life and "life on the screen," see: Turkle, S. (1995), *Life on the screen: Identity in the age of the Internet* (New York: Simon & Schuster). Rheingold, H. (1993), *The virtual community (Reading, MA: Addison-Wesley).*

page 8. Evidence that we tend to approach daily life with acceptance rather than doubt is summarized in: Gilbert, D.T. (1991), How mental systems believe, *American Psychologist,* 46(2), 107–119. Langer, E. (1989), *Mindfulness* (Reading, MA: Addison-Wesley).

page 8. For a discussion of how difficult it can be to learn tools with arbitrary convention, see: Norman, D. (1990), *The design of everyday things* (Garden City, NY: Doubleday).

page 11. For a discussion of media presentations as symbols, see: Worth, S., & Gross, L. (1974), Symbolic strategies, *Journal of Communication, 24,* 27–39.

page 12. For examples of how evolution is discussed in psychology, see: Barkow, J.H., Cosmides, L., & Tooby, J. (Eds.) (1992), *The adapted mind: Evolutionary psychology and the generation of culture* (New York: Oxford University Press). Buss, D.M. (1994), *The evolution of desire: Strategies of human mating* (New York: Basic Books). Konner, M. (1982), *The tangled wing: Biological constraints on the human spirit* (New York: Holt, Rinehart, & Winston). Messaris, P. (1994), *Visual "literacy": Image, mind, and reality* (Boulder, CO: Westview Press). Pinker, S. (1994), *The language instinct: How the mind creates language* (New York: HarperPerennial). Shepard, R.N. (1990), *Mind sights: Original visual illusions, ambiguities, and other anomalies, with a commentary on the play of mind in perception and art* (Ypsilanti, MI: W.H. Freeman Publishing).

page 12. Discussions of automatic behavior in daily life can be found in: Bargh, J.A. (1988), Automatic information processing: Implications for communication and affect, in: L. Donohew, H.E. Sypher, & E.T. Higgins (Eds.), *Communication, social cognition, and affect* (pp. 377–390) (Hillsdale, NJ: Lawrence Erlbaum). Bargh, J.A. (1992), The generality of the automatic attitude activation effect, *Journal of Personality and Social Psychology, 62*(6), 893–912. Langer, E. (1989), *Mindfulness* (Reading, MA: Addison-Wesley).

Chapter 2: Politeness

page 19. For a more formal presentation of the experiments discussed in this chapter, see: Nass, C., Moon, Y., Morkes, J., Kim, E-Y., & Fogg, B.J. (in press), Computers are social actors: A review of current research, in: B. Friedman (Ed.), *Moral and ethical issues in human-computer interaction* (Stanford, CA: CSLI Press). Nass, C., Steuer, J.S., & Tauber, E. (1994), Computers are social actors, *Proceeding of the CHI Conference* (Boston, MA).

page 19. The use of the quotation "How am I doing?" is discussed in Koch, E.I. (with Rauch, W.A.) (1984), *Mayor* (New York: Simon & Schuster).

page 19. For examples of politeness universals, see: Brown, P. (1987), *Politeness: Some universals in language use* (Cambridge: Cambridge University Press). Holmes, J. (1992), *Women, men, and politeness* (Harlow, Essex, England: Longman). Sifianou, M. (1992), *Politeness phenomena in England and Greece: A cross-cultural perspective* (Oxford: Clarendon Press).

page 19. The importance of mastering politeness, as well as other social norms, is discussed in: Goleman, D. (1995), *Emotional intelligence* (New York: Bantam Books).

page 20. A demonstration that people who ask questions relevant to themselves get more positive answers than people who ask questions about others can be found in: Finkel, S.E., Guterbock, T.M., & Borg, M.J. (1991), Race-of-interviewer effects in a pre-election poll: Virginia 1989, *Public Opinion Quarterly, 55,* 313–330. Kane, E.W. (1993), Interviewer gender and gender attitudes, *Public Opinion Quarterly, 57,* 1–28.

page 20. For the argument that homogeneous responses reflect less honesty, see: Kiesler, S., & Sproull, L. (1986), Response effects in the electronic survey, *Public Opinion Quarterly, 50,* 402–413.

page 21. For a demonstration that people are more honest to computers than to other people, see: Martin, C.L., & Nagao, D.H. (1989), Some effects of computerized interviewing on job applicant responses, *Journal of Applied Psychology, 74,* 72–80.

page 22. For a discussion of the power of limited cues of humanness, see: McCloud, S. (1993), *Understanding comics—The invisible art* (Northampton, MA: Kitchen Sink Press).

page 22. For a discussion of the link between contingency and perceived humanness, see: Nass, C., & Steuer, J.S. (1993), Voices, boxes, and sources of messages: Computers and social actors, *Human Communication Research, 19*(4), 504–527. Rafaeli, S. (1986), Para-social interaction and the human-computer relationship, Doctoral dissertation, Stanford University, Stanford, CA. Rafaeli, S. (1990), Interacting with media: para-social interaction and real interaction, in: B.D. Ruben & L.A. Lievrouw (Eds.), *Mediation, information, and communication: Information and behavior,* Vol. 3 (pp. 125–181) (New Brunswick, NJ: Transaction Press).

page 27. A discussion of "willing suspension of disbelief" in human-computer interaction can be found in: Laurel, B. (1993), *Computers as theater* (Reading, MA: Addison-Wesley).

page 27. The idea that people intentionally think about a computer programmer is discussed in: Dennett, D.C. (1987), *The intentional stance* (Cambridge, MA: MIT Press).

page 28. The prevalence of automatic behavior in daily life is discussed in: Bargh, J.A. (1992), The generality of the automatic attitude activation effect, *Journal of Personality and Social Psychology, 62*(6), 893–912. Langer, E. (1989), *Mindfulness* (Reading, MA: Addison-Wesley).

page 28. The interaction approach to politeness can be found in: Brown, P. (1987), *Politeness: Some universals in language use* (Cambridge: Cambridge University Press).

page 29. Grice's Maxims are outlined in: Grice, H.P. (1967), Logic and conversation, in: P. Cole & J. Morgan (Eds.), *Syntax and semantics 3: Speech acts* (pp. 41–58) (New York: Academic Press). For another approach to the application of Grice's Maxims to human-computer interaction, see: Brennan, S. E. (1990), Conversation as direct manipulation: An iconoclastic view, in: B. Laurel (Ed.), *The art of human-computer interface design* (pp. 393–404) (Reading, MA: Addison-Wesley).

page 33. Popular sources of politeness rules include: Carnegie, D. (1964), *How to win friends and influence people* (New York: Simon & Schuster). Martin, J. (1982), *Miss Manners' guide to excruciatingly correct behavior* (New York: Warner Books). Post, E. (1955), *Etiquette: The blue book of social usage* [9th ed.] (New York: Funk & Wagnalls).

page 33. The disappearing character occurred in the Apple Guides project. It is described in: Oren, T., Salomon, G., Kreitman, K., & Don, A. (1990), Guides: Characterizing the interface, in: B. Laurel (Ed.), *The art of human-computer interface design* (Reading, MA: Addison-Wesley).

page 34. For evidence that when people look at a face, they spend approximately half of their time looking at the eyes, see: Ekman, P. (Ed.) (1973), *Darwin and facial expression: A century of research in review* (New York: Academic Press). Ekman, P., Friesen, W.V., & Ellsworth, P. (1972), *Emotion in the human face: Guide-lines for research and an integration of findings* (New York: Pergamon Press).

page 36. A discussion of caveats for international travelers can be found in: Donovan, J. (1971), *The businessman's international travel guide* (New York: Stein & Day).

Chapter 3: Interpersonal Distance

page 37. The research results discussed in this chapter were originally presented in: Reeves, B., Lombard, M., & Melwani, G. (1992), Faces on the screen: Pictures or natural experience, Paper presented to the International Communication Association, Miami.

page 37. Space determines the duration of interactions: Konecni, V.J., Libuser, L., Morton, H., & Ebbesen, E.B. (1975), Effects of a violation of personal space on escape and helping responses, *Journal of Experimental Psychology, 11,* 288–299.

page 37. Space determines the emotional tenor of interactions: Mehrabian, A. (1968), Inference of attitude from the posture orientation and distance of a communicator, *Journal of Consulting and Clinical Psychology, 32,* 296–308.

page 37. Studies that examine negative influences of unwanted advances include the following: Baron, R.A., & Byrne, D. (1984), *Social psychology: Understanding human interaction,* 4th ed. (Boston: Allyn & Bacon). Evans, G.W., & Howard, R.B. (1972), A methodological investigation of personal space, in: W.J. Mitchell (Ed.), *Environmental design: Research and practice (EDRA 3)* (Los Angeles: University of California). Middlemist, R.D., Knowles, E.S., & Matter, C.F. (1976), Personal space invasions in the lavatory: Suggestive evidence for arousal, *Journal of Personality and Social Psychology, 33,* 541–546.

page 37. A study that examines positive responses to closeness is: Storms, M.D., & Thomas, G.C. (1977), Reactions to physical closeness, *Journal of Personality and Social Psychology, 35,* 412–418.

page 38. For a review of research about the relationship between attention, emotion, and physiology, see: Lang, P.J. (1995), The network model of emotion: Motivational connections, in: R.S. Wyer & T.K. Srull (Eds.), *Advances in social cognition,* Vol. 6. (Hillsdale, NJ: Lawrence Erlbaum Associates).

page 38. Faces, particularly eyes, reveal a person's intentions. Hence, people focus on faces when arousal is high: Ekman, P. (Ed.) (1973), *Darwin and facial expression: A century of research in review* (New York: Academic Press). Matsumoto, D. (1989), Face, culture, and judgments of anger and fear: Do the eyes have it? *Journal of Nonverbal Behavior, 13,* 171–188. Mertens, I., Siegmund, H., & Grusser, O.J. (1993), Gaze motor asymmetries in the perception of faces during a memory task, *Neurophysologia, 31,* 989–998. Reeve, J. (1993), The face of interest, *Motivation and Emotion, 17,* 353–375.

page 38. Eyes, mouth, and eyebrows are the most important features in an interpersonal encounter: Ekman, P., Friesen, W.V., & Ellsworth, P. (1972), *Emotion in the human face: Guide-lines for research and an integration of findings* (New York: Pergamon Press).

page 42. For a discussion of the secondary task reaction time method, see: Basil, M.D. (1994), Secondary reaction-time measures, in: A. Lang (Ed.), *Measuring psychological responses to media* (pp. 85–98) (New York: Lawrence Erlbaum Associates).

page 42. A good summary of the notion of limited mental capacity can be found in: Anderson, J.R. (1995), *Cognitive psychology and its implications,* 4th ed. (pp. 75–105) (Ypsilanti, MI: W.H. Freeman Publishing).

page 43. For a discussion of the differences between recall and recognition memory, see: Bower, G.H., & Clapper, J.P. (1989), Experimental methods in cognitive science, in: M.I. Posner (Ed.), *Foundations of cognitive science* (Cambridge, MA: MIT Press).

page 49. For a detailed discussion of the mental translation of information from one symbol system into another, see: Salomon, G. (1979), *Interaction of media, cognition and learning: An exploration of how symbolic forms cultivate mental skills and affect knowledge acquisition* (San Francisco: Jossey-Bass).

page 49. Appearance affects social interactions: Ritts, V., Patterson, M.L., & Tubbs, M.E. (1992), Expectations, impressions, and judgments of physically attractive students: A review, *Review of Education Research, 62*(4), 413–426. Sternberg, R.J., Conway, B.E., Ketron, J.L., & Bernstein, M. (1981), People's conception of intelligence, *Journal of Personality and Social Psychology, 41*(1), 37–55.

page 51. For a discussion of the use of close-ups, see: Bordwell, D., & Thompson, K. (1990), *Film art: An introduction,* 3rd ed. (New York:

McGraw-Hill). Foss, B. (1992), *Filmmaking: Narrative and structural techniques* (Los Angeles: Silman-James Press).

Chapter 4: Flattery

page 53. The results presented here are also discussed in: Fogg, B.J., & Nass, C. (in press), Silicon sycophants: The effects of computers that flatter, *International Journal of Human-Computer Studies*.

page 53. The argument that everyone is a sucker for praise and flattery is presented in: Cialdini, R.B. (1993), *Influence: Science and practice*, 3rd ed. (New York: HarperCollins).

page 53. People like flatterers more than people who say nothing: Berscheid, E., & Walster, E.H. (1978), *Interpersonal attraction*, 2nd ed. (Reading, MA: Addison-Wesley). Byrne, D., Rasche, L., & Kelley, K. (1974), When "I like you" indicates disagreement: An experimental differentiation of information and affect, *Journal of Research in Personality, 8*, 207–217. Jones, E.E. (1964), *Ingratiation* (New York: Appleton-Century-Crofts). Jones, E.E., & Wortman, C. (1973), *Ingratiation: An attributional approach* (Morristown, NJ: General Learning Press). People also think that flatterers have positive qualities, such as intelligence: Pandey, J., & Kakkar, S. (1982), Supervisors' affect: Attraction and positive evaluation as a function of enhancement of others, *Psychological Reports, 50*, 479–546. Pandey, J., & Singh, P. (1987), Effects of Machiavellianism, other-enhancement, and power-position on affect, power feeling, and evaluation of the ingratiator, *Journal of Psychology, 121*(3), 287–300.

page 53. Discussions of the match between flattery and true praise include: Berscheid, E., & Walster, E.H. (1978), *Interpersonal attraction*, 2nd ed. (Reading, MA: Addison-Wesley). Byrne, D., Rasche, L., & Kelley, K. (1974), When "I like you" indicates disagreement: An experimental differentiation of information and affect, *Journal of Research in Personality, 8*, 207–217. Cialdini, R.B. (1993), *Influence: Science and practice*, 3rd ed. (New York: HarperCollins). Jones, E.E. (1964), *Ingratiation* (New York: Appleton-Century-Crofts).

page 53. When people hear positive things about themselves, they think the information is accurate: Cialdini, R.B. (1993), *Influence: Science and practice*, 3rd ed. (New York: HarperCollins). Jones, E.E. (1964), *Ingratiation* (New

York: Appleton-Century-Crofts). Jones, E.E. (1990), *Interpersonal perception* (Ypsilanti, MI: W.H. Freeman Publishing).

page 54. There are three interrelated theories that explain why flattery is accepted but unwarranted criticism is rejected: (1) People process messages in the way that most enhances self-image: Kunda, Z. (1987), Motivated inference: Self-serving generation and evaluation of causal theories, *Journal of Personality and Social Psychology, 53*(4), 636–647. (2) People tend to embrace positive messages and reject negative ones: Swann, W. B., & Schroeder, D. G. (1995), The search for beauty and truth: A framework for understanding reactions to evaluations, *Personality and Social Psychology Bulletin, 21*(12), 1307–1318. (3) People scrutinize messages only when they have a motivation to do so: Fiske, S., & Taylor, S.E. (1984), *Social cognition* (Reading, MA: Addison-Wesley).

page 54. For a discussion of the self-serving bias, see: Nisbett, R.E., & Ross, L. (1980), *Human inference: Strategies and shortcomings of social judgment* (Englewood Cliffs, NJ: Prentice-Hall). Ross, M., & Fletcher, G.J.O. (1985), Attribution and social perception, in: G. Lindzey & E. Aronson (Eds.), *The handbook of social psychology,* Vol. 2, 3rd ed. (New York: Random House).

page 61. Praise is most effective when it is a "judicious blend of the bitter and the sweet," Jones, E.E. (1964), *Ingratiation* (New York: Appleton-Century-Crofts). However, as long as an ulterior motive is not suspected, even effusive praise can be effective: Berscheid, E., & Walster, E.H. (1978), *Interpersonal attraction,* 2nd ed. (Reading, MA: Addison-Wesley).

page 62. For discussions of how confidence affects responses to flattery, see: Berscheid, E., & Walster, E.H. (1978), *Interpersonal attraction,* 2nd ed. (Reading, MA: Addison-Wesley). Wortman, C., & Linsenmeier, J. (1977), Interpersonal attraction and techniques of ingratiation in organizational settings, in: B. Shaw & G. Salancik (Eds.), *New directions in organizational behavior* (pp. 133–179) (Chicago: St. Clair).

Chapter 5: Judging Others and Ourselves

page 65. This research is discussed in: Nass, C., & Steuer, J.S. (1993), Voices, boxes, and sources of messages: Computers are social actors, *Human Communication Research, 19*(4), 504–527. Nass, C., Steuer, J.S., Henriksen, L., &

Dryer, D.C. (1994), Machines and social attributions: Performance assessments of computers subsequent to "self-" or "other-" evaluations, *International Journal of Human-Computer Studies, 40*, 543–559.

page 65. For a demonstration that people believe that praised performances are successful, see Meyer, W.U., Mittag, W., & Engler, U. (1986), Some effects of praise and blame on perceived ability and affect, *Social Cognition, 4*(3), 293–308.

page 65. People like others who praise: Folkes, V.S., & Sears, D.O. (1977), Does everybody like a liker? *Journal of Experimental Social Psychology, 13*, 505–519. Mason, L., & Nass, C. (1989), Partisan and non-partisan readers' perceptions of political enemies and newspaper bias, *Journalism Quarterly, 66*, 564–570.

page 65. For evidence that people tend to accept information, regardless of expertise, see: Gilbert, D.T. (1991), How mental systems believe, *American Psychologist, 46*(2), 107–119. Gilbert, D.T., Tafarodi, R.W., & Malone, P.S. (1993), You can't not believe everything you read, *Journal of Personality and Social Psychology, 65*(2), 221–233.

page 65. Criticized performances are perceived as bad: Meyer, W.U., Mittag, W., & Engler, U. (1986), Some effects of praise and blame on perceived ability and affect, *Social Cognition, 4*(3), 293–308.

page 66. People who criticize are disliked: Mason, L., & Nass, C. (1989), Partisan and non-partisan readers' perceptions of political enemies and newspaper bias, *Journalism Quarterly, 66*, 564–570. Powers, T.A., & Zuroff, D.C. (1988), Interpersonal consequences of overt self-criticism: A comparison of neutral and self-enhancing presentations of self, *Journal of Personality and Social Psychology, 54*(6), 1054–1062.

page 66. Critics are perceived as more intelligent than are people who praise: Amabile, T.M. (1983), Brilliant but cruel: Perceptions of negative evaluators, *Journal of Personality and Social Psychology, 19*, 146–156. Amabile, T.M., & Glazebrook, A.H. (1981), A negativity bias in interpersonal evaluation, *Journal of Personality and Social Psychology, 18*, 1–22.

page 66. Praise of others is more credible than praise of self: Wilson, W., & Chambers, W. (1989), Effectiveness of praise of self versus praise of others, *Journal of Social Psychology, 129*, 555–556.

page 67. People who criticize themselves are liked better than people who criticize others: Powers, T.A., & Zuroff, D.C. (1988), Interpersonal consequences of overt self-criticism: A comparison of neutral and self-enhancing presentations of self, *Journal of Personality and Social Psychology, 54*(6), 1054–1062.

page 72. For a discussion of the importance of social intelligence, see: Goleman, D. (1995), *Emotional intelligence* (New York: Bantam Books).

Chapter 6: Personality of Characters

page 75. Formal descriptions of the studies discussed in this chapter are referenced where the particular studies are introduced.

page 75. For an example of how psychologists compress rich personalities into a few simple dimensions, see: Cattell, R.B. (1945), The description of personality: Principles and findings in a factor analysis, *American Journal of Psychology, 58*, 69–90. Digman, J.M. (1990), Personality structure: Emergence of the five-factor model, *Annual Review of Psychology, 41*, 417–440.

page 75. For definitions of dominance and submissiveness, see: Kiesler, D.J. (1983), The 1982 interpersonal circle: A taxonomy for complementarity in human transactions, *Psychological Review, 90*, 185–214. Nass, C., Moon, Y., Fogg, B.J., Reeves, B., & Dryer, D.C. (1995), Can computer personalities be human personalities? *International Journal of Human-Computer Studies, 43*, 223–239.

page 76. A review of the key words for the personality dimensions can be found in: McCrae, R.R., & John, O.P. (1992), An introduction to the five-factor model and its applications, *Journal of Personality, 60*, 175–215. Wiggins, J.S. (1979), A psychological taxonomy of trait-descriptive terms: The interpersonal domain, *Journal of Personality and Social Psychology, 37*, 395–412.

page 76. The procedure by which a list of adjectives is converted into a set of personality dimensions is described in: Costa, P.T., Jr., & McCrae, R.R. (1988), From catalog to classification: Murray's needs and the five-factor model, *Journal of Personality and Social Psychology, 55*, 258–265. Goldberg, L.R. (1981), Language and individual differences: The search for universals in personality lexicons, in: L. Wheeler (Ed.), *Review of personality and social psychology,* Vol. 2 (pp. 141–165) (Beverly Hills, CA: Sage).

page 76. For evidence that there are five basic dimensions of personality, see: Digman, J.M., & Takemoto-Chock, N.K. (1981), Factors in the natural language of personality: Re-analysis, comparison, and interpretation of six major studies, *Multivariate Behavioral Research, 16,* 149–170. Fiske, D.W. (1949), Consistency of the factorial structures of personality ratings from different sources, *Journal of Abnormal and Social Psychology, 44,* 329–344.

page 76. Evidence that the first two dimensions of personality, dominance and friendliness, are the most important for interpersonal interaction can be found in: McCrae, R.R., & Costa, P.T., Jr. (1989), The structure of interpersonal traits: Wiggins's circumplex and the five-factor model, *Journal of Personality and Social Psychology, 56,* 586–595. McCrae, R.R., & John, O.P. (1992), An introduction to the five-factor model and its applications, *Journal of Personality, 60,* 175–215. Wiggins, J.S., & Broughton, R. (1985), The interpersonal circle: A structural model for the integration of personality research, in: R. Hogan (Ed.), *Perspectives in Personality,* Vol. 1 (pp. 1–47). Williams, J.E., Munick, M.L., Saiz, J.L., & Formy-Duval, D.L. (1995), Psychological importance of the "Big Five": Impression formation and context effects, *Personality and Social Psychology Bulletin, 21,* 818–826.

page 76. For adjectives that define the two key personality dimensions, see: Kiesler, D.J. (1983), The 1982 interpersonal circle: A taxonomy for complementarity in human transactions. *Psychological Review, 90,* 185–214.

page 76. For a description of the five personality dimensions, see the above note about the five basic dimensions of personality.

page 76. For evidence that the basic personality dimensions appear across cultures, see: Isaka, H. (1990), Factor analysis of trait terms in everyday Japanese language, *Personality and Individual Differences, 11,* 115–124. John, O.P., Goldberg, L.R., & Angleitner, A. (1984), Better than the alphabet: Taxonomies of personality-descriptive terms in English, Dutch, and German, in: H. Bonarius, G. van Heck, & N. Smid (Eds.), *Personality psychology in Europe: Theoretical and empirical developments* (Berwyn, PA: Swetz North America).

page 76. For references to the "Big Five," see the above note concerning the five basic dimensions of personality.

page 76. For a discussion of the application of the personality dimensions to the description of other people, see: Anderson, C.A., & Sedikides, C. (1991),

Thinking about people: Contributions of a typological alternative to associationistic and dimensional models of person perception, *Journal of Personality and Social Psychology, 60*, 203–217.

page 76. The way that people identify personality dimensions is discussed in: McCrae, R.R., & John, O.P. (1992), An introduction to the five-factor model and its applications, *Journal of Personality, 60*, 175–215. Williams, J.E., Munick, M.L., Saiz, J.L., & Formy-Duval, D.L. (1995), Psychological importance of the "Big Five": Impression formation and context effects, *Personality and Social Psychology Bulletin, 21*, 818–826.

page 77. The first personality study was: Reeves, B., & Greenberg, B. (1977), Children's perceptions of television characters, *Human Communication Research, 3*, 113–117.

page 78. For a more detailed discussion of developmental issues related to person perception, see: Reeves, B. (1979), Children's understanding of television people, in: E. Wartella (Ed.), *Children communicating: Media and development of thought, speech and understanding* (pp. 115–156) (Beverly Hills, CA: Sage). Wartella, E., & Reeves, B. (1987), Communication and children: Development of language, communicative competence, and understanding of media, in: C. Berger & S. Chaffee (Eds.), *Handbook of Communication Science* (pp. 619–650) (Beverly Hills, CA: Sage).

page 79. For discussions of multidimensional scaling, see: Shepard, R.N., Romney, A.K., & Nerlove, S.B. (Eds.) (1972), *Multidimensional scaling: Theory and applications in the behavioral sciences* (New York: Seminar Press). Torgerson, W.S. (1958), *Theory and methods of scaling* (New York: Wiley).

page 79. For a discussion of the primitive basis of similarity and difference, see: Shepard, R.N., Romney, A.K., & Nerlove, S.B. (Eds.) (1972), *Multidimensional scaling: Theory and applications in the behavioral sciences* (New York: Seminar Press).

page 80. For a similar finding that extraversion is the most important dimension, see: Williams, J.E., Munick, M.L., Saiz, J.L., & Formy-Duval, D.L. (1995), Psychological importance of the "Big Five": Impression formation and context effects, *Personality and Social Psychology Bulletin, 21*, 818–826.

page 80. The replication of the first study was: Reeves, B., & Lometti, G.

(1979), The dimensional structure of children's perceptions of television characters: A replication, *Human Communication Research, 5,* 247–256.

page 81. This discussion of Study 2 is the only available report of these data. The research was conducted by Nass, C., Reeves, B., & Dryer, D.C. in 1994.

page 83. Personality is a fundamental classifier of any social representation: Dryer, D.C., Nass, C., Steuer, J.S., & Henriksen, L. (1993), Interpersonal responses to computers programmed to function in social roles. Poster presented at the annual meeting of the Western Psychological Association, Phoenix, AZ. Nass, C., Moon, Y., Fogg, B.J., Reeves, B., & Dryer, D.C. (1995), Can computer personalities be human personalities? *International Journal of Human-Computer Studies, 43,* 223–239.

page 83. For a discussion of how personality governs affect, expectations, and interactions, see: Dryer, D.C. (1993), Interpersonal goals and satisfaction with interactions, Doctoral dissertation, Stanford University, Stanford, CA.

page 84. A demonstration that people like identifiable personalities can be found in: Vonk, R. (1994), Trait inferences, impression formation, and person memory: Strategies in processing inconsistent information about persons, in: W. Stroebe & M. Hewstone (Eds.), *European Review of Social Psychology* (pp. 111–149) (New York: Wiley). Vonk, R. (1995), Effects of inconsistent behaviors on person impressions: A multidimensional study, *Personality and Social Psychology Bulletin, 21,* 674–685.

page 84. The cues that people use to determine personality are discussed in: Kiesler, D.J. (1983), The 1982 interpersonal circle: A taxonomy for complementarity in human transactions, *Psychological Review, 90,* 185–214. Wiggins, J.S. (1979), A psychological taxonomy of trait-descriptive terms: The interpersonal domain, *Journal of Personality and Social Psychology, 37,* 395–412.

page 84. A discussion of how characters are developed can be found in: Thomas, F., & Johnston, O. (1981), *Disney animation: The illusion of life* (New York: Abbeville Press).

page 85. The distribution of people across the major dimensions of personality is discussed in: deRaad, B. (1995), The psycholexical approach to the structure of interpersonal traits, *European Journal of Personality, 9*(2) 89–102. Eysenck, H.J., & Eysenck, S.B.G. (1975), *Manual of the Eysenck personality questionnaire* (London: Hodder & Stoughton). Hill, O.W., & Clark, J.L. (1993), The personality typology of Black college students: Evidence for a characteristic cognitive style? *Psychological Reports, 72*(3), 1091–1097.

page 86. For a general discussion of the research on media and social reality, see: Gerbner, G., Gross, L., Morgan, M., & Signorielli, N. (1986), Living with television: The dynamics of the cultivation process, in: J. Bryant & D. Zillmann (Eds.), *Perspectives on media effects* (pp. 17–40) (Hillsdale, NJ: Lawrence Erlbaum Associates).

page 86. The study of priming with media personalities is discussed in: Reeves, B., & Garramone, G. (1982), Children's person perception: Generalization from television to real people, *Human Communication Research, 8*, 317–326.

page 87. The concept of psychological priming is described in: Berkowitz, L., & Rogers, K. H. (1986), A priming effects analysis of media influences, in: J. Bryant & D. Zillmann (Eds.), *Perspectives on media effects* (pp. 57–81) (Hillsdale, NJ: Lawrence Erlbaum Associates).

Chapter 7: Personality of Interfaces

page 89. A more formal presentation of this research can be found in: Moon, Y., & Nass, C. (in press), How "real" are computer personalities? Psychological responses to personality types in human-computer interaction, *Communication Research*. Nass, C., Moon, Y., Fogg, B.J., Reeves, B., & Dryer, D.C. (1995), Can computer personalities be human personalities? *International Journal of Human-Computer Studies, 43*, 223–239.

page 90. The law of similarity-attraction is documented in: Byrne, D., & Nelson, D. (1965), Attraction as a linear function of proportion of positive reinforcements, *Journal of Personality and Social Psychology Bulletin, 4*, 240–243. Examples include: (1) liking of strangers: Griffitt, W.R. (1966), Interpersonal attraction as a function of self-concept and personality similarity-dissimilarity, *Journal of Personality and Social Psychology, 4*, 581–584; (2) friendships: Duck, S.W., & Craig, G. (1978), Personality similarity and the development of friendship, *British Journal of Social and Clinical Psychology, 17*, 237–242; (3) college roommate assignments: Carli, L.L., Ganley, R., & Pierce-Otay, A. (1991), Similarity and satisfaction in roommate relationships, *Personality and Social Psychology Bulletin, 17,* 419–426; (4) marital satisfaction: Eysenck, H.J., & Wakefield, J.A. (1981), Psychological factors as predictors of marital satisfaction, *Advances in Behaviour Research and Therapy, 3,* 151–192; Richard, L.S., Wakefield, J.A., & Lewak, R. (1990), Similarity of personality variables as predictors of marital satisfaction: A Minnesota Multiphasic Personality Inventory (MMPI) item analysis, *Personality and Individual Differences, 11,* 39–43.

page 90. For an example of an attempt to give personality to computers, see: Oren, T., Salomon, G., Kreitman, K., & Don, A. (1990), Guides: Characterizing the interface, in: Laurel, B. (Ed.), *The art of human-computer interface design* (pp. 367–381)(Reading, MA: Addison-Wesley).

page 90. Discussions of the difficulty in creating personality can be found in: Maes, P. (1993/1994), Modeling adaptive autonomous agents, *Journal of Artificial Life, 1(1/2)* (Cambridge, MA: MIT Press). Maes, P. (1995), Artificial life meets entertainment: Likelike autonomous agents, *Communications of the ACM, 38*(11), 108–114.

page 92. The exact items used to determine personality were derived from a subset of the Bem Sex Role Inventory. The Inventory provides a measure of dominance and submissiveness: Bem, S.L. (1974), The measurement of psychological androgeny, *Journal of Consulting and Clinical Psychology, 42,* 155–162. Wiggins, J.S., & Broughton, R. (1985), The interpersonal circle: A structural model for the integration of personality research, in: R. Hogan (Ed.), *Perspectives in Personality, 1,* 1–47.

page 92. The guidelines for how to manifest dominance and submissiveness were derived from: Kiesler, D.J. (1983), The 1982 interpersonal circle: A taxonomy for complementarity in human transactions, *Psychological Review, 90,* 185–214.

page 94. The Desert Survival Problem is described in: Lafferty, J.C., & Eady, P.M. (1974), *The desert survival problem* (Plymouth, MI: Experimental Learning Methods).

page 94. The Desert Survival Problem is commonly used in the study of interaction: Dryer, D.C. (1993), Interpersonal goals and satisfaction with interactions, Doctoral dissertation, Stanford University, Stanford, CA.

page 95. The adjectives used to assess the computer's personality were derived from the Bem Sex Role Inventory: Bem, S.L. (1974), The measurement of psychological androgeny, *Journal of Consulting and Clinical Psychology,* *42*, 155–162.

page 97. For a discussion of the correlation between personality and intelligence, see: Baron, J. (1982), Personality and intelligence, in: R.J. Sternberg (Ed.), *Handbook of human intelligence* (Cambridge: Cambridge University Press).

page 98. For the list of adjectives used to assess the personality dimensions, see: Nass, C., Moon, Y., Fogg, B.J., Reeves, B., & Dryer, D.C. (1995), Can computer personalities be human personalities? *International Journal of Human-Computer Studies, 43,* 223–239.

page 98. The distribution of people across the major dimensions of personality is discussed in: deRaad, B. (1995), The psycholexical approach to the structure of interpersonal traits, *European Journal of Personality, 9*(2) 89–102. Eysenck, H.J., & Eysenck, S.B.G. (1975), *Manual of the Eysenck personality questionnaire* (London: Hodder & Stoughton). Hill, O.W., & Clark, J.L. (1993), The personality typology of Black college students: Evidence for a characteristic cognitive style? *Psychological Reports, 72*(3), 1091–1097.

Chapter 8: Imitating Personality

page 101. The research in this chapter is more formally presented in: Moon, Y., & Nass, C. (in press), How "real" are computer personalities? Psychological responses to personality types in human-computer interaction, *Communication Research.*

page 101. Evidence that we like people better when they change to conform to us as compared to when they are consistently like us can be found in: Aronson, E., & Linder, D. (1965), Gain and loss of esteem as determinants of interpersonal attractiveness, *Journal of Experimental Social Psychology, 1,* 156–171. Mettee, D.R. (1971), The true discerner as a potent source of positive affect, *Journal of Experimental Social Psychology, 7,* 292–303. Mettee, D.R., Taylor, S.E., & Friedman, H. (1973), Affect conversion and the gain-loss effect, *Sociometry, 36,* 505–519.

page 101. The terms "gain-loss theory" and "gain theory" were coined by: Aronson, E., & Linder, D. (1965), Gain and loss of esteem as determinants of interpersonal attractiveness, *Journal of Experimental Social Psychology, 1,* 156–171.

page 102. Permanent versus temporary changes in personality are the difference between traits and states. The difference is discussed in: Allport, G.W., & Odbert, H.S. (1936), Trait names: A psycho-lexical study, *Psychological Monographs, 47*(211). John, O.P. (1990), Basic dimensions of personality: A review and critique, in: P. McReynolds, J.C. Rosen, & G.J. Chelune (Eds.), *Advances in Psychological Assessment,* Vol. 7 (New York: Plenum Press).

page 105. Most experiments fail to demonstrate loss effects, even when they are predicted: Mettee, D.R., Taylor, S.E., & Friedman, H. (1973), Affect conversion and the gain-loss effect, *Sociometry, 36,* 505–519. For an exception, see Clore, G.L., Wiggins, N.H., & Itkin, S. (1975), Gain and loss in attraction: Attributions from nonverbal behavior, *Journal of Personality and Social Psychology, 31,* 706–712.

page 105. For a discussion of traditional methods for manipulating personality, see: Dryer, D.C. (1993), Interpersonal goals and satisfaction with interactions, Doctoral dissertation, Stanford University, Stanford: CA. Moon, Y., & Nass, C. (in press), How "real" are computer personalities? Psychological responses to personality types in human-computer interaction, *Communication Research.*

Chapter 9: Good versus Bad

page 111. This chapter is based on the following study: Reeves, B., Lang, A., Thorson, E., & Rothschild, M. (1989), Emotional television scenes and hemispheric specialization, *Human Communication Research, 15,* 493–508.

page 111. For a review of the literature about grouping adjectives, see: Osgood, C.E., Suci, G.J., & Tannenbaum, P.H. (1957), *The measurement of meaning* (Urbana: University of Illinois Press).

page 112. For evidence that people scrutinize faces, see: Ekman, P. (Ed.) (1973), *Darwin and facial expression: A century of research in review* (New York: Academic Press).

page 113. One study that used a drug to inhibit communication in the brain is: Sackeim, H.A., Greenberg, M.S., Weiman, A.L., Gur, R.C., Honogerbuhler, J.P., & Geschwind, N. (1982), Hemispheric asymmetry in the expression of positive and negative emotion, *Archives of Neurology, 39*, 687–692.

page 113. Lesions and hemispheric specialization are discussed in: Davidson, R.J. (1984), Hemispheric asymmetry and emotion, in: K.R. Scherer & P. Ekman (Eds.), *Approaches to emotion* (pp. 39–58) (Hillsdale, NJ: Lawrence Erlbaum Associates).

page 113. The experience of extreme levels of good and bad and the relationship to hemispheric specialization are discussed in: Tucker, D.M. (1981), Lateral brain function, emotion, and conceptualization, *Psychological Bulletin, 89*, 19–46.

page 113. Imaging effects on hemispheric specialization are discussed in: Koff, E., Borod, J.C., & White, B. (1983), A left hemisphere bias for visualizing emotional situations, *Neuropsychologia, 21*(3), 273–275.

page 113. The experience of sour and sweet taste and hemispheric specialization is discussed in: Davidson, R.J. (1984), Hemispheric asymmetry and emotion, in: K.R. Scherer & P. Ekman (Eds.), *Approaches to emotion* (pp. 39–58) (Hillsdale, NJ: Lawrence Erlbaum Associates).

page 113. The experience of smiling and frowning faces is discussed in: Reuter-Lorenz, P.A., & Davidson, R.J. (1981), Differential contribution of the two cerebral hemispheres to the perception of happy and sad faces, *Neuropsychologia, 19*, 609–613.

page 115. For a discussion of the use of EEG to measure hemispheric specialization, see: Rothschild, M., Thorson, E., Reeves, B., Hirsch, J., & Goldstein, R. (1986), EEG activity and the processing of television commercials, *Communication Research, 13*, 182-220.

page 116. For a discussion of the generalization of media stimuli to larger categories of stimuli, see: Reeves, B., & Geiger, S. (1994), Designing experiments that assess psychological responses to media messages, in: A. Lang (Ed.), *Measuring psychological responses to media* (pp. 165–180) (Hillsdale, NJ: Lawrence Erlbaum Associates).

Chapter 10: Negativity

page 119. This chapter is based on a number of published studies. Each study is referenced at the point at which it is introduced.

page 119. The law of hedonic asymmetry and other laws of emotion are reviewed in: Frijda, N.H. (1988), The laws of emotion, *American Psychologist*, *43*(5), 349–358.

page 120. For discussions of how negative events demand attention, see: Cannon, W.B. (1927), The James-Lange theory of emotions: A critical examination and an alternative theory, *American Journal of Psychology, 39*, 106–124. Cannon, W.B. (1929), *Bodily changes in pain, hunger, fear and rage: An account of researches into the function of emotional excitement*, 2nd ed. (New York: Appleton-Century-Crofts). Gilligan, S.G., & Bower, G.H. (1984), Cognition and emotion: Concept and action, in: C.E. Izard, J. Kagan, & R.B. Zajonc (Eds.), *Emotion, cognition, and behavior* (pp. 547–588) (Cambridge: Cambridge University Press). Izard, C.E. (1977), *Human emotions* (New York: Plenum Press). Leventhal, H. (1974), Emotions: A basic problem for social psychology, in: C. Nemeth (Ed.), *Social psychology: Classic and contemporary integrations* (pp. 1–51) (Chicago: Rand McNally).

page 120. For a discussion of negativity and attention as they relate to primitive responses, see: Lang, P.J. (1995), The emotion probe: Studies of motivation and attention, *American Psychologist, 50*(5), 372–385.

page 120. For a discussion of the Pollyanna Effect, see: Fiske, S., & Taylor, S.E. (1984), *Social cognition* (Reading, MA: Addison-Wesley).

page 120. For a more detailed discussion of the psychological literature on negativity and memory, and the application of the literature to media, see: Lang, A., & Friestad, M. (1993), Emotion, hemispheric specialization, and visual and verbal memory for television messages, *Communication Research, 20*(5), 647–670. Thorson, E., & Friestad, M. (1985), The effects of emotion on episodic memory for television commercials, in: P. Cafferata & A. Tybout (Eds.), *Advances in consumer psychology* (pp.131–136) (Lexington, MA: Lexington).

page 121. For more information about proactive and retroactive interference in the processing of media, see: Thorson, E., & Reeves, B. (1985),

Memory effects of over-time measures of viewer liking and activity during programs and commercials, in: R.J. Lutz (Ed.), *Advances in consumer research*, Vol. XII (New York: Association for Consumer Research). Thorson, E., Reeves, B., Schleuder, J., Lang, A., & Rothschild, M. (1985), Effects of program context on the processing of television commercials, in: N. Stephens (Ed.), *Proceedings of the American Academy of Advertising* (Tempe: Arizona State University).

page 121. Exposure to disfigured faces inhibits rehearsal for prior material and causes lower recall: Christianson, S., & Loftus, E. (1987), Memory for traumatic events, *Applied Cognitive Psychology, 1,* 225–239.

page 123. Experiment 1 is presented in more detail in: Newhagen, J., & Reeves, B. (1991), Emotion and memory responses to negative political advertising, in: F. Biocca (Ed.), *Television and political advertising: Psychological processes* (pp. 197–220) (Hillsdale, NJ: Lawrence Erlbaum Associates).

page 125. Experiment 2 is presented in more detail in: Reeves, B., Newhagen, J., Maibach, E., Basil, M.D., & Kurz, K. (1991), Negative and positive television messages: Effects of message type and message context on attention and memory, *American Behavioral Scientist, 34,* 679–694.

page 125. Experiment 3 is presented in: Newhagen, J., & Reeves, B. (1992), This evening's bad news: Effects of compelling negative television news images on memory, *Journal of Communication, 42,* 25–41.

page 129. For a discussion of negativity in politics, see: Ansolabehere, S., & Iyengar, S. (1996), *Going Negative: How political advertisements shrink and polarize the electorate* (New York: Free Press).

page 130. For a discussion of how psychologists produce emotional experience using words and imaging tasks, see: Lang, P.J. (1987), Image as action: A reply to Watts and Blackstock, *Cognition & Emotion, 1*(4), 407–426.

Chapter 11: Arousal

page 131. This chapter is based on the following study: Detenber, B., & Reeves, B. (in press), Motion and image size effects on viewer responses to pictures: Application of a bio-information theory of emotion, *Journal of Communication.*

page 131. For a general discussion of arousal, see: Fisk, S.T. (1981), Social cognition and affect, in: J.H. Harvey (Ed.), *Cognition, social behavior and the environment* (pp. 227–251) (Hillsdale, NJ: Lawrence Erlbaum Associates). Lang, P.J. (1995), The emotion probe: Studies of motivation and attention, *American Psychologist, 50*(5), 372–385.

page 132. The two-dimensional conception of arousal and valence is taken from: Lang, P.J. (1995), The emotion probe: Studies of motivation and attention, *American Psychologist, 50*(5), 372–385.

page 133. The independence of arousal and valence and implications for studying media are discussed in: Bradley, M.M., Greenwald, M.K., Petry, M.C., & Lang, P.J. (1992), Remembering pictures: Pleasure and arousal in memory, *Journal of Experimental Psychology: Learning, Memory, & Cognition, 18*(2), 379–390. Lang, A. (1994), What can the heart tell us about thinking? in A. Lang (Ed.), *Measuring psychological responses to media* (pp. 99–111) (New York: Lawrence Erlbaum Associates).

page 133. The relationship between arousal and memory for pictures is discussed in: Bradley, M.M., Greenwald, M.K., Petry, M., & Lang, P.J. (1992), Remembering pictures: Pleasure and arousal in memory, *Journal of Experimental Psychology: Learning, Memory, & Cognition, 18*, 379–390. Some researchers now argue that arousal is the only important dimension of emotion when considering memory. Their point is that highly negative information is usually arousing: Lang, P.J. (1995), The emotion probe: Studies of motivation and attention, *American Psychologist, 50*(5), 372–385.

page 134. The method of measuring arousal and valence, called the SAM (Self Assessment Mannequin), is taken from: Lang, P.J. (1980), Behavioral treatment and bio-behavioral assessment: Computer applications, in: J.B. Sidowski, J.H. Johnson, & T.A. Williams (Eds.), *Technology in mental health care delivery systems* (pp.119–137) (Norwood, NJ: Ablex).

page 135. The distribution of images across the dimensions of emotion (as well as gender differences in the distribution) is consistent with the distribution of other stimulus sets as reported in: Lang, P.J. (1995), The emotion probe: Studies of motivation and attention, *American Psychologist, 50*(5), 372–385.

page 137. For an example of the different materials used in psychological experiments about emotion, see: Gross, J.J., & Levenson, R.W. (1995), Emotion elicitation using films, *Cognition and Emotion, 9*(1), 87–108.

page 137. For a discussion on how arousal accumulates, see: Zillmann, D. (1971), Excitation transfer in communication-mediated aggressive behavior, *Journal of Experimental Social Psychology, 7,* 419–434. Zillmann, D. (1991), Television viewing and physiological arousal, in: J. Bryant & D. Zillmann (Eds.), *Responding to the screen: Reception and reaction processes* (pp. 103–133) (Hillsdale, NJ: Lawrence Erlbaum Associates).

page 137. For a general discussion of the interdependence of time units in the processing of media, see: Reeves, B., & Thorson, E. (1986), Watching television: Experiments on the viewing process, *Communication Research, 13,* 343–36l.

page 138. For a discussion of the relationship between emotional content in television programs and the ads that appear within the programs, see: Thorson, E., Reeves, B., Schleuder, J., Lang, A., & Rothschild, M. (1985), Effects of program context on the processing of television commercials, in: N. Stephens (Ed.), *Proceedings of the American Academy of Advertising* (Tempe: Arizona State University).

page 138. Media are used to excite and unwind: Zillmann, D. (1991), Television viewing and physiological arousal, in: J. Bryant & D. Zillmann (Eds.), *Responding to the screen: Reception and reaction processes* (pp. 103–133) (Hillsdale, NJ: Lawrence Erlbaum Associates).

Chapter 12: Specialists

page 143. The first study presented in this chapter is also discussed in: Nass, C., Reeves, B., & Leshner, G. (1996), Technology and roles: A tale of two TVs, *Journal of Communication, 46*(2), 121–128. The second study is presented in: Leshner, G., Reeves, B., & Nass, C. (1996), Switching channels: The effects of television channels on the mental representation of television news, unpublished manuscript.

page 144. People believe specialists more than generalists: Bochner, S., & Insko, C.A. (1966), Communicator discrepancy, source credibility, and opinion change, *Journal of Personality and Social Psychology, 4,* 614–621. Petty, R.E.,

Cacioppo, J.T., & Goldman, R. (1981), Personal involvement as a determinant of argument-based persuasion, *Journal of Personality and Social Psychology, 41,* 847–855.

page 144. Arbitrary labeling of specialists is effective: Zimbardo, P., & Leippe, M.R. (1991), Shortcuts to acceptance: Using heuristics instead of systematic analysis, in: P. Zimbardo and M.R. Leippe (Eds.), *The psychology of attitude change and social influence* (New York: McGraw-Hill).

page 144. A discussion of how categorization simplifies interaction can be found in: Fiske, S., & Taylor, S.E. (1984), *Social cognition* (Reading, MA: Addison-Wesley).

page 144. Evidence that people are biased toward believing can be found in: Gilbert, D.T. (1991), How mental systems believe, *American Psychologist, 46*(2), 107–119. Gilbert, D.T., Krull, D.S., & Malone, P.S. (1990), Unbelieving the unbelievable: Some problems in the rejection of false information, *Journal of Personality and Social Psychology, 59*(4), 601–613.

page 151. For a discussion of the link between a celebrity's role and people's belief in their endorsements, see: Ohanian, R. (1991), The impact of celebrity spokespersons' perceived image on consumers' intention to purchase, *Journal of Advertising Research, 31,* 46–54.

Chapter 13: Teammates

page 153. The research presented in this chapter is also reported in: Nass, C., Fogg, B.J., & Moon, Y. (in press), Can computers be teammates? *International Journal of Human-Computer Studies.*

page 153. It takes very little to make people feel a part of a group: Tajfel, H. (1982), *Social identity and intergroup behavior* (Cambridge: Cambridge University Press).

page 154. People perceive teammates to be more similar to themselves: Allen, V.L., & Wilder, D.A. (1979), Group categorization and attribution of belief similarity, *Small Group Behavior, 10,* 73–80. Mackie, D.M. (1986), Social identification effects in group polarization, *Journal of Personality and Social Psychology, 50,* 720–728.

page 154. Members of a team are perceived as superior to non-members:

Brock, T.C. (1965), Communicator-recipient similarity and decision change, *Journal of Personality and Social Psychology, 1,* 650–654. Mackie, D.M., Worth, L.T., & Asuncion, A.G. (1990), Processing of persuasive in-group messages, *Journal of Personality and Social Psychology, 58,* 812–822.

page 154. People cooperate and conform more with team members: Abrams, D., Wetherell, M., Cochrane, S., Hogg, M.A., & Turner, J.C. (1990), Knowing what to think by knowing who you are: Self-categorization and the nature of norm formation, conformity and group polarization, *British Journal of Social Psychology, 29,* 97–119. Deutsch, M., & Gerard, H.B. (1955), A study of normative and information social influences upon individual judgement, *Journal of Abnormal and Social Psychology, 51,* 629–636.

page 154. A discussion of "groupthink" is presented in: Janis, I.L. (1982), *Groupthink: Psychological studies of policy decisions and fiascoes,* 2nd ed. (Boston: Houghton-Mifflin).

page 154. The group identity/teammate link is demonstrated in: Mackie, D.M., & Cooper, J. (1984), Group polarization: The effects of group membership, *Journal of Personality and Social Psychology, 46,* 575–585. Turner, J.C. (1982), Toward a cognitive redefinition of the social group, in: H. Tajfel (Ed.), *Social identity and intergroup behavior* (pp. 15–40) (Cambridge: Cambridge University Press). Wilder, D.A. (1990), Some determinants of the persuasive power of in-groups and out-groups: Organization of information and attribution of independence, *Journal of Personality and Social Psychology, 59,* 1202–1213.

page 154. The interdependence/teammate link is demonstrated in: Allen, V.L. (1965), Situational factors in conformity, in: L. Berkowitz (Ed.), *Advances in experimental social psychology,* Vol. 2 (pp. 133–176) (Orlando, FL: Academic Press). Horwitz, M., & Rabbie, J.M. (1982), Individuality and membership in the intergroup system, in: H. Tajfel (Ed.), *Social identity and intergroup relations* (pp. 241–274) (Cambridge: Cambridge University Press). Lewin, K. (1948), *Resolving social conflicts* (New York: Harper).

page 158. For an excellent summary of the breadth and depth of teammate responses, see: Tajfel, H. (Ed.) (1982), *Social identity and intergroup behavior* (Cambridge: Cambridge University Press).

page 159. For discussions of "one-down" versus "one-up" in computing, see: Friedman, B., & Kahn, P. H., Jr. (1992), Human agency and responsible computing: Implications for computer system design, *Journal of Systems and Software, 17*(10), 7–15. Weizenbaum, J. (1976), *Computer power and human reason: From judgment to calculation* (Ypsilanti, MI: W.H. Freeman Publishing). For examples of the relative emphasis on "one-down" versus "one-up," see: Minsky, M. (1986), *The society of mind* (New York: Knopf). Norman, D. (1993), *Things that make us smart: Defending human attributes in the age of the machine* (Reading, MA: Addison-Wesley). Schneiderman, B. (1992), *Designing the user interface: Strategies for effective human-computer interaction* (Reading, MA: Addison-Wesley). Zuboff, S. (1988), in: *In the age of the smart machine: The future of work and power* (New York: Basic Books).

Chapter 14: Gender

page 161. The first study in this chapter is also discussed in: Nass, C., Moon, Y., & Green, N. (1996), Are computers gender-neutral? Gender-stereotypic responses to computers, Paper presented to the International Communication Association, Chicago. The second study is presented in: Voelker, D.H. (1994), The effects of image size and voice volume on the evaluation of represented faces, Doctoral dissertation, Stanford University, Stanford, CA.

page 162. For a general discussion of gender stereotypes, see: Spence, J.T., Deaux, K., & Helmreich, R.L. (1985), Sex roles in contemporary American society, in: G. Lindzey & E. Aronson (Eds.), *The handbook of social psychology,* Vol. 2, 3rd ed. (New York: Random House).

page 162. For evidence that praise from males is taken more seriously than praise from females, see: Eagly A.H., & Wood, W. (1982), Inferred sex differences in status as a determinant of gender stereotypes about social influence, *Journal of Personality and Social Psychology, 43,* 915–928.

page 162. For a discussion of gender stereotypes with respect to knowledge, see: Heilman, M.E. (1979), High school students' occupational interest as a function of projected sex ratios in male-dominated occupations, *Journal of Applied Psychology, 64,* 275–279.

page 162. Women are expected to exhibit less dominant behavior than men: Costrich, N., Feinstein, J., Kidder, L., Maracek, J., & Pascale, L. (1975), When stereotypes hurt: Three studies of penalties in sex-role reversals, *Journal of Experimental Social Psychology, 11,* 520–530. Deutsch, C.J., & Gilbert,

L.A. (1976), Sex role stereotypes: Effect on perceptions of self and others and on personal adjustment, *Journal of Counseling Psychology, 23,* 373–379. McKee, J.P., & Sheriffs, A.C. (1959), Men's and women's beliefs, ideals, and self-concepts, *American Journal of Sociology, 64,* 356–363.

page 162. For a discussion of the origins of gender stereotypes, see: Fiske, S., & Taylor, S.E. (1984), *Social cognition* (Reading, MA: Addison-Wesley).

page 162. Men and women show few differences in most gender stereotyping: Deaux, K., & Emsweiler, T. (1974), Explanations of successful performance on sex-linked tasks: What is skill for the male is luck for the female, *Journal of Personality and Social Psychology, 29,* 80–85. Rosenkrantz, P.S., Voegel, S.R., Bee, H., Broverman, I.K., & Broverman, D.M. (1968), Sex role stereotypes and self concepts in college students, *Journal of Consulting and Clinical Psychology, 32,* 287–295.

page 163. Voices are assigned a gender rapidly: Coleman, R.O. (1971), Male and female voice quality and its relationship to vowel formant frequencies, *Journal of Speech and Hearing Research, 14,* 565–577. Coleman, R.O. (1976), A comparison of the contributions of two voice quality characteristics to the perception of maleness and femaleness in the voice, *Journal of Speech and Hearing Research, 19,* 168–180. Gunzburger, D., Bresser, A., & Keurs, M.T. (1987), Voice identification of prepubertal boys and girls by normally sighted and visually handicapped subjects, *Language & Speech, 30,* 47–58.

page 163. Masculine and feminine voices are gender-stereotyped: Robinson, J., & McArthur, L.Z. (1982), Impact of salient vocal qualities on causal attribution for a speaker's behavior, *Journal of Personality and Social Psychology, 43,* 236–247.

page 163. Examinations of gender in media content include: Meehan, D.M. (1983), *Ladies of the evening: Women characters of prime-time television* (Metuchen, NJ: Scarecrow Press). National Commission on Working Women. (1985), *Report on women in the media and television* (Washington, DC).

page 163. Ratios of men to women in traditional media can be found in: Gerbner, G., Gross, L., Morgan, M., & Signorielli, N. (1986), Living with television: The dynamics of the cultivation process, in: J. Bryant and D. Zillmann (Eds.), *Perspectives on media effects* (pp. 17–48) (Hillsdale, NJ: Lawrence Erlbaum Associates).

page 163. Discussions of the ways in which media portrayals can create and sustain gender stereotypes can be found in: Gerbner, G., Gross, L., Morgan, M., & Signorielli, N. (1986), Living with television: The dynamics of the cultivation process, in: J. Bryant & D. Zillmann (Eds.), *Perspectives on media effects* (pp. 17–48) (Hillsdale, NJ: Lawrence Erlbaum Associates). Gerbner, G., Gross, L., Morgan, M., & Signorielli, N. (1994), Growing up with television: The cultivation perspective, in: J. Bryant and D. Zillmann (Eds.), *Media effects: Advances in theory and research* (pp. 17–42) (Hillsdale, NJ: Lawrence Erlbaum Associates).

page 166. Males are perceived as having more instrumental qualities, such as drive and assertiveness, than women: Rosenkrantz, P.S., Vogel, S.R., Bee, H., Broverman, I.K., & Broverman, D.M. (1968), Sex role stereotypes and self concepts in college students, *Journal of Consulting and Clinical Psychology, 32*, 287–295.

page 166. Males are perceived as more intellectually competent than women: Goldberg, P.A. (1968), Are women prejudiced against women? *Transaction*, April, 28–30.

page 166. Evaluations from males are seen as more influential than evaluations from females: Nass, C., Moon, Y., & Green, N. (1996), Are computers gender-neutral? Gender-stereotypic responses to computers, Paper presented to the International Communication Association, Chicago.

page 168. For a discussion of how people use stereotypes to guide their attitudes and behaviors, see: Fiske, S., & Taylor, S.E. (1984), *Social cognition* (Reading, MA: Addison-Wesley).

page 168. For evidence that people do not like gender-ambiguous voices, see: Crabtree, M., Mirenda, P., & Beukelman, D.R. (1990), Age and gender preferences for synthetic and natural speech, *AAC: Augmentative & Alternative Communication, 6*, 256–261. Mirenda, P., Eicher, D., & Beukelman, D.R. (1989), Synthetic and natural speech preferences of male and female listeners in four age groups, *Journal of Speech and Hearing Research, 32*, 175–183.

page 168. People assign many demographic characteristics to voices: Mencel, E., Moon, J., & Leeper, H.A. (1978), Speaker race identification of North American Indian children, *Folia Phoniatrica, 40*, 175–182. Scherer, K.R. (1978), Personality inference from voice quality: The loud voice of extroversion, *European Journal of Social Psychology, 8,* 467–487. Walton, J.H., & Orlikoff, R. (1994), Speaker race identification from acoustic cues in the vocal signal, *Journal of Speech and Hearing Research, 37,* 738–745.

page 169. The issue of gender in traditional media has received a great deal of attention: Meehan, D.M. (1983), *Ladies of the evening: Women characters of prime-time television* (Metuchen, NJ: Scarecrow Press). National Commission on Working Women (1985), *Reports on women in the media and television* (Washington, DC).

page 169. An example of studies that examine gender portrayals is: Gerbner, G., Gross, L., Morgan, M., & Signorielli, N. (1986), Living with television: The dynamics of the cultivation process, in: J. Bryant and D. Zillmann (Eds.), *Perspectives on media effects* (pp. 17–48) (Hillsdale, NJ: Lawrence Erlbaum Associates).

Chapter 15: Voices

page 171. More formal presentation of the experiments presented in this chapter can be found in: Nass, C., & Steuer, J.S. (1993), Computers, voices, and sources of messages: Computers are social actors, *Human Communication Research, 19*(4), 504–527. Steuer, J.S. (1994), Vividness and source of evaluation as determinants of social responses toward mediated representations of agency, Doctoral dissertation, Stanford University, Stanford, CA.

page 172. For evidence that human voices are distinguished from all other sounds, see: Kreiman, J., & vanLancker, D.R. (1988), Hemispheric specialization for voice recognition: Evidence from dichotic listening, *Brain and Language, 34*(2), 246–252. Moore, B.C.J. (1982), *An introduction to the psychology of hearing,* 2nd ed. (London: Academic Press).

page 172. Evidence that people can discriminate multiple voices coming from the same location can be found in: Moore, B.C.J. (1982), *An introduction to the psychology of hearing,* 2nd ed. (London: Academic Press).

page 172. Evidence that the same voice coming from different locations is thought of as the same person can be found in: Geiselman, R.E., & Bellezza, F. (1976), Long-term memory for speaker's voice and source location, *Memory & Cognition, 4*(5), 483–489. McGurk, H., & Lewis, M. (1974), Space perception in early infancy: Perceptions within a common auditory-visual space? *Science, 186,* 649–650.

Chapter 16: Source Orientation

page 181. The experiment described in this chapter is presented more formally in: Nass, C., & Sundar, S.S. (1996), Are computers social actors? Are programmers psychologically relevant to human-computer interaction? Unpublished manuscript.

page 181. Even when people know that a communicator was *arbitrarily* assigned to present a particular position on an issue, they nevertheless infer that the communicator agrees somewhat with the position: Brockner, J., & Nova, M. (1979), Further determinants of attitude attributions: The perceived effects of assigned behavior on post-behavior attitudes, *Personality and Social Psychology Bulletin, 5,* 311–315. Jones, E.E., & Harris, V.A. (1967), The attribution of attitudes, *Journal of Experimental Social Psychology, 3,* 1–24. Miller, R.L. (1976), Mere exposure, psychological reactance, and attitude change, *Public Opinion Quarterly, 40,* 229–233. Miller, A.G., Baier, R., & Schonberg, P. (1979), The bias phenomenon in attitude attribution: Actor and observer perspectives, *Journal of Personality and Social Psychology, 37,* 1421–1431.

page 181. People have a tendency to hold messengers responsible for a message. This tendency occurs regardless of whether or not the presenter expresses personal agreement with the content of the news: Small, W.J. (1970), *To kill a messenger: Television news and the real world* (New York: Hastings House). Stone, V.A., & Beell, T.L. (1975), To kill a messenger: A case of congruity, *Journalism Quarterly, 52,* 111–114.

page 182. Limitations in human-encoding capacity allow increased absorption of one type of information only at the cost of less absorption of the other types: McConnell, J.D. (1970), Do media vary in effectiveness? *Journal of Advertising Research, 10,* 19–22. Pool, I. de S. (1983), Tracing the flow of information, *Science, 221,* 609–613. McGuire, W.J. (1961), Some factors influencing the effectiveness of demonstrational films, in: A.A. Lumsdaine (Ed.), *Student response in programmed instruction* (pp. 187–207) (Washington, DC: National Academy of Sciences).

page 182. For discussions of what happens when people are asked to process more information than they can handle, see: Bettman, J.R. (1975), Issues in designing consumer information environments, *Journal of Consumer Research, 2,* 169–177. Kanouse, D.E., & Hayes-Roth, B. (1981), Cognitive considerations in the design of product warnings, in: L.A. Morris, M.B. Mazis, and I. Barofsky (Eds.), *Product labeling and health risks* (pp. 147–164) (New York: Banbury). Scammon, D.L. (1977), "Information overload" and consumers, *Journal of Consumer Research, 4,* 148–155.

page 182. An individual that is forced to give a particular speech is perceived as agreeing with the content of the speech: Brockner, J., & Nova, M. (1979), Further determinants of attitude attributions: The perceived effects of assigned behavior on post-behavior attitudes, *Personality and Social Psychology Bulletin, 5,* 311–315. Jones, E.E., & Harris, V.A. (1967), The attribution of attitudes, *Journal of Experimental Social Psychology, 3,* 1–24.

page 182. Celebrity endorsements work: McCracken, G. (1989), Who is the celebrity endorser? Cultural foundations of the endorsement process, *Journal of Consumer Research, 16,* 310–321. Ohanian, R. (1991), The impact of celebrity spokespersons' perceived image on consumers' intention to purchase, *Journal of Advertising Research, 31,* 46–54. Tripp, C., Jensen, T.D., & Carlson, L. (1994), The effects of multiple product endorsements by celebrities on consumers' attitudes and intentions, *Journal of Consumer Research, 20,* 535–547.

page 183. The study about differences in the perception of sources in television and print news is: Newhagen, J., & Nass, C. (1989), Differential criteria for evaluating credibility of newspapers and TV news, *Journalism Quarterly, 66,* 277–284.

page 183. People tend to trust TV news more than newspapers: Westley, B.H., & Severin, W.J. (1964), Some correlates of media credibility, *Journalism Quarterly, 41,* 325–335.

page 187. The original discussion of the "willing suspension of disbelief" can be found in: Coleridge, S.T. (1889), *Biographia literaria, or, biographical sketches of my literary life and opinions* (London: George Bell). For an application of the theory to human-computer interaction, see: Laurel, B. (1993), *Computers as theater* (Reading, MA: Addison-Wesley).

page 187. For a similar argument that the perception of a computer's intelligence is more important than its actual intelligence, see: Turkle, S. (1995),

Life on the screen: Identity in the age of the Internet (New York: Simon & Schuster). *Working Notes: AAAI Spring Symposium Series, Believable Agents.* Symposium conducted at the AAAI spring symposium, Stanford, CA.

page 187. Discussions about the real similarities between thinking machines and thinking people can be found in: Hofstadter, D.R., & Dennett, D.C. (Eds.) (1981), *The mind's I* (Toronto: Bantam). Simon, H.A. (1969), *Sciences of the artificial* (Cambridge, MA: MIT Press). Weizenbaum, J. (1976), *Computer power and human reason: From judgment to calculation* (Ypsilanti, MI: W.H. Freeman Publishing). Winograd, T., & Flores, C. (1987), *Understanding computers and cognition: A new foundation for design,* (Reading, MA: Addison-Wesley).

page 187. A discussion of Searle's Chinese Room can be found in: Searle, J.R. (1980), Minds, brains, and programs, *The Behavioral and Brain Sciences, 3,* 417-424.

page 187. For a discussion of the differences between actual and perceived intelligence, including people's inability to accurately assess intelligence, see: Sternberg, R.J. (1986), Inside intelligence, *American Scientist, 74,* 137–143. Sternberg, R.J., Conway, B.E., Ketron, J.L., & Bernstein, M. (1981), People's conceptions of intelligence, *Journal of Personality and Social Psychology, 41*(1), 37–55.

page 188. For a discussion of how people perceive intelligence, see: Baron, J. (1982), Intelligence as a perceived trait, in: R.J. Sternberg & P. Ruzgis (Eds.), *Personality and intelligence* (Cambridge: Cambridge University Press). Sternberg, R.J., Conway, B.E., Ketron, J.L., & Bernstein, M. (1981), People's conceptions of intelligence, *Journal of Personality and Social Psychology, 41*(1), 37–55

page 188. The description of the Turing Test was initially presented in: Turing, A.M. (1950), Computer machinery and intelligence, *Mind,* LIX(236).

page 188. The idea that people re-orient when they encounter confusions in software can be found in: Winograd, T., & Flores, C. (1987) *Understanding computers and cognition: A new foundation for design* (Reading, MA: Addison-Wesley).

Chapter 17: Image Size

page 193. Formal reports of the two studies discussed in this chapter are referenced when they are first discussed.

page 194. One study about the influence of size on infants is: Fantz, R.L., Fagan, J.F., & Miranda, S.B. (1975), Early visual selectivity, in: L.B. Cohen & P. Salapatek (Eds.), *Infant perception: From sensation to cognition*, Vol. 1 (New York: Academic Press).

page 194. For the link between height and physical attractiveness, see: Jackson, L.A. (1992), *Physical appearance and gender* (Albany: State University of New York Press).

page 194. For a study about size and perceived productivity at work, see: Josephs, R.A., Gielser, R.B., & Silvera, D.H. (1994), Judgment by quantity, *Journal of Experimental Psychology: General, 123*(1), 21-32.

page 194. For a more detailed discussion of the relationship between stimulus size and arousal, see: Detenber, B., & Reeves, B. (in press), Motion and image size effects on viewer responses to pictures: Application of a bio-information theory of emotion, *Journal of Communication*.

page 195. For a discussion of the relationship between peripheral vision and arousal responses, see: Livingstone, M., & Hubel, D. (1988), Segregation of form, color, movement, and depth: Anatomy, physiology, and movement, *Science, 240,* 740–749. There is some evidence that video screen size contributes to differences in viewer's sensation of reality: Hatada, T., Sakata, H., & Kusaka, H. (1980), Psychological analysis of the sensation of reality induced by a visual wide field display, *SMPTE Journal, 89(8),* 560–569.

page 197. Study 1 is published as: Detenber, B., & Reeves, B. (in press), Motion and image size effects on viewer responses to pictures: Application of a bio-information theory of emotion, *Journal of Communication*.

page 197. Screen sizes are reported in the serial: *Television and cable factbook* (Washington, DC: Television Digest).

page 197. The method of measuring arousal, called the SAM (Self Assessment Mannequin), is taken from: Lang, P.J. (1980), Behavioral treatment and bio-behavioral assessment: Computer applications, in: J.B. Sidowski,

J.H. Johnson, & T.A. Williams (Eds.), *Technology in mental health care delivery systems* (pp.119–137) (Norwood, NJ: Ablex).

page 198. The report for Study 2 is: Reeves, B., Detenber, B., & Steuer, J.S. (1993), New televisions: The effects of big pictures and big sound on viewer responses to the screen, Paper presented to the Information Systems Division of the International Communication Association, Washington, DC.

page 198. For a discussion of the history of image size, see: Belton, J. (1992), *Wide screen cinema* (Cambridge, MA: Harvard University Press).

page 201. For a discussion about the transference of excitement from one activity to another, see: Zillmann, D. (1991), Television viewing and physiological arousal, in: J. Bryant & D. Zillmann (Eds.), *Responding to the screen: Reception and reaction processes* (pp.103–133) (Hillsdale, NJ: Lawrence Erlbaum Associates).

page 201. For discussions of how arousal accumulates, see: Zillmann, D. (1971), Excitation transfer in communication-mediated aggressive behavior, *Journal of Experimental Social Psychology, 7*, 419–434. Zillmann, D. (1991), Television viewing and physiological arousal, in: J. Bryant & D. Zillmann (Eds.), *Responding to the screen: Reception and reaction processes* (pp. 103–133) (Hillsdale, NJ: Lawrence Erlbaum Associates).

Chapter 18: Fidelity

page 203. This chapter is based on the following study: Reeves, B., Detenber, B., & Steuer, J.S. (1993), New televisions: The effects of big pictures and big sound on viewer responses to the screen, Paper presented to the Information Systems Division of the International Communication Association, Chicago.

page 203. For a more detailed discussion of visual acuity as it relates to the perception of mediated information, see: Hochberg, J.E. (1986), Representation of motion and space in video and cinematic displays, in: K.R. Boff, L. Kaufman, & J.P. Thomas (Eds.), *Handbook of perception and human performance* (Chapter 22) (New York: Wiley).

page 204. For a discussion of the perceptual issues related to high-definition television, see: Fukuda, T. (1990), New electronic media and the human interface, *Ergonomics, 33*(6), 687–706.

page 206. Two other studies that have found no differences in visual fidelity are: Lang, A. (1995), Defining audio/video redundancy from a limited-capacity information processing model perspective, *Communication Research, 22*(1), 86–115. Neuman, W.R., Crigler, A.C., & Bove, V.M. (1991), Television sound and viewer perceptions, *Proceedings of the Joint IEEE/Audio Engineering Society*, February.

page 206. For a discussion of the best predictors of the video images that people prefer, see: Kolb, F. (1989), Bibliography: Psychophysics of image evaluation, *SMPTE Journal, 98*(8), 594–598. Teunissen, K., & Westerink, J. (1996), A multidimensional evaluation of the perceptual quality of television sets, *SMPTE Journal, 105*(1), 31–43.

page 207. Preferences for horizontal formats are discussed in: Eisenstein, S. (1970), The dynamic square, in: J. Leyda (Ed.), *Film essays and a lecture* (pp. 48–65) (New York: Praeger). Nystrom, B.D. (1992), Perceived image quality of 16:9 and 4:3 aspect ratio video displays, *Journal of Electronic Imaging, 1*(1), 99–103.

page 207. For evidence that information in peripheral vision is more arousing, see: Livingstone, M., & Hubel, D. (1988), Segregation of form, color, movement, and depth: Anatomy, physiology, and movement, *Science, 240*, 740–749.

page 207. A discussion of letterboxing can be found in: Pitts, K. (1992), How acceptable is letterbox for viewing widescreen pictures? *IEEE Transactions on Consumer Electronics, 38*(3), XLIII–LI.

page 208. For articles on the role of audio quality in movies and virtual reality, see: Holman, T. (1994), Motion-picture theater sound system performance: New studies of the B-chain, *SMPTE Journal, 103*(3), 136–149. McEwan, J.A. (1994), Real-time 3-D: The sound of the times, *GEC Review, 9*(2), 67–80. Perrott, D.R., Cisneros, J., McKinley, R.L., & D'Angelo, W.R. (1995), Aided detection and identification of visual targets, *Proceedings of the Human Factors and Ergonomics Society, 1*, 104–108.

page 209. For a discussion of the role of audio quality in the experience of motion pictures, see: Reeves, B., Detenber, B., & Steuer, J.S. (1993), New televisions: The effects of big pictures and big sound on viewer responses to the screen, Paper presented to the Information Systems Division of the International Communication Association, Chicago.

page 210. The finding that good audio influenced judgments about the quality of video was also found in another study about the relationship between audio and video fidelity: Neuman, W.R., Crigler, A.C., & Bove, V.M. (1991), Television sound and viewer perceptions, *Proceedings of the Joint IEEE/Audio Engineering Society*, February.

Chapter 19: Synchrony

page 211. The present chapter is based on the following study: Reeves, B., & Voelker, D.H. (1993), Effects of audio-video asynchrony on viewer's memory, evaluation of content, and detection ability. Unpublished research report prepared for Pixel Instruments, Stanford University, Stanford, CA.

page 211. For a general discussion of how small units of time influence psychology, see: Newell, A. (1990), *Unified theory of cognition* (Cambridge, MA: Harvard University Press).

page 211. For a discussion of how timing influences interpersonal communication, see: Clark, H.H., & Clark, E.V. (1977), *Psychology and language: An introduction to psycholinguistics* (New York: Harcourt Brace).

page 213. For a discussion of the effects of technical transmission difficulties (or signal detection problems) on psychological processing, see: Boyle, E.A., Anderson, A.H., & Newlands, A. (1994), The effects of visibility on dialogue and performance in a cooperative problem solving task, *Language & Speech*, 37(1), 1–20.

page 216. The concept of back channel responses is reviewed in: Blau, A.F. (1987), Communication in the back-channel: Social structural analysis of nonspeech/speech conversations, *Dissertation Abstracts International*, 47 (9–A) 3237. Boyle, E.A., Anderson, A.H., & Newlands, A. (1994), The effects of visibility on dialogue and performance in a cooperative problem solving task, *Language & Speech*, 37(1), 1–20. Hess, L.J., & Johnston, J.R. (1988), Acquisition of back channel listener responses to adequate messages, *Discourse Processes*, 11(3), 319–335. Mott, H., & Petrie, H. (1995), Workplace interactions: Women's linguistic behavior, *Journal of Language & Social Psychology*, 4(3), 324–336.

Chapter 20: Motion

page 219. This chapter is based on the following study: Reeves, B., Thorson, E., Rothschild, M., McDonald, D., Hirsch, J., & Goldstein, B. (1985), Attention to television: Intrastimulus effects of movement and scene changes on alpha variation over time, *International Journal of Neuroscience, 27*, 241–255.

page 219. For a discussion about the importance of movement in visual processing, see: Bolivar, V.J., & Barresi, J. (1995), Giving meaning to movement: A developmental study, *Ecological Psychology, 7*(2), 71–97. Brown, E.L., & Defenbacher, K. (1979), *Perception and the senses* (New York: Oxford University Press). Haber, R.N., & Hershenson, M. (1973), *The psychology of visual perception* (New York: Holt, Rinehart, and Winston). Kolers, P.A. (1972), *Aspects of motion perception* (Elmsford, NY: Pergamon Press).

page 219. For a discussion of the psychological importance of objects that loom in front of people, see: Schiff, W. (1965), The perception of impending collision: A study of visually-directed avoidance behavior, *Psychological Monographs, 79*(604).

page 219. For a more detailed discussion of orienting responses in general and in relation to media, see: Reeves, B., Thorson, E., & Schleuder, J. (1986), Attention to television: Psychological theories and chronometric measures, in: J. Bryant & D. Zillmann (Eds.), *Perspectives on media effects* (Hillsdale, NJ: Lawrence Erlbaum Associates).

page 219. For a discussion of motion in cinematic presentations, see: Hochberg, J.E. (1986), Representation of motion and space in video and cinematic displays, in: K.R. Boff, L. Kaufman, & J.P. Thomas (Eds.), *Handbook of perception and human performance* (New York: Wiley).

page 220. Scholars of communication often distinguish between information that is viewed for its interpretive significance and information that demands action. For example, see: Worth, S., & Gross, L. (1974), Symbolic strategies, *Journal of Communication, 24*, 27–39.

page 220. For a discussion of EEG and the measurement of orienting responses, see: Reeves, B., Thorson, E., & Schleuder, J. (1986), Attention to television: Psychological theories and chronometric measures, in: J. Bryant and D. Zillmann (Eds.), *Perspectives on media effects* (Hillsdale, NJ: Lawrence Erlbaum Associates).

page 225. For a discussion of how different contexts interact with different time units, see: Newell, A. (1990), *Unified theories of cognition* (Cambridge, MA: Harvard University Press).

page 225. For a discussion of how people tune out messages, see: Petty, R.E., & Cacioppo, J.T. (1986), *Communication and persuasion: Central and peripheral routes to attitude change* (New York: Springer-Verlag).

page 225. For demonstrations that motion in peripheral vision is more arousing, see: Livingstone, M., & Hubel, D. (1988), Segregation of form, color, movement, and depth: Anatomy, physiology, and movement, *Science, 240*, 740–749. Shapiro, K.L., & Johnson, T.L. (1987), Effects of arousal on attention to central and peripheral visual stimuli, *Acta Psychologica, 66*, 157–172.

page 226. For a discussion of the amount of motion necessary to cause changes in attention, see: Smith, A.J. (1994), Direction identification on thresholds for second-order motion in central and peripheral vision, *Journal of the Optical Society of America, A, Optics, Image Science, and Vision, 11*, 506–514.

Chapter 21: Scene Changes

page 227. This chapter is based on several different published experiments. Each study is referenced at the point in the chapter where the study is discussed.

page 227. For a discussion of cuts in film aesthetics, see: Eisenstein, S. (1975), *The film sense* (New York: Harcourt Brace Jovanovich).

page 227. For a discussion of cuts in the psychological literature, see: Hochberg, J.E. (1986), Representation of motion and space in video and cinematic displays, in: K. Boff, L. Kaufman, & J. Thomas (Eds.), *Handbook of perception and human performance*, Vol. 2 (New York: Wiley).

page 228. Study 1 is based on an experiment reported in: Reeves, B., Thorson, E., Rothschild, M., McDonald, D., Hirsch, J., & Goldstein, B. (1985), Attention to television: Intrastimulus effects of movement and scene changes on alpha variation over time, *International Journal of Neuroscience, 27*, 241–255.

page 228. Research about visual orienting responses is reviewed in Chapter 20 and in: Ohman, A. (1979), The orienting response, attention, and learning: An information-processing perspective, in: H.D. Kimmel, E.H. Van Olst, & J.F. Orlebeke (Eds.), *The orienting reflex in humans* (Hillsdale, NJ: Lawrence Erlbaum Associates).

page 228. For a discussion of the use of EEG to study visual orientating, see Chapter 20 and the literature review in: Reeves, B., Thorson, E., Rothschild, M., McDonald, D., Hirsch, J., & Goldstein, B (1985), Attention to television: Intrastimulus effects of movement and scene changes on alpha variation over time, *International Journal of Neuroscience, 27,* 241–255.

page 229. Study 2 is based on: Geiger, S., & Reeves, B. (1993), The effects of scene changes and semantic relatedness on attention to television, *Communication Research, 20,* 155–175.

page 231. Study 3 is based on the following reference: Thorson, E., Reeves, B., & Schleuder, J. (1985), Message complexity and attention to television, *Communication Research, 12,* 427–454.

page 233. Study 4 is described in the following paper: Geiger, S., & Reeves, B. (1991), Evaluation and memory for political candidates in televised commercials, in: F. Biocca (Ed.), *Television and political advertising: Psychological processes* (pp. 125–144) (Hillsdale, NJ: Lawrence Erlbaum Associates).

page 234. Study 5 is described in: Geiger, S., & Reeves, B. (1993), We interrupt this program: Attention for television sequences, *Human Communication Research, 19,* 368–387.

page 235. For a discussion of how activation of networks is associated with thinking, see: Anderson, J.R. (1995), *Cognitive psychology and its implications,* 4th ed. (pp. 75–105) (Ypsilanti, MI: W.H. Freeman Publishing).

page 236. For a discussion of whether people must learn the conventions of film and video production, see: Messaris, P. (1994), *Visual "literacy": Image, mind, and reality* (Boulder, CO: Westview Press).

page 237. Film-makers increasingly use techniques, such as cuts, that rely on primitive instincts: Anderson, D.R., & Burns, J. (1991), Paying attention to television, in: J. Bryant & D. Zillmann (Eds.), *Responding to the screen: Reception and reaction processes* (Hillsdale, NJ: Lawrence Erlbaum Associates).

Bordwell, D., & Thompson, K. (1990), *Film art: An introduction,* 3rd ed. (New York: McGraw-Hill).

page 238. For an example of a study that measures the relationship of visual breaks and memory for information, see: Britton, B.K., Holdredge, T.S., Curry, C., & Westbrook, R.D. (1979), Uses of cognitive capacity in reading identical tests with different amounts of discourse level meaning, *Journal of Experimental Psychology: Human Learning and Memory, 5,* 262–270.

Chapter 22: Subliminal Images

page 241. This discussion is based on the following study: Reeves, B., Biocca, F., Pan, Z., Oshagan, H., & Richards, J. (1989), Unconscious processing and priming with pictures: Effects on emotional attributions about people on television. Unpublished manuscript, Institute for Communication Research, Stanford University.

page 241. For a comprehensive review of the literature on subliminal effects, and a discussion of the major research paradigms in psychology that are mentioned in this chapter, see: Holender, D. (1986), Semantic activation without conscious identification in dichotic listening, parafoveal vision, and visual masking: A survey and appraisal, *The Behavioral and Brain Sciences, 9,* 1–66.

page 243. The best examples of popular literature about subliminal persuasion are: Key, B.W. (1981), *Subliminal seduction: Ad media's manipulation of a not so innocent America* (New York: New American Literature). Packard, V. (1985), *The hidden persuaders* (New York: Pocket Books).

page 245. The concept of priming is described in: Berkowitz, L., & Rogers, K.H. (1986), A priming effects analysis of media influences, in: J. Bryant & D. Zillmann (Eds.), *Perspectives on media effects* (pp. 57–81) (Hillsdale, NJ: Lawrence Erlbaum Associates).

Chapter 23: Conclusions about the Media Equation

page 254. The metaphor of the restaurant versus the supermarket was proposed by Karen Fries.

page 255. For a discussion of how difficult it can be to learn tools with arbitrary conventions, see: Norman, D. (1990), *The design of everyday things* (New York: Doubleday).

Author Index

The numbers following the authors' names refer to the chapters where their work is referenced. The exact citations are listed in the Chapter References beginning on page 259.

Britton, B.K., 21
Brock, T.C., 13
Brockner, J., 16
Broughton, R., 6, 7
Broverman, D.M., 14
Broverman, I.K., 14
Brown, E.L., 1, 20
Brown, P., 2
Burns, J., 21
Buss, D.M., 1
Byrne, D., 3, 4, 7

Cacioppo, J.T., 12, 20
Cannon, W.B., 10
Carli, L.L., 7
Carlson, L., 16
Carnegie, D., 2
Cattell, R.B., 6
Chambers, W., 5
Christianson, S., 10
Cialdini, R.B., 4
Cisneros, J., 18
Clapper, J.P., 3
Clark, E.V., 19
Clark, H.H., 19
Clark, J.L., 6, 7
Clore, G.L., 8
Cochrane, S., 13
Coleman, R.O., 14
Coleridge, S.T., 16
Conway, B.E., 3, 16
Cooper, J., 13
Cosmides, L., 1
Costa, P.T., Jr., 6
Costrich, N., 14
Crabtree, M., 14

Craig, G., 7
Crigler, A.C., 18
Curry, C., 21

D'Angelo, W.R., 18
Davidson, R.J., 9
Deaux, K., 14
Defenbacher, K., 1, 20
Dennett, D.C., 2, 16
deRaad, B., 6, 7
Detenber, B., 11, 17, 18
Deutsch, C.J., 14
Deutsch, M., 13
Digman, J.M., 6
Don, A., 2, 7
Donovan, J., 2
Dryer, D.C., 5, 6, 7, 8
Duck, S.W., 7

Eady, P.M., 7
Eagly A.H., 14
Ebbesen, E.B., 3
Eicher, D., 14
Eisenstein, S., 18, 21
Ekman, P., 2, 3, 9
Ellsworth, P., 2, 3
Emsweiler, T., 14
Engler, U., 5
Evans, G.W., 3
Eysenck, H.J., 6, 7
Eysenck, S.B.G., 6, 7

Fagan, J.F., 17
Fantz, R.L., 17
Feinstein, J., 14
Finkel, S.E., 1, 2

Martin, C.L., 2
Martin, J., 2
Mason, L., 1, 5
Matsumoto, D., 3
Matter, C.F., 3
McArthur, L.Z., 14
McCloud, S., 2
McConnell, J.D., 16
McCracken, G., 16
McCrae, R.R., 6
McDonald, D., 1, 20, 21
McEwan, J.A., 18
McGuire, W.J., 16
McGurk, H., 15
McKee, J.P., 14
McKinley, R.L., 18
McQuail, D., 1
Meehan, D.M., 14
Mehrabian, A., 3
Melwani, G., 3
Mencel, E., 14
Mertens, I., 3
Messaris, P., 1, 21
Mettee, D.R., 8
Meyer, W.U., 5
Middlemist, R.D., 3
Miller, A.G., 16
Miller, R.L., 16
Minsky, M., 13
Miranda, S.B., 17
Mirenda, P., 14
Mittag, W., 5
Moon, J., 14
Moon, Y., 1, 2, 6, 7, 8, 13, 14
Moore, B.C.J., 15
Morgan, M., 6, 14

Morkes, J., 1, 2
Morton, H., 3
Mott, H., 19
Munick, M.L., 6

Nagao, D.H., 2
Nass, C., 1, 2, 4, 5, 6, 7, 8, 12, 13, 14, 15, 16
National Commission on Working Women, 14
Nelson, D., 7
Nerlove, S.B., 6
Neuman, W.R., 18
Newell, A., 19, 20
Newhagen, J., 10, 16
Newlands, A., 19
Nisbett, R.E., 4
Norman, D., 1, 13, 23
Nova, M., 16
Nystrom, B.D., 18

Odbert, H.S., 8
Ohanian, R., 12, 16
Ohman, A., 21
Oren, T., 2, 7
Orlikoff, R., 14
Osgood, C.E., 9
Oshagan, H., 22

Packard, V., 22
Pan, Z., 22
Pandey, J., 4
Pascale, L., 14
Patterson, M.L., 3
Perrott, D.R., 18
Petrie, H., 19